SOUTHWOLD RIVER

GEORGIAN LIFE IN THE BLYTH VALLEY

Rachel Lawrence

SUFFOLK BOOKS

First published 1990 by Suffolk Books

British Library Cataloguing-in-Publication Data
Lawrence, Rachel
Southwold River: Geeorgian Life in the Blyth Valley.
1. Suffolk. Blyth Valley. Social life.
I. Title
942.641
ISBN 0 86055-144-X

Printed and bound in Great Britain by BPCC Wheatons Ltd, Exeter

SUFFOLK BOOKS

Official Publishers to Suffolk County Council Arts and Libraries Department
An imprint of Wheaton Publishers Ltd,
a member of the Maxwell Communication Corporation plc

Wheaton Publishers Ltd
Hennock Road, Exeter, Devon EX2 8RP
Tel: 0392 411131

SALES
Direct sales enquiries to Suffolk Books at the address above

CONTENTS

ACKNOWLEDGEMENTS

I AM MOST GRATEFUL TO THE SUFFOLK RECORD OFFICE at Ipswich not only for accepting this book for publication but also because a great deal of the material I have used was supplied by their staff who gave me so much valuable advice and assistance. I would like also to thank the staff at the Public Record Office, the Norfolk and Lowestoft Record Offices, the British Library, the Guildhall Library, the Greater London Record Office, the House of Lords Record Office; and also the Curator and Librarian of Southwold Museum. I am particularly indebted to Southwold Town Council and their Clerk for allowing me frequent access to their splendid collection of documents.

Messrs Adnams plc kindly gave me access to their papers, as did Messrs Watney Combe Reid & Truman, and Mr Margarson of Cross Ram, Solicitors, Halesworth. I have drawn considerably on the work of E. R. Cooper and am grateful to his daughter, Judith Cooper, who not only let me look at his papers but also gave me lunch!

Many other people have lent documents or helped in other ways but in particular I am indebted to Alan Bottomley for so much scholarly assistance over Southwold history of which he is the master.

I would like to thank the Suffolk Institute of Archaeology and History for willingly allowing me to reuse material I published in their *Proceedings*. Their generosity is typical of the attitude of Suffolk historians to a newcomer like myself. Above all I cannot adequately express my thanks to Norman Scarfe not only for his inspiring encouragement but also for finding time to comment fully on the manuscript.

I am also greatly indebted to the late Dr W. J. Reader for making a great many constructive criticisms, and indeed I shall always be in his debt for tuition in research over many years. I appreciate very much the expertise with which the staff of Suffolk Books have designed and produced the book.

Without Berta Browett who first typed the draft and then taught me how to use the word processor, I would have made no progress. Still less would I have done so without the very substantial help and unfailing support of my husband.

Illustrations

For photographic work I am much indebted to R. W. Page, also to John Burrage, Burt Horrocks and Peter Punchard. I would like to thank the following for permission to use illustrations from their collections:

Cambridge University Collection: copyright reserved: pp. 53, 77 John Collins: p.75; Controller HMSO, British Crown copyright/MOD & Cambridge University Collection, copyright reserved: p. 8; Courtauld Institute of Art: p. 60; GGS Photography, Norwich: pp. 35, 43; John Hill: pp. 25, 27; Barrett Jenkins: p. 82 (top); David Lee: p. 98; National Maritime Museum, Greenwich: pp. 6 (top), 67; R. W. Page: pp. 18 (top), 21, 87 (bottom), 91, 119; R. A. Paterson: p. 79 (bottom); Peter Punchard: pp. 29 (bottom), 87 (top); Michael Seago, Great Yarmouth Maritime Museum collection: p. 6 (bottom); Southwold Museum: pp. 11, 13, 29 (top), 47, 71 (top); Southwold Town Council: p. 73 (top); Suffolk Record Office, Ipswich: pp. 39, 45, 59; Suffolk Records Society: p.3.

Maps

I am indebted to Moss Fuller for drawing the base map for the map on p. 4. Suffolk Record Office provided photographs of the map on p. 3 and also of the Halesworth Tithe Map on which the map on p. 116 is based. The maps on pp. 22 (bottom) and 124 are included in PP1845XVI.

Artwork for the maps on pp. 4, 22–3 and 116 was drawn by Andrew Nadolski.

The illustration on the jacket, 'Southwold Harbour 1822' by William Daniell, is reproduced by courtesy of Southwold Museum and the Orwell Bookshop, Southwold.

LIST OF ILLUSTRATIONS

LIST OF SUBSCRIBERS

G. P. and M. J. Acock, The White Cottage, Hillside Road, Reydon, Southwold
Jonathan Adnams, Elms Farm, Rissemere Lane, Reydon, Southwold
Adnams & Co plc, Sole Bay Brewery, Southwold
Mr and Mrs J. W. Alington, White Lodge, South Green, Southwold
Elsie K. Bally, St Francis, Walberswick
John David Barber, 19 The Crescents, Wangford Road, Reydon, Southwold
Gwyneth E. J. Barker, 38 East Street, Southwold
Dr Monica Barnett, 30 Gowers End, Glemsford, Sudbury
A. Barrett Jenkins, 12 Pier Avenue, Southwold
Bill and Elizabeth Barrett, Pip's Peace, Kenton, Stowmarket
Dr A. Beetlestone, 'Thrums', 7 Acre Lane, Walberswick
Mr C. L. Booth, 7 Queen Street, Southwold
Alan Farquhar Bottomley, M.A., Eversley, Southwold
Mrs Boult, 23 North Parade, Southwold
Penelope Bray, 28 South Green, Southwold
Mr S. H. Broadbent, 12 Loftus Avenue, Reydon, Southwold
Mr J. R. G. Brown, c/o The Saltings, Bridge Road, Reydon, Southwold
Mrs M. Brown, 30 High Street, Southwold
Peter A. Brown, 60 Rosmore Court, Park Road, London
Sally Brown, 23 Stradbroke Road, Southwold
Mrs Bryceson, Field Stile Road, Southwold
D. C. and M. E. Burke, Sea Green Cottage, Walberswick
Doris M. Burley, 8 Long Marsh Close, Reydon, Southwold
Peggy P. Cave, Dolphin House, Centre Cliff, Southwold
Margaret Chadd, Mardle House, Wangford
Mrs P. M. Cheeseman, 46 Victoria Street, Southwold
Dr Ronald Church, 3 Centre Cliff, Southwold
J. C. Coleman, Reydon, Southwold
Winston and Mary Colloby, The Dutch Barn Restaurant, Ferry Road, Southwold
Miss J. E. Cooper, 73 Old Barrack Road, Woodbridge
Dr R. N. Cooper, 6 Bartholomew Green, Southwold
Stephan R. Cooper, 72 Victoria Street, Southwold
Philip P. Coppen, 16 Upway , Rayleigh, Essex
J. A. Courtney, 116 Wangford Road, Reydon, Southwold
David Craddock, 13 Ditchling Close, Stopsley, Luton, Bedfordshire
J. C. Cragie, 'Saint Kilda', The Street, Wenhaston, Halesworth
R. D. Crombie
Warwick M. Cross, Froxfield, Marlborough Road, Southwold

Janet Croston, 6 Market Place, Kessingland
M. Danielsen and E. Okell, Ross on Wye
Mr and Mrs A. M. Davies, Lane Corner, Walberswick
David R. Davies, 16 Crab Hill, Beckenham, Kent
Louise Dawson, Reydon Grange, Wangford
Mr and Mrs W. J. Dawson, Fairfield, 42 Hotson Road, Southwold
Mr H. J. Dean, 43 Hotson Road, Southwold
Nettie de Montmorency, Southwold
J. W. Denny, The Boathouse, Ferry Road, Southwold
D. Dixon, 11 Cautley Road, Southwold
Mr Robert W. A. Downes, 13 Crowland Close, Ipswich
Gordon S. Downey, 14 Cannon House, Queen Street, Hitchin, Hertfordshire
Mrs J. Doy, 7 Elliott Avenue, Reydon, Southwold
Reverend and Mrs John W. Draper, 52 Pier Avenue, Southwold
D. and J. Drummond, Moat House, Mill Green, Saxtead, Woodbridge
Mrs J. Durham, 4 Orwell Court, York Road, Southwold
R. L. Easterbrook, Wayland, Walberswick
Caroline and John Ellis, Surlingham, Norfolk
Dr and Mrs M. B. Ellis, 31 Marlborough Road, Southwold
Mr and Mrs H. Evans, Camden Leigh, Wilderness Road, Chislehurst, Kent
Nesta Evans, Tostock, Suffolk
Maurice J. Everson, 48 London Road, Halesworth
Mrs Ewen Mount, Little Court, Chartham, Canterbury, Kent
Mrs P. J. Feather, c/o the Saltings, Bridge Road, Reydon, Southwold
Dr and Mrs Peter Fells, 29 East End Road, Church End, Finchley, London
Mr and Mrs Alan Fletcher, 26 Hollies Close, Royston, Hertfordshire
Mr M. Forbes, Veralam House, 2 Greens Lane, Reydon, Southwold
M. E. Fordham, 58 Old Station Road, Halesworth
M. R. Foster, 51 Cross Deep Gardens, Twickenham, Middlesex
Mr and Mrs N. L. Fry, 14 The Crescents, Reydon, Southwold
John F. Garrood, Grey Tiles, Cumberland Road, Southwold
Matthew C. C. Garrard, Wangford
Reverend and Mrs N. J. H. Garrard, Lancaster
Barbara Gautrey, 15 East Cliff, Southwold
B. Gingell, 7 North Parade, Southwold
A. Ginn, 7 Kingfisher Crescent, Reydon, Southwold
Wilma Gordon, 63 North Road, Southwold
Peter C. Green, 42 Burns Place, Dollard des Ormeaux, Quebec, Canada
Mr and Mrs Paul Griffin, 1 Strickland Place, Southwold
H. W. G. Griggs, 2 Fairfield Villas, Fairfield Road, Reydon, Southwold
Mr and Mrs. M. E. Gooch, Gothic House, Halesworth
Halesworth Middle School, Harrisons Lane, Halesworth
Betty and Jack Harkness, 1 Bank Alley, Southwold
Doris L. Hatfield MBE, 5 Cautley Road, Southwold
Brian Haward, The Rope House, Station Road, Southwold
F. F. Hawkins, 64 Pier Avenue, Southwold
Mr and Mrs W. Haydn Davies, Basildon, Essex
J. E. B. Hill, Watermill Farm, Wenhaston, Halesworth
Peter F. Hills, 5 Blackshore, Southwold
Mr P. S. Hobbs, 37 Baden Powell Crescent, Carleton Park, Pontefract, Yorkshire
Donald Hollingworth, Corn Store, Bartholomew Green, Southwold
David Holmes, Walpole
S. and R. Hooper, 19 Nicholas Drive, Reydon, Southwold

Mr and Mrs Trader Horne, South Cottage, Kemsing, Kent
Donald and Irene Horwood, Southwold
Ben and Melanie Horwood, Eastbridge
Matthew and Jane Horwood, Southwold
Mrs S. G. Howe Browne, Homeleigh, The Common, Southwold
Mr and Mrs Eric Huggins, 18 Chester Road, Southwold
Mike and Joyce Hyslop, 10 Market Place, Southwold
Jack Jellicoe, 3 Queen Street, Southwold
Felicity J. Jelliff, Heron Cottage, Wenhaston
Dame Jennifer Jenkins, 2 Kensington Park Gardens, London
Keith Norman Johnceline, Blackheath, Wenhaston, Halesworth
Harold Kemp, 1 Wymering Road, Southwold
Philip W. Kett, Common Edge, Church Lane, Walberswick
John S. Kiff, 61 Pier Avenue, Southwold
E. M. King, 37 Pier Avenue, Southwold
Mary J. King, Dutch House, Walberswick, Southwold
Graham Langley, County Councillor for Southwold, 98 Wangford Road, Reydon, Southwold
Anne Lee, South Cliff Cottage, South Green, Southwold
David M. Lee, 21 High Street, Southwold
A. G. Leguen de La Croix, The Old Vicarage, Halesworth, Suffolk
Simon Loftus, Bulcamp
Miss G. Long, 5 Pier Avenue, Southwold
Alan Mackley, 1 Angel Lane, Blythburgh, Halesworth, Suffolk
Stephen Maddox, 49 Marlborough Road, Suffolk
Anne Manly, 2a High Street, Southwold
Joan and Stafford May, Fallow Corner, South Ridge, St George's Hill, Weybridge
Mr K. R. May, 11 Mallard Road, Reydon, Southwold
Mrs Rosalyn McDermott, 39 Stradbroke Road, Southwold
Mrs A. E. McIsaac, Sorrel Cottage, Broad Chalke, Salisbury
Mr and Mrs M. Medland, 36 Stradbroke Road, Southwold
Diane E. Miller, 29 Brecon Road, Brooke, Norwich
F. Mills, 17 North Parade, Southwold
J. G. Morris, Market Square, Petworth, W. Sussex
Mr Robin A. S. Moser, Mill End, Clavering, Saffron Waldon, Essex
Mr D. E. Moyse, Westerland, School Lane, Reydon, Southwold
Mr and Mrs M. W. Naunton, Basildon, Essex
Peter Northeast, Rattlesden, Suffolk
Millicent Overon, 41 Marlborough Road, Southwold
R. N. and J. Phillips, The Elms, Little Blakenham, Ipswich
Dr O. G. Pickard CBE, Little Dingle Cottage, Dunwich, Saxmundham
Richard Pither, 45 Ferry Road, Southwold
Donald Pope, 3 Lowestoft Road, Reydon, Southwold
Mrs Vivian G. Pratt
John R. Pretty, 10 Nightingale Avenue, Reydon, Southwold
B. A Priestman, Creek Cottage, Walberswick, Southwold
Pri-Med Developments Ltd, Oaklands, Blackwater Covert, Southwold
Dr A. F. Prior, Rodings, Salisbury Road, Southwold
Beryl Pulham, 82 Roundwood Road, Ipswich
D. H. and Z. C. Randall, 20 Stradbroke Road, Southwold
Mary Ransome, 73 Victoria Street, Southwold
Julia Reisz, The Old Tea Room, Walberswick
B. L. and E. M. Richardson, Lake House, North Road, Southwold
Mr and Mrs J. P. C. Richardson, 122 North End House, Fitzjames Avenue, London

Mrs W. M. Riddell, Briar Cottage, The Green, Walberswick
Stanley D. Roach, Walmer Way, Jermyns Road, Southwold
Toby V. Robinson
Mr M. Rockall, Stradbroke Road, Southwold
Mr and Mrs W. J. Rolfe, Uplands, 27a North Parade, Southwold
Mrs Elizabeth Rowley, Wantage House, The Common, Southwold
Robert G. Ruthven, 42 Windsor Road, Southwold
Judith and Graeme Salmon, 34 Hilltop Road, Oxford
Frederica Sanderson, 13 High Street, Southwold
Norman Scarfe, Woodbridge
Mrs E. Scott, 28 Park Lane, Southwold
Richard Scott, Samphire Cottage, Walberswick, Suffolk
Paul Scriven, Frostenden, Suffolk
Miss J. M. Sheldon, Over The Way, Palmers Lane, Walberswick
H. M. Shore, Reydon, Southwold
Tizzy Simpson, Hidden House, Walberswick, Southwold
Baron Slobovitch, Field Stile Road, Southwold
D. C. Smith, Crossways, Gorse Lane, Reydon, Southwold
M. J. Solomon, 35 Field Stile Road, Southwold
Southwold Town Council, Town Hall, Southwold
Mary Spencer, Northwood, Middlesex
E. Stainton, The Common, Southwold
M. L. Stansall, The Bell Hotel, Walberswick
Christopher N. Stokes, Rickling, Essex
Betty Storey, Cranbrook, The Common, Southwold
Michael S. Sutcliffe, 26 Park Lane, Southwold
Mr and Mrs C. R. Tapper, 54 Parklands Avenue, Cowes, Isle of Wight
P. F. & K. E. Taylor, Fairwinds, 7 Evans Close, Reydon, Southwold
Mrs R. Taylor, Holly Tree House, Sotherton, Wangford
A. H. Teece, 1 Westgate Street, Long Melford, Sudbury
Mrs Doreen Thompson, Windy Peak, Gun Hill, Southwold
Horace Townsend, 7 Cautley Road, Southwold
P. Anne Tozer, 36 Langleys Road, Selly Oak, Birmingham
Mr and Mrs Twallin, 5 North Parade, Southwold
Mrs Vera Underwood, Flat B, 54 Pier Avenue, Southwold
Mary Usherwood, Laurel Cottage, The Green, Walberswick
Miss N. L. Vallis, Chekkers, 7 Loftus Avenue, Reydon, Southwold
Mrs V. G. Vinten, Manor Garden Cottage, Woodleys Yard, Southwold
Mrs Carole P Warren, 7 Hunters Close, Borehamwood, Hertfordshire
Judith Waters, 73 Blenheim Crescent, London
Scrivener Waters, 10 East Green, Southwold
W. Webb, Seascape, Walberswick Green, Southwold
Michael Wells, 1 Buckenham Court, Mill Lane, Southwold
Mrs E. West, Southfield House, Wangford Road, Reydon, Southwold
Michael J. West, 25 North Road, Southwold
Mr and Mrs Q. Weston, Spring Place, Bitchet Green, Sevenoaks, Kent
Kenneth and Mary Westrope, Berrywood, 32 Hotson Road, Southwold
Leslie and Louise Wheeler, 4 Centre Cliff, Southwold
Brenda and Maurice Wilde, 21 Station Road, Southwold
Dr and Mrs H. G. M. Williamson, The Camp, Chester Road, Southwold
John R. Winter, 43 St Edmunds Road, Southwold
Mr and Mrs A. Wright, 53 Westwood Gardens, Chandlers Ford, Hampshire
A. R. Wythe, 10 Manor Close, Walberswick, Southwold

INTRODUCTION

by Norman Scarfe

WHEN THE LATE PROFESSOR EMERITA OF HARVARD, Helen Cam, wrote the introduction to her seminal collection of local studies, *Liberties and Communities in Medieval England*, she headed it 'In Defence of the Study of Local History'. If we no longer feel the need to be defensive about local history, we owe it largely to such pioneering books as hers, published by Cambridge University Press in 1944.

The book I am very proud to be introducing to you forty-six years later, is the work of one of Helen Cam's pupils at Cambridge, whose professional researches into business history have included such serious business as that of ICI, of the electricity industry, and of the Institute of Electrical Engineers. I feel that her present work may be even more 'serious' because the subject is more the history of a whole natural environment; the story of a river valley and its inhabitants, especially in those activities most central to their lives: their attempts to improve and to safeguard their livelihoods – the transporting of their produce, their luxuries and their raw materials along a river not ideal for 'navigation', and through a harbour mouth as notoriously unreliable, indeed treacherous, as any round our coast.

When Rachel Lawrence and her husband chose to retire to Southwold some ten years ago, it was a stroke of very good fortune for all of us who love not only Southwold but the various distinctive districts that make up the life-story of Suffolk. Like her tutor, Rachel Lawrence has that rare combination of gifts: the inclination and the stamina to work patiently through the available original records in the local and national archives and in the printed sources; a professional judgement about the balance of economic, social and simply personal forces in the history of the neighbourhood; and finally, and perhaps rarest, the gift of knowing when, and how, to write the story itself.

'The enviable qualities', she writes, 'of initiative and self-confidence which emerged so strongly in eighteenth-century Britain were not confined to those who produced cast iron and steam-engines . . . they were apparent in many back yards and out-of-the-way places. The characters in the Blyth valley whose achievements and failures are described in this book had a full share of them.'

The valley setting is so unforgettable. At the river-mouth, Southwold, with its lighthouse and brewery, its high street heading for the cliff edge and veering off into an assortment of village greens, and its magnificent medieval church in a side street: oh, and the great views, out to sea, and south to the frail harbour mouth that this book is so much about, and to Walberswick. Then, at the head of the estuary, a few miles inland, Blythburgh, saying nothing of its association with the early royal house of East Anglia, its ancient market-place scarcely discernible beneath the cottages, and only its indescribably beautiful great church to speak of its position as a former market and staithe. In this book it features as one quay on the Blyth river navigation making another market town accessible from the sea.

Joseph Hodskinson's Map of Suffolk in 1783, in the middle of the period of this book, has the advantage that it names and marks many of the features in the story; not only Black Shore, but the Reydon 'New Key' now very hard to trace on the ground: it also gives a good idea of the proximity of the various parks and their grandees who play a leading part in the story. At Benacre, the Gooches were curiously not very prominent. From Sotterley, the recently arrived city-rich and shrewd Barnes played a very forceful lead-part in both harbour and Navigation, and theirs was that 'New Key' at Reydon. At Heveningham, the Vannecks (also city magnates), were more peripherally involved, but promoted Goldsmith in the Halesworth theatre! At Cockfield Hall, Yoxford, the Bloises, too, were merchants (in this case from medieval Ipswich) who moved out 'into land'. In the 1664–8 *Visitation of Suffolk*, there is William Bloys of Grundisburgh, Knight, marrying first a daughter of Sir Robert Brooke of Yoxford (Cockfield) and, second, a Barnardiston of Kedington, one of the oldest, and certainly the richest, of the merchant landed families in seventeenth-century Suffolk: anyway, that is how the Bloises came to be at Cockfield.

Hodskinson's map shows one of the 'oldest' Suffolk landed families, the Rouses of Dennington, seated at Henham, virtually beside the river just north of Blythburgh. They bought Henham from the medieval Hopton family in 1544. Naturally the Rouses are very much at the heart of developments along 'their' river in these years. The Vannecks, Barnes and Rouses are now deploying at least part of their enterprise in Australia, but retain firm links here, among their old neighbours the Bloises and Gooches.

Hodskinson not only names the estates of grandees, but shows, for instance, where Mr Badeley lived in Walpole. Who? This is where Rachel Lawrence comes into her own. She links superbly the stories of the larger entrepreneurs with those of the lesser merchants, clergy, attorneys and tradespeople, forging them into the kind of local history we have long been waiting for. (Her story of the origins of the Crisp family is a good instance.) She describes the remaining fragments of Reydon 'New Key' and furthermore knows where to find the chalk caves that supplied the chalk for the local lime kilns. Of the lanes leading to New Key she writes: 'Up these lanes lumbered heavy wagons with coal for Henham Hall . . . well-to-do farmers and tradesmen, for blacksmiths' forges and brickmakers' kilns. They made the return journey laden with farm produce – wheat, peas, beans, but above all with barley . . . for the best pale malt, the brewers wanted the short plump thin-skinned barley from Norfolk and Suffolk.'

She knows who lived where in Southwold and in Halesworth, who owned each of the pubs, and where the serious meetings were held. She knows how the local economy was affected by the 'improvements' so many of her characters brought about, and how many were bankrupted by the wars and, of these, who recovered. Her final irresistible chapters show the first Scottish newcomer taking on the local 'establishment' and losing politically though certainly not economically: the Patrick Stead Hospital he founded at Halesworth still flourishes.

Two people I wish were still alive to read this book: Sir Charles Tennyson, the poet's grandson and biographer, who loved Southwold and its river, and whose son Julian wrote *Suffolk Scene* before he was killed in the war in Burma. My other regret is that Helen Cam is no longer alive to enjoy, and doubtless gently criticize, her distinguished pupil's admirable work, so thoroughly informed and vividly written.

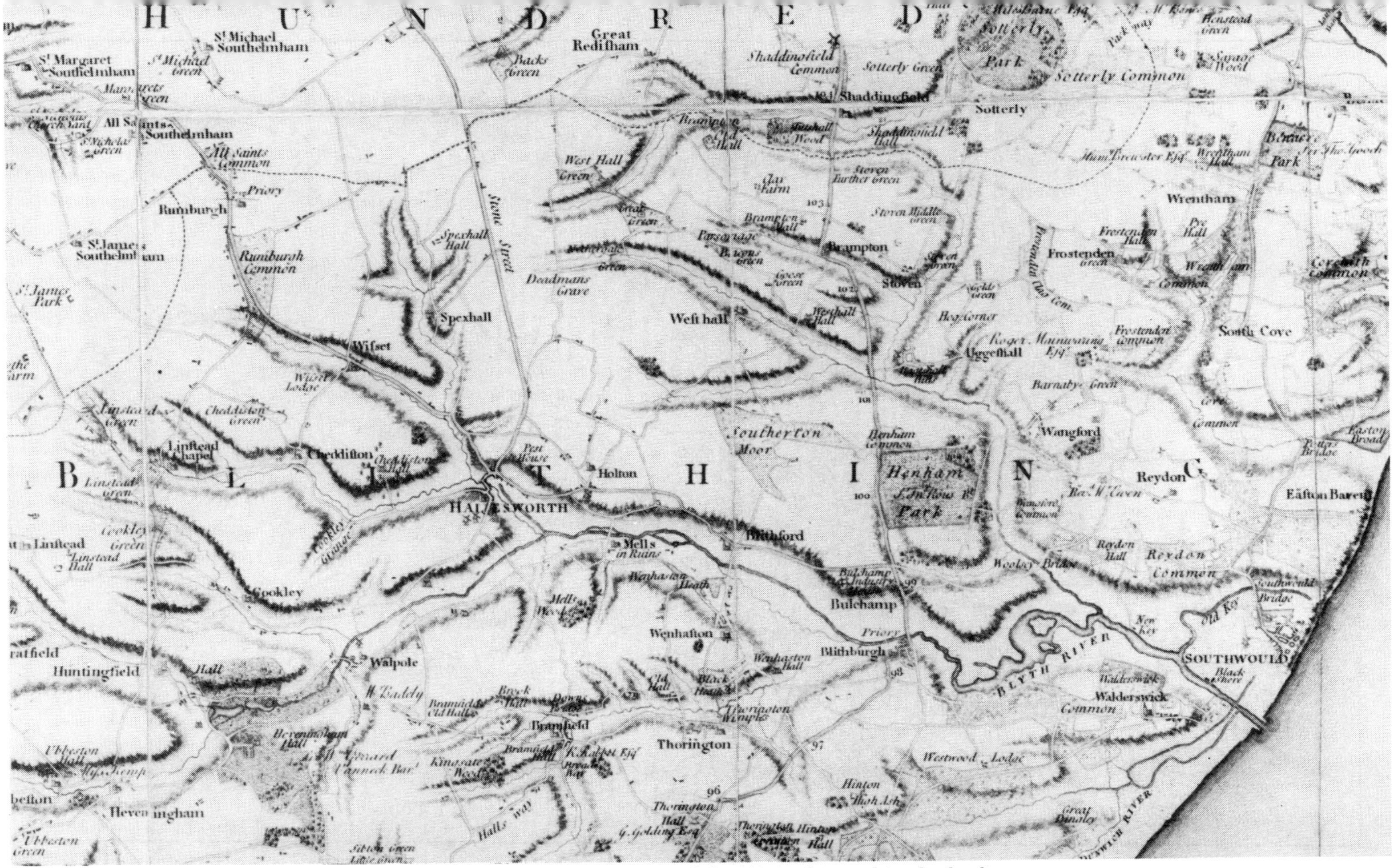

Part of Joseph Hodskinson's Map of Suffolk, 1783, which shows many of the places featured in the book.

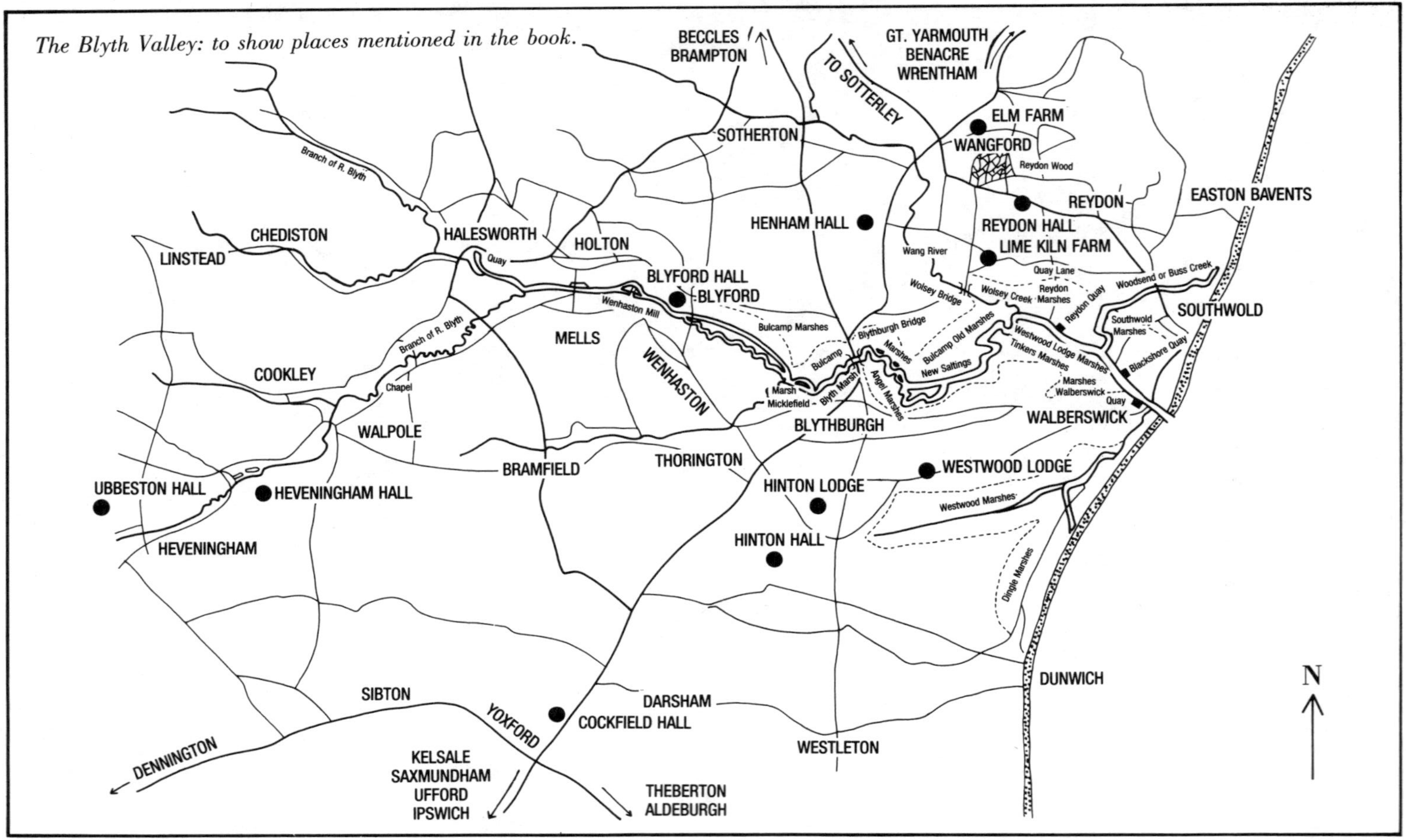

The Blyth Valley: to show places mentioned in the book.

PROLOGUE

THEN AND NOW

THE EAST ANGLIAN COAST IS RIMMED by small havens where solid warehouses and merchants' houses bear witness to past wealth. Crowded with sail and prosperous in Medieval and Tudor times, some ports and creeks were facing setbacks and decline in the later seventeenth century, only to find new vitality a hundred years later as increased traffic began to ply up and down the coast. The coastal trade of Norfolk and Suffolk in coal and corn, fish and dairy produce, had been very long established, but in the later eighteenth century when hearths and furnaces were multiplying and London's demand for food grew more insistent, the ancient ports came alive with more and larger collier brigs arriving from Newcastle and Sunderland and brigs and schooners loading up with corn and malt, peas and beans. In the seventy years after 1760 the tonnage of ships in the coastal trade grew at least fourfold, and for much of this period east coast ports were predominant. Coal was the largest business and next in importance was the shipping of grain. In the 1780s all but one of the ten leading British ports sending grain coastwise were on the east coast, while in the 1820s six out of the ten leading ports in this trade were in East Anglia, with Yarmouth heading the list. This trade in coal and grain found its way also into small east coast havens including little Suffolk ports – Woodbridge, Aldeburgh, Southwold. At the same time the mounting need to transport heavy loads of coal into the country behind and to bring bulky agricultual produce to the ships brought boats and barges on to the meandering estuarial rivers and provided the impulse for river improvement.[1]

The advent of the railways ended the heyday of coastal and river transport. The railways killed many river navigations and compelled many small harbours to be content with fishing boats so that it is easy to forget their past glories. It is difficult now to picture the River Blyth Navigation and Southwold harbour at the river mouth as they once were.

The Blyth nowadays trickles reluctantly under the bridge in the town of Halesworth and moves slowly, almost unnoticed, behind factory yards and buildings into the flat meadows beyond where it is joined by a branch bringing water from Ubbeston, Heveningham and Walpole. The river passes quietly by the old mill at Wenhaston and under Blyford bridge. It attracts attention only when it reaches the village of Blythburgh where the tidal waters ebb and flow over wide stretches of mud flats and provide a spectacular setting for Blythburgh's great fifteenth-century church. In the last reaches

'Colliers off Harwich' by Francis Swaine, 1770.

Wherries at a Norfolk staithe.

the waters gather strength and depth before they arrive at the long straggling harbour of Southwold, half an hour's walk from Southwold town to the north but close to the village of Walberswick which is scattered behind its southern bank. The road from the town of Southwold runs beside marshy meadows to the old quay at Blackshore overlooked by an ancient brick warehouse and the Harbour Inn which has suffered many changes of name over the years. From Blackshore the harbour stretches on to the south-east for nearly a mile, flanked on both sides by flat grass and sandy verges with slipways and untidy wooden jetties. As it nears the sea the river is confined by concrete walls with an opening on the south side to receive the water from the Dunwich and Westwood marshes. Beyond these walls are the present concrete piers built out into the sea.

Only pleasure boats and fishing boats now lie in the harbour but a hundred and fifty years ago two-masted brigs and schooners berthed there. Between 400 and 500 merchant vessels passed in or out of Southwold harbour each year from 1836 to 1850 (Table 3): most came in with coal from Newcastle and other north-east ports; a few brought chalk and porter from London, rock salt from Liverpool or bone dust from Ipswich; boats headed out carrying grain or malt to London or loaded with ballast to stabilize an empty voyage to the coal ports. About thirty-six vessels belonged to the port of Southwold itself and the ownership of these was usually shared amongst local people including the Master. Most of the boats were small, with seventy to eighty tons carrying capacity in theory, although this was often exceeded in practice. Boats heavy with coal had a draught of eight or nine feet and those loaded with corn sometimes also had a nine-foot draught which meant in both cases that they could not find enough water to ride any distance up river.[2]

A very shallow draught was needed to fetch and carry heavy loads higher up the Blyth and this was the great asset of the black-sailed wherries. Clinker-built with high masts easily lowered, the wherries had the capacity to carry twenty-five tons or more. Because of their handier rig they were quicker and easier to manage than the heavier keels which were first used on the Blyth Navigation: the keels had their masts amidships and a square sail but the wherry mast was set in the bows and had a loose-footed gaff sail. Wherries could make the journey from Halesworth to Southwold and back in two days and they were soon a familiar sight on the Blyth, as they were also on the Waveney and on the east Norfolk rivers.[3]

The days when merchandise was carried on the sea by sailing craft and transported on rivers by wherries have long gone. The Navigation of the River Blyth was wound up locally in the 1880s and extinguished by Parliament in 1934; the future of Southwold harbour itself is now uncertain; but from the mid eighteenth century till the coming of the railways the water carriage they provided played a key role in the economic life of merchants, farmers and landowners in the Blyth valley and high hopes and expectations were pinned on both harbour and river.

The pioneers who made possible these expectations were men of their time – a time of extraordinary enterprise. The industrial revolution may have passed Suffolk by, but Suffolk like Norfolk was in the van of the revolution in agricultural practice – the revolution which made it possible to feed the increasing population in the country. The enviable qualities of initiative and self-confidence which emerged so strongly in eighteenth-century Britain were not confined to those who produced cast iron and steam engines, nor indeed to agricultural giants like Turnip Townsend or Robert Bakewell; they were apparent in many backyards and out-of-the-way places. The characters in the Blyth valley whose achievements and failures are described in this book had a full share of them.

The River Blyth where it enters the sea at Southwold harbour. To the left and on the south side is the village of Walberswick, Blackshore quay is up river on the north bank. (British Crown copyright/MOD).

GREAT EXPECTATIONS

CHAPTER 1

Thomas Gardner's World

THE EARLY MEANDERINGS OF THE RIVER BLYTH twist through the clay soil district of 'high' Suffolk until the river finds its way into the sandy maritime district so much admired by Arthur Young, Secretary to the Board of Agriculture during the Napoleonic Wars. It was not so much the soil which this celebrated agricultural expert acclaimed, as the high standard of farm management attained by the farmers whom he met here and with whom he corresponded. François de La Rochefoucauld who accompanied Young on a brief tour of Suffolk in 1784 was amazed by the intelligence and expertise of the farmers – 'The knowledge possessed by all these farmers is incredible' – and was also deeply impressed by the lively interest in their properties taken by many English landlords. Farming, he wrote, was regarded as an honourable estate because 'the highest in the land are engaged in it'.[1] Knowledgeable, forward-looking men of this sort were already by the mid eighteenth century striving by means of sluices, marsh walling and drains to contain the estuarial floods which poured over the flat marshes at high tides, and thus to increase their pastureland. The encroachments on the River Blyth and its generous marshes which were to gather speed towards the end of the century had already begun.

With similar enterprise, men in the Blyth valley at this time were urging plans to stabilize and improve Southwold harbour and to make the river navigable up to Halesworth. Both river and harbour had rendered valuable service to the people of Southwold, Walberswick and Blythburgh over many centuries. Boats on the river had carried heavy loads of corn, hay and timber and the harbour had provided a vital route to the sea. The wandering mouth of the River Blyth brought great prosperity to Walberswick and Southwold in the fifteenth and sixteenth centuries as it moved northward towards them, leaving the once great port of Dunwich ever more stranded. But it was an exasperating mouth, unfixed at any certain spot and frequently blocked. At the mercy of tide and sea which heaped up beach and shingle according to the changing winds, the haven was always a hazardous entrance for seamen.

By the end of the seventeenth century fortune had deserted the Blyth valley. The Dutch had snatched away the fishing; Dunkirk pirates had repeatedly harassed ships and boats; the Dutch wars had imposed heavy burdens and had taken away able-bodied men; disastrous fires had consumed houses at Blythburgh and Walberswick and destroyed a great portion of the town of Southwold. Economic recovery was impeded by the unsatisfactory condition of the harbour and yet the men of Southwold who had assumed superintendence of the haven felt that their salvation lay with this outlet to the sea.[2]

Despite the somnolent, rather depressed atmosphere in the early eighteenth century new hopes were kindling in east Suffolk. As the trade in coal and agricultural produce along the east coast gathered impetus it began to affect small ports and their hinterland and as the years passed hopefulness was encouraged by the buoyant demand for food from the growing urban population in the country and the upward trend of corn prices from mid century.

The Southwold Harbour Act of 1746 and the River Blyth Navigation Act of 1757 signalled a determination to take advantage of increasing opportunities for trade. The crashing of oaks and firs, felled for posts and pilings, and the hammering of nails which these Acts initiated were the product of new expectations. These private Acts were also indications of the new approach to transport administration. In typical eighteenth-century fashion both Acts handed over control of the work and of the finances to bodies of Commissioners – reputable local men named under the Acts but with power to fill vacancies as they wished.[3]

In 1754 Thomas Gardner published his historical account of Dunwich, Blythburgh and Southwold – a classic for local historians – and he dedicated this great work to the recently appointed Commissioners of the Haven of Southwold. Surveying the scene from his viewpoint as Deputy Controller of the Customs, Gardner saw in the new regime at the harbour promise of great benefit to the 'Traffick and Commerce of our Town' and benefit to the neighbourhood 'upon Account of Exportation and Importation of Commodities' and lastly 'a certain Benefit to the Landowners by draining their Marshes and Meadows'.

Casting his glass over Southwold and the villages round, Gardner's general impression was of decline and decay. This 'decay' (a favourite word of his) he attributed chiefly to the decline of the fisheries. Blythburgh, once 'the Residence of Merchants and good reputable persons; well frequented upon Account of its Trade and divers other Affairs . . . especially the Fishery' now had but twenty-one houses and 124 souls. Walberswick which even in the seventeenth century had a ship-building industry and a flourishing trade shipping butter and cheese to London, now had but twenty dwelling houses; Reydon, the large scattered village stretching west and north behind Southwold, had lost its Hall, its park and also, Gardner tells us, a market; Easton Bavents, perched on the grass cliffs a mile to the north, formerly large and well peopled, had been reduced by the sea to two dwelling houses.

Like the other coastal towns and villages Southwold had declined with the 'Decay of the Fishery'. But in 1750 new life had come to Southwold with the Government decision to make the town a centre for the *Free British Fishery*, a national effort, set up to try to overcome the menacing Dutch dominance of the herring fisheries. Gardner found that in 1750 there were only forty dwelling houses and 666 souls in Southwold 'but since that Time, the Encouragement given by the Free British Fishery induced many People of different Occupations to come hither from divers Parts of Great Britain'.

Gardner's enthusiasm for 'this grand Undertaking' and his pleasure in the bustling excitement it was bringing – 'This year sixty-three busses rendez-voused at this Port' – led him to deal rather scantily with the coasting and foreign trade which none the less was bringing prosperity to some merchants in Southwold and also in neighbouring villages. In a brief paragraph he listed traffic in salt, export of red herrings and red sprats, malt and corn, import of coals, cinders, timbers, lime; and he added that there were one brigantine and nine sloops belonging to Southwold men.[4] Understandably his attention was rivetted on the new Fishery and there was nothing novel to remark about this coastal and foreign trade. As far as the well-being of the harbour is concerned, however, it was much more important than the Fishery which in any case lasted only twenty-one years. It was the merchants engaged in the shipping trade who recognized their dependence on a viable

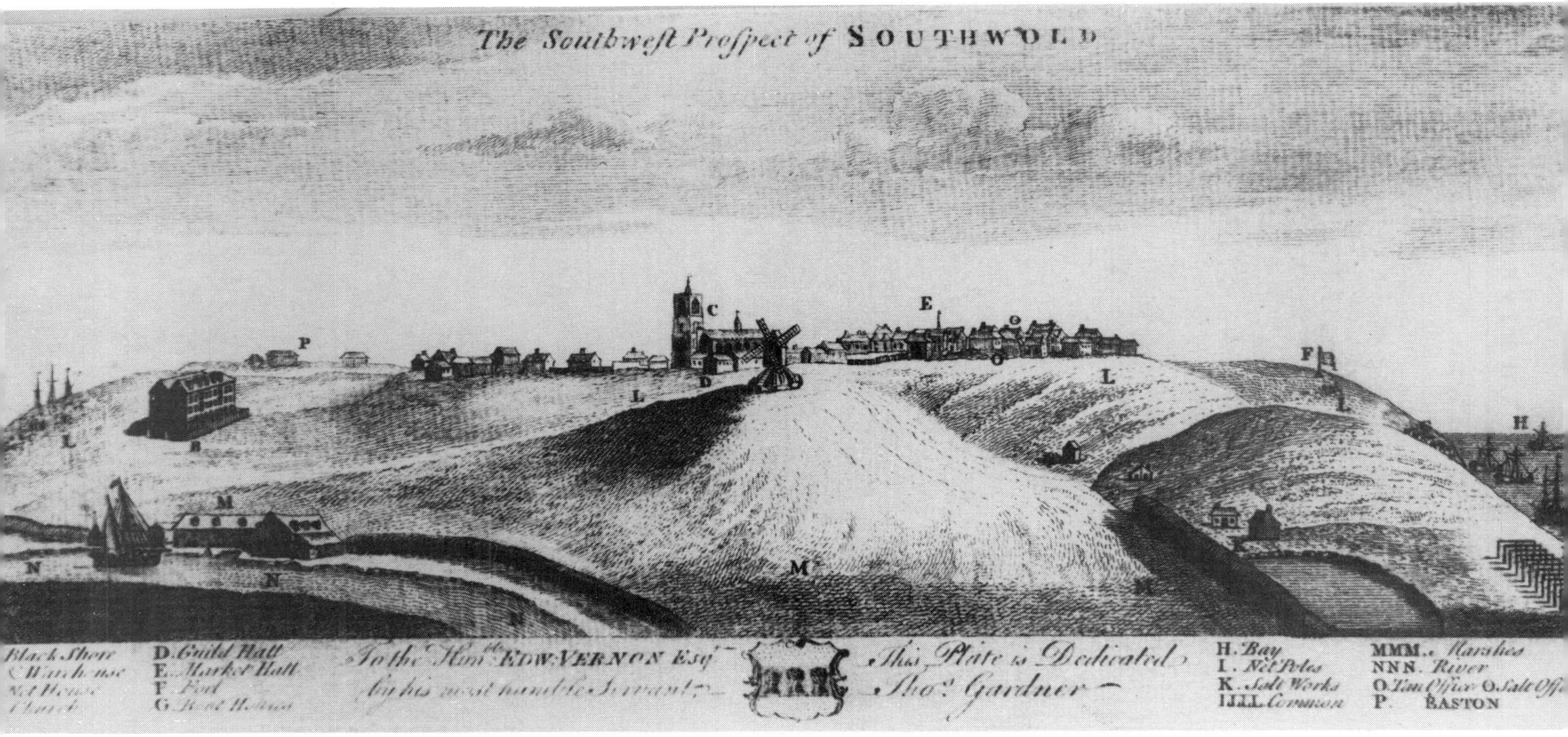

'The Southwest Prospect of Southwold': plate dedicated by Thomas Gardner to the Hon. Edward Vernon Esq., c. 1754.

haven and who, till the end of the century, committed themselves to the task of supervising the endless repair work on the vulnerable timber piers.

Gardner did not follow the River Blyth above Blythburgh. Wenhaston, Blyford and Halesworth were inland places little concerned about King Herring. The Reverend Richard Canning, writing about ten years later, described Halesworth as a well-built town with a considerable weekly market on Thursdays and a good fair for lean cattle on the Feast-day of Saint Luke. Halesworth was a centre for farmers in the 'high farming' land where according to Defoe, writing in 1724, 'the whole country is employed in dairies and in feeding of cattle'. These dairy farmers, for whom the Halesworth inn The Red Cow was tactfully named, often had a side interest in hemp and its products. They drove to Halesworth market from villages such as Cookley, Linstead, Heveningham and Sibton, where their herds of polled Suffolk cows produced milk for butter and cheese and the dairy-maids spun hemp in their spare moments. Halesworth was part of a pattern of farming and a way of life which belonged to the slow-moving years of the early eighteenth century; a time of stationary, rather low agricultural prices.[5]

If we look back on the valley of the Blyth in this earlier time we can picture the river winding its way from Halesworth through buttercup meadows, wooded groves and wet pastureland. Below Blyford the river was flanked by marsh which gave way to bronze reed beds. The incoming tide flowed over the salt marshes and in later years a marshman described cutting reeds for thatch near Blythburgh and falling asleep on a heap of rushes only to wake and find himself in the midst of the water which he said covered the whole so that the water looked as bright as the river all over.[6] The reed beds gave way to generous mud flats where any man with a craft was free to go pinpatching for winkles as he pleased.[7] The valuable rights of laying oysters in the estuary were, of course, reserved. Sir John Rous had beds near Wolsey Creek; near Reydon quay Miles Barne had the right and profit of laying oysters; there were also oyster beds further down the river near Woodsend Creek.[8] But the poor man could still dab for flounders lying on the bottom of the river and in the winter months, armed with a pick, could track the abundant eels along the ditches and creeks. Although, no doubt, landowners claimed rights of fishing and wildfowling this was an easy-going time and poaching was not yet regarded as a heinous offence. It was the age of Crabbe's Squire Asgill:

Of Heaven's free Gifts he took no special care
He never quarrel'd for a simple Hare[9]

In any case the pattern of landholding along the Blyth in the mid eighteenth century was not conducive to rigorous game preserving. Amongst the farms, marshes and meadows held by the larger local landowners – Rous and Blois, and from 1746 Miles Barne – were scattered holdings with a variety of owners. The rural saver usually invested his money in land and indeed had little satisfactory alternative. After he died the acres he had bought might be divided or part sold to provide for debts, widow, dependent children; often they were mortgaged. Several of the landowners along the Blyth were absentees. William Chapman of Loudham Hall near Woodbridge owned Wenhaston Mill and land at Wenhaston and Blyford; William Plumer, living in Hertfordshire, had inherited land along the river at Wenhaston and Halesworth. Cuts for the Navigation were made on his ground and that of three Halesworth townsfolk. The river margins by Blythburgh had several owners. Thomas Raymond, a surgeon living near Stradbroke, owned 250 acres of marsh and other land at Bulcamp. Indeed at this time the holdings of the Rous family at Bulcamp were interspersed with those of other owners: John Colston of Walpole; the Parish of Sibton; John Block of Ipswich. To the west Reginald Rabett of Bramfield Hall also owned land at Bulcamp as well as at Blyford and Wenhaston.[10]

The haphazard pattern and the easy-going atmosphere did not last. In the second half of the eighteenth century the larger landowners gradually bought up acres as they came on the market and consolidated their estates, while at the same time, in combination with enterprising tenants, they began in earnest to reclaim land from the copiously flooding river.

This new vigour on the river bank and in the surrounding country was one important part of the economic and social changes which gathered pace in the Blyth valley as the years ran on to the end of the eighteenth and into the nineteenth centuries. These were rousing and exciting years. New opportunities and new obstacles threw out challenges to courage and initiative; and the men whose stories are told in later pages, met those challenges in very different ways.

But before turning to these characters we need to look first at the new harbour venture and the genesis of the Navigation. Both signalled the advent of a changed atmosphere and in both cases the way they came about profoundly affected future developments. To look at the beginnings of both is a valuable introduction to the subsequent scene.

River Blyth, looking towards Southwold: pencil drawing by H. Davy, c. 1824.

CHAPTER 2

The Harbour Initiative

Swoul and Dunwich and Walderswick
All go in at one lousy creek[1]

WITH THIS HEART-FELT JINGLE HARASSED SEAMEN summed up a long history of frustrations and dangers. They had no reason to love the wandering estuary of the River Blyth. Here over centuries masters and crews had been faced with an unpredictable coastline, blocked entrances and shifting bars of shingle and sand.

It was a very old problem but it became increasingly intolerable in the eighteenth century. Trade on the east coast was expanding; more corn was being shipped from East Anglian ports; more and more collier brigs were bringing down coal from the north-east ports.[2] The Grand Assemblies of Southwold Corporation accordingly found themselves passing a growing number of resolutions to improve their haven – resolutions which came to little for the Corporation had no spare money. In January 1741 the Assembly agreed 'to procure and get a new haven' and stop up the old one. For financial help they turned as they had turned in the decades before to 'the gentlemen in the country' but this was to be the last time that they made an appeal of this kind. It was becoming obvious that these casual contributions were outdated and would never provide adequate funds for the project on which most minds were now fixed – the building of piers to stabilize the harbour permanently. If the country landowners was going to provide money for an enterprise of this kind they would demand a proper financial return on their investment together with security and adequate control.[3]

The eventual solution to the financial impasse was a very typical eighteenth-century arrangement and resembled the method already being used to finance the new turnpike roads. Responsibility for the harbour was taken out of the hands of the impecunious town and handed over to the powers in the neighbourhood from whom, it was recognized, most of the money needed must come. In 1746 under the first Southwold Harbour Act, twenty-two Commissioners were appointed to take charge of the opening, cleansing, repairing and improving of Southwold haven. They were empowered to claim dues from every ship sailing in or out of the harbour and from ships loading or unloading according to the cargo – one shilling per chaldron of coals, one penny per ton of chalk for lime burning, one shilling per last of corn. Under the Act they could raise money by issuing interest-bearing mortgages secured on the proceeds of the dues and so they could at once get in money and go ahead without delay.

By the autumn of 1751 £2000 had been subscribed and towards this the Corporation of Southwold had managed to raise only £100, although an additional £210 came from individual Southwold merchants. More than half the money came from the three big landowners in the neighbourhood – Sir John Rous, the invalid Sir Charles Blois and the newly arrived and affluent Miles Barne of Sotterley. Admiral Edward Vernon, Member of Parliament for Ipswich and a strong supporter of the harbour scheme, subscribed £150 and the remaining money came in small sums mainly from a few local landowners like Alexander Bence of Thorington Hall, Charles Scrivener of Sibton and Reginald Rabett of Bramfield. No doubt the five per cent originally offered on the mortgages must have made the investment attractive at a time when there were few outlets for rural savings.[4]

Southwold Corporation themselves had taken the initiative over the new harbour project and in 1745 they had instructed their Clerk, Peter Pullyn, to press forward with the business of procuring the Act and voted him £50 towards the expenses.[5] But when the following year the list of Commissioners was printed in the Act, Southwold town was swamped by the landed interest. Only the two bailiffs of Southwold were to be Commissioners and the other twenty were all drawn from the gentry. From amongst these local landowners there were always some who were ready to take their responsibilities seriously. Over the years a few gentlemen were usually prepared, some of them with impressive regularity, to ride or drive to the Swan at Southwold for the Harbour Commission meetings; to go down to the harbour to view the havoc wrought by winter storms; above all to keep a watchful eye on the haven finances and when there was convincing need to put their hands in their pockets again.

Much more, however, was needed than this, and it is very clear that from the start these baronets and esquires were absolutely dependent on the skill and commitment of the local merchants who were prepared to come forward to organize and superintend the endless work involved in propping up the fragile harbour structures. These men needed the harbour and they came forward not as paid officials but in accordance with the accepted eighteenth-century idea of self-help. Civil engineers were called in and departed with their fees but it was the local merchants who shouldered the main responsibilities till the end of the century.

In the early days the Commissioners relied chiefly on William Lenney, a merchant of Reydon, the village whose boundaries embraced so much of Southwold and stretched along the north bank of the Blyth. Like other east coast port authorities faced with the same problems, the Southwold Commissioners decided to stabilize the harbour by using piers to deflect the sand-carrying waves and concentrate the internal scour in a narrow channel. It was Lenney who supervised the securing, strengthening and extending of the old existing pier on the north and it was he who, in 1751, was asked to watch over the work of John Reynolds, the Civil Engineer, who erected the new south pier.[6] Lenney was a man who dealt in timber and understood it, and timber was the vital material on which the harbour piers depended; none the less his prominence at this time must have been a sharp reminder to the Southwold merchants that the harbour was no longer a perquisite of the town. Lenney's granaries and timber yard were at the new upstart quay at Reydon, a mile up river from the recognized harbour quay at Blackshore. At Reydon quay Lenney, supported by his new landlord, Miles Barne, was as we shall see (pp.61–2) upstaging the Southwold quay – a state of affairs which was bitterly resented in the town.

William Lenney, however, died in 1753 and from that time on Southwold merchants took his place in the front line. The urgent need for their services was recognized by the Commission when they elected Samuel Nunn a Commissioner in October 1751 and followed this by electing John May in 1754.[7] Both Nunn and May were substantial Southwold merchants who knew that the harbour was essential to their business and who were therefore prepared to care for it and give it their time and know-how. This indeed was a crisis time for the haven since already the new structures were in serious trouble and both the reconstructed north pier and the recently built south pier had been weakened by strong winds and seas and by the ravages of sea worms who devoured the timber. Money was short and Miles Barne, the largest mortgage holder, was alienated. He had resigned from the Commission in 1752 and in 1754 refused to accept a proposal to reduce the interest on mortgages to four per cent.

From 1754 to 1757 Nunn and May, manfully assisted by Christopher Smear, the Curate of Southwold, and helped by a loan from Admiral Vernon, handled affairs as best they could and with a determination to save the harbour. The provisions of the 1746 Act on finance and administration were loose and undefined and in many ways during these years affairs at the harbour seem to have been handled much as they had been under the old Southwold regime and before the establishment of the Commission. At one point indeed a scheme was put forward for responsibility for the south pier to be farmed out to May who agreed to maintain it for twenty-one years in return for the sum of £1200 down.[8]

Miles Barne found this situation profoundly unsatisfactory and the action he took forms part of his story (pp.62–3). He clashed with the Southwold merchants and they were made to feel his authority and their need for his money. The clash finally brought home to the town their dependence on the landowners and eventually there was reconciliation. Barne got the financial and administrative reforms which he wanted incorporated in the second Harbour Act of 1757 and from then on was outstanding among the landowners in his attention to harbour affairs.[9] At the same time Southwold merchants continued the vital task of superintending the never-ending work to keep the harbour viable. The two sides learnt to respect each other and the further history of the harbour till the end of the eighteenth century is, generally speaking, one of mutual co-operation.

CHAPTER 3

The Launch of the Navigation

IN THE WINTER OF 1759 THE EQUIVALENT OF modern bulldozers descended on the River Blyth. Otters and herons were frightened from their haunts as forty or more men equipped with spades and iron-shod wheelbarrows were marshalled by James Colleson, the illiterate contractor, to make the Navigation. The river was turned by great dams and a horsemill was used to throw off water. Colleson had undertaken to dig new cuts and deepen and scour long stretches before midsummer. There were over five miles of river to be tackled above Blythburgh bridge; and in the meadows at Halesworth as well as new cuts there was to be a waste-gate to hold up a head for a reservoir – the new quay basin. While the navigators dug, carpenters and bricklayers were at work on bridges, sluices and locks. Two brick locks were made at Halesworth and at Wenhaston Mill; and wood faggots were used for the other three locks at Mells Chapel, Blyford and Bulcamp. The following autumn work began on widening the river below Blythburgh bridge and a new cut was made across Sir John Rous's marsh; while Blythburgh bridge which was reported to be in a very ruinous state was rebuilt and heightened to allow wherries to pass underneath. The current fashion for river improvement had hit the Blyth valley and on 1 April 1757 Royal Assent had been given to the Act to make the River Blyth navigable from Halesworth bridge into the Haven of Southwold.[1]

Optimistic enthusiasm and a degree of feverish excitement characterized the launching of the Blyth Navigation scheme. It was very different from the more sober harbour project. In the background was gathering national zeal for the construction of river navigations which would enable barges and wherries to carry grain from country villages and towns to wider markets and in return to bring back the cheap coal now increasingly needed for the furnaces of developing rural industries. Locally men in the Blyth valley could see the success of recent efforts to facilitate navigation on the Stour, the Lark and the Brandon rivers and close at hand on the River Waveney. The Blyth pioneers thrust the Brandon and Waveney Act on the House of Commons draftsman as a model for their proposed bill.[2]

The concept of the Blyth Navigation lit up imaginations and kindled hopes; and prominent amongst the most hopeful was the leading spirit in the enterprise, Thomas Knights, a Halesworth brewer. Knights needed the Navigation. Undeterred by inadequate capital, he had been building up a brewer's empire in Halesworth based on

A jolly party at the skeleton remnants of Bulcamp Lock.

The remains of the first lock – Halesworth Lock – built with brick.

mortgages and optimism and by 1750 he was in serious financial trouble (p.84). He had land by the river and he saw the Navigation through rose-coloured spectacles as a waterway of lucrative trade which would solve his financial problems and bring new prosperity to Halesworth.

We do not know how long Knights may have been hatching his ideas but in May 1753 he noted in his pocket-book the names of sixteen gentlemen, landowners, 'who signed for making the river navigable'. Most of these gentlemen were hardly in the first rank but the list was headed by Sir John Rous who throughout lent his support to the scheme. In the same year Benjamin Reeve drew a plan of the river from Halesworth bridge to Blythburgh bridge, including for good measure the branch to Ubbeston, and on 4 May John Reynolds surveyed the river and submitted an estimate of £4614 for making it navigable from Blythburgh to Halesworth including three locks.[3]

One of the most enthusiastic and interested supporters of the Navigation scheme was the Reverend Robert Buxton, Vicar of Darsham and married to Rous's widowed mother. In November 1753 he wrote to Knights urging him not to delay with the promotion of the bill for the Navigation but despite this three years elapsed before Knights was actively in touch with the House of Commons Clerk. He and his supporters may well have been temporarily frightened off by the formidable amount of Reynold's estimate.[4]

In Halesworth town itself there was only limited support for Tom Knights' project. As we have seen, Halesworth at this time was a small inland market town and few of the craftsmen and shopkeepers who made their living there were roused to enthusiasm by the Navigation scheme. Halesworth, however, did also have a surprising number of professional men and it was amongst them that Knights found his allies in the town: Thomas Forster, the Rector; Dr Charles Hay who built up a flourishing practice both in Halesworth and among the County families and reputedly made 400 or 500 pounds a year from his patients;[5] Samuel Rye a wealthy surgeon; and several influential attorneys. Between them they managed to persuade a good number of shopkeepers and innkeepers to agree to subscribe a guinea or half a guinea towards the cost of the Act of Parliament, though James Jermyn, the attorney, was not sanguine about the money actually being handed in. 'Doubtless we shall fall short by some person being backward at paying though forward enough to subscribe their names' he wrote to Knights in London in 1757.[6]

When it came to more substantial support only a few Halesworth drapers and craftsmen were prepared to put their money in the Navigation, and it was fortunate for the project, which required a substantial amount of capital, that it appealed to the imagination of so many people farther afield. The harbour was financed by mortgaging the profits of the dues but the money for the Navigation was obtained by a flotation of shares. Shares were issued at five per cent annual interest and by June 1761 subscriptions had brought in £3587. Of this money, only £255 came from Halesworth tradesmen – an ironmonger, a hatter, a plumber and glazier, a glover and a grocer and draper. Like the Harbour Commissioners Knights had to look to the country gentlemen for money and a large number were caught up by the enthusiasm. Most of the harbour investors had obvious connections with the Blyth estuary but for the Navigation money came in from a wide scattering of places ranging from Mendham and Cookley to the west, Brampton to the north and Kelsale to the south. Gentlemen occupying the 'neat seats' at Yoxford contributed between them £500. Joshua Vanneck of Heveningham subscribed £300. Reputedly one of the richest merchants in Europe, he could no doubt afford a gamble – for a gamble it turned out to be and a very unprofitable one. No dividend was paid till 1769 and though the shareholders did better in the seventies there were only two payments in the eighties before payment ceased for about fifty years.[7]

Knights and his cronies hatched their scheme in their club. English eighteenth-century towns, and even small country places, were full of these clubs, congenial masculine gatherings in local public houses where the necessary 'steaming Bowl or foaming Tankard' would be constantly at hand. Knights' club must surely have met in the Angel tavern of which he was then the owner.[8]

Some of Tom Knights' friends were prepared to invest substantially in the Navigation. Thomas Forster, the Rector, Dr Charles Hay and the surgeon, Samuel Rye, all subscribed £100. Knights himself bought no shares and indeed he was in no position to do so as he was urgently in need of money at this time and with his property already heavily mortgaged he was searching for some means of raising a further loan (p.85).

Perhaps some talk of Thomas Knights' financial predicaments had reached the ears of the Reverend Robert Buxton at Darsham and perhaps the talk had been heavily embroidered. In February 1757 the calm of the club was shattered when a most alarming letter from Buxton was read out to the assembled company. Knights was not present for by this time he was already installed at the Bell Inn, Smithfield, and consulting with the House of Commons Clerk and with Sir Cordell Firebrace, the County Member, who was to sponsor the bill. Now Buxton alleged that Knights was 'endeavouring to get the Duties and Tolls of the River to be assigned . . . to him and his heirs only unless Dr Hay chooses to be joined with him'. Buxton, moreover, claimed 'undoubted authority' for his assertions which must have sent waves of panic through the club. Fortunately, however, the Rector was present and dealt admirably with the situation. He immediately penned a letter to Knights on behalf of the club requesting 'a steady . . . observance of every particular settled and agreed upon at our last meeting' and an assurance that the agreed trustees would be appointed and given the power to determine the duties and tolls. Forster was also careful to tell Knights that the Halesworth men were so fearful that they had also written direct to Firebrace repeating their instructions. Dr Charles Hay who had been most unpleasantly implicated in the rumours and had found himself pressed at the club for 'an explanation of what I am entirely ignorant of' wrote also, hoping it was all a mistake and asking Knights urgently to clear the matter up 'for the sake of your own reputation and mine'.[9]

Whether there was any truth at all in Buxton's rumours is a matter for conjecture but Thomas Forster handled the situation calmly and showed no desire to distrust Knights who at that time was his churchwarden. 'When the affair was first mentioned and all the time before you answered his letter no person could be more tender of a gentleman's character than Mr Forster was of yours' Knights' cousin, William Norford, wrote to him in London. Knights and Firebrace both wrote back promptly from London and effectively scotched the rumours. No one was more relieved than Dr Hay who hastened round the streets of Halesworth showing their letters to as many inhabitants as he could find.[10]

These very disagreeable personal accusations were not the only difficulties with which Knights had to contend. A serious hiccup over the bill was brought about by the vacillations of the Southwold Harbour Commissioners. Several of the local landed gentry who supported the Navigation, including Sir John Rous, were also Harbour Commissioners. A new bill for the harbour was being discussed at this time (p.63) and it was mutually agreed by Halesworth and Southwold to combine the two into one bill which the Halesworth men expected would lessen the expense. Arrangements for this went forward and on 8 February 1757 the House of Commons order read: 'That leave be given to bring in a Bill for making the River Blyth navigable from Halesworth Bridge, in the County of Suffolk, into the Haven of Southwold; and also for enlarging the Term and altering several Powers granted by an Act, made in the 20th Year of his present Majesty's Reign, for opening, cleansing, repairing and improving the Haven of Southwold.' Then at the last moment, early in March, there was a separation. The Halesworth bill received its first reading alone on 4 March and the Harbour bill had its first reading on 23 March.[11]

I have been unable to discover the reasons underlying the decision to separate the two bills. Knights in his diary noted only: 'Halesworth and Southwold joined in one petition but Southwold was opposed so Halesworth was obliged to get one separate'. A joint bill did not necessarily suppose a joint administration and this does not seem to have been proposed at the time; but the separation of the bills serves to underline the split between the two ends of the River Blyth – a split which led eventually to bitter disputes. No doubt there were always those among the Harbour Commissioners who would resist any proposal to saddle their Commission with the risky Navigation enterprise and as the financial problems of the Halesworth men became increasingly apparent they must have felt fully justified and would have had little sympathy with the proposition mooted at Halesworth in 1777 to amalgamate the two Commissions (p.28). The wherry trade was then but a small part of the total trade at Southwold and they could not have anticipated that the situation would change in later years and that eventually the merchants using the Navigation would be the main contributors to the harbour dues.

Knights and his supporters also had a continuous undercurrent of opposition to contend with. The *Ipswich Journal* in July 1761 congratulated 'those Gentlemen who actuated by a generous Zeal for the public Utility, dared embark in this Undertaking; nor feared to stem the Torrent of Malice, Prejudice, and Interest, to bring about so general a Benefit.' Samuel Nunn, merchant of Southwold, writing to Knights in December 1759, congratulated him that the work on the Navigation had begun 'to the shame of all its enemies which I believe are many from party spirit or from being afraid it should hurt them in their trade'. Nunn himself looked forward to seeing Halesworth wherries collecting coals from Blackshore Quay.[12]

In Halesworth itself, feeling was so strong that in 1764, three years after the Navigation was completed, the Commissioners were informed that 'some merchants had endeavoured to discourage trade upon the river and had refused to receive the farmers' corn in Halesworth'. They therefore drew up and signed a Resolution:

> *The sum of £4000 and upwards having been expended in making the River Blyth Navigable in order to promote the general benefit of the adjacent Country, it is with some Concern that the Commissioners have observed an unfriendly design of some Merchants to disappoint their reasonable Expectations by discouraging in some Measure the Trade which the convenient situation of that River justly Challenges. They have therefore this Day resolved at a publick Meeting to have no Commercial Dealings with any but those who shall for the future do all in their power to promote this laudable Undertaking In which Resolution they hope to be joined by all such Gentlemen, Farmers and others who either by property Residence or otherwise are Interested in carrying on so useful a Navigation.*[13]

The new cut and the quay basin at Halesworth, flanked by the well-built second warehouse: c. 1913.

A Plan of the River Blyth, taken by Benjamin Reeve, 1753.

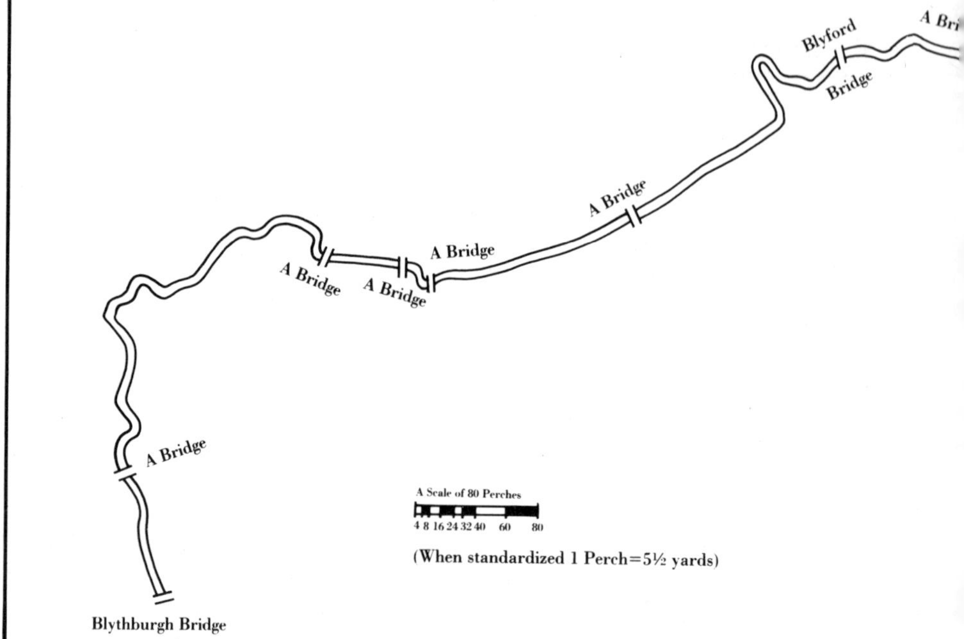

(When standardized 1 Perch=5½ yards)

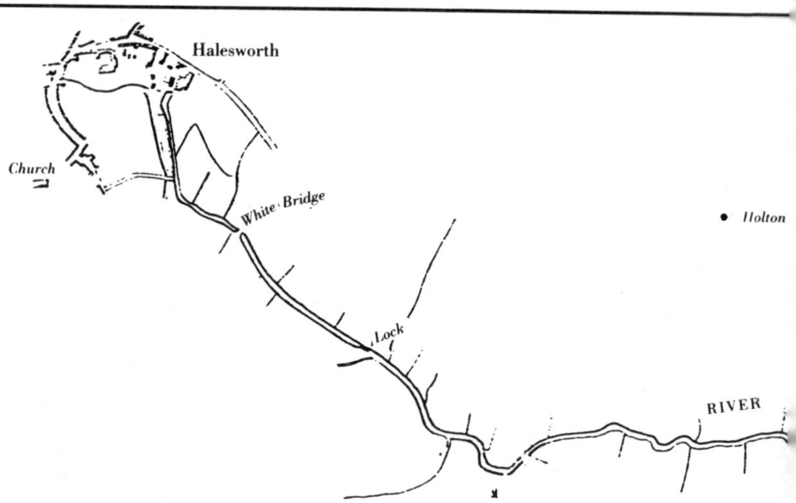

The River Blyth Navigation from Blyford Bridge to Halesworth, surveyed by A. T. Clarke in 1831. Four of the locks are shown but the lock (or tidal staunch) at Bulcamp was further down river. The map was included in the First Report of the Tidal Harbours Commission, 1845 (PP1845XVI).

The scale used is of One Nautic Mile or 2028 yards as under:

507 Yards 1014 Yards 1 Nautic Mile

The River Blyth from Blyford Bridge to Halesworth, surveyed by A. T. Clarke, 1831.

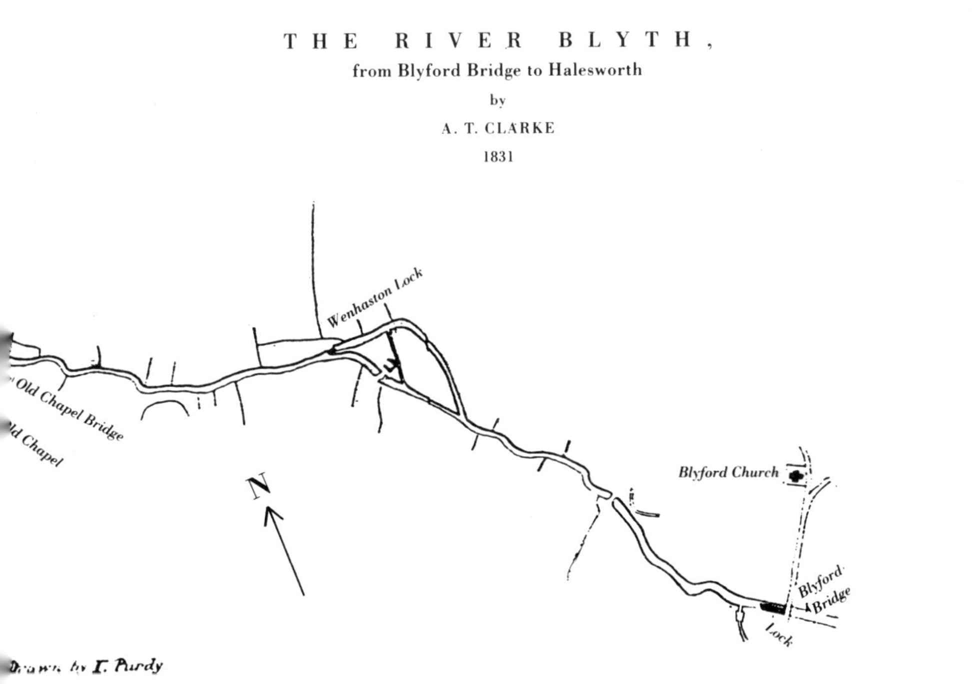

CHAPTER 4

Creating the Waterway: Frustrations and Delays

FOR THE TOWNSFOLK OF HALESWORTH THE NAVIGATION was an alien growth. Southwold harbour by contrast was part of the intrinsic inheritance of Southwold men. They had always had to care for it and under the new regime they continued to come forward, so that till the end of the eighteenth century there were always Southwold merchants prepared to watch over the harbour structures and to superintend construction and repairs. There were no comparable men in Halesworth to care for the Navigation works and the River Commissioners were obliged to depend heavily on the services of paid surveyors and supervisors.

In June 1757 at the first General Meeting, held at the Angel in Halesworth, Sir John Rous presided over an assembly which was dominated by clergymen, medical men and attorneys. Prominent among them was John Ingham of Yoxford, attorney and steward to the Lord of the Manor of Halesworth, William Plumer, who himself lived away in Hertfordshire. Ingham undertook to find a surveyor and at the meeting two months later he introduced Langley Edwards from Lynn in Norfolk, who had already carried out a survey and was prepared with a scheme to make the Navigation from Blythburgh bridge to Halesworth for a total sum of £3000.

On the strength of this estimate the Commissioners opened their subscription list for shares and by June 1759 £3100 had been promised. After an abortive attempt to obtain a cheaper estimate, the Commissioners wrote to Edwards in July and told him that the required money was subscribed and that they had agreed to rely on him. Probably in hopes of a reduced estimate they asked him to make a re-survey but although Edwards obliged, he arrived again at the sum of £3000. In the autumn of 1759 the Commissioners agreed to accept his plans and went ahead with advertising for contractors, arrangements for purchasing land and an application to the Justices for the rebuilding of Blythburgh bridge.[1] From the first Edwards saw that the water-mill at Wenhaston would be a major obstacle in the path of the Navigation but although he strongly advised the Commissioners to purchase the mill or at least obtain the tenancy they never succeeded in doing either, and in consequence until 1771, when the mill was converted to a breast-mill, which required less water from the river, they were deluged by complaints about delays to the wherries caused by the millers drawing off the water.[2]

John Ingham who acted for the Blois family as well as for Plumer was, as we shall see,

Wenhaston Mill in the 1920s.

a man who carried heavy responsibilities (p.101). He was a man of affairs who was not going to walk along the river and overlook the work as it went along. He and his fellow Commissioners seem to have expected altogether too much of Langley Edwards who having drawn up the plans was very reluctant to do much more despite the £100 he asked for superintending the works. He rode away to the north leaving an inadequate assistant, Mr Samuel Jones, in his place. In the summer of 1760 the Commissioners found 'great Defects in the Bridges' and after indignantly asking Jones why Edwards did not attend more closely to the works sent the surveyor an angry letter. Still Edwards did not appear at Halesworth and the Commissioners were reduced to calling in a stonemason from Norwich to examine the defective brickwork in the bridges. It was not until they had resolved to send their Clerk to fetch him that eventually in September Edwards turned up. He now presented his design for the new bridge at Blythburgh and plans for the work below Blythburgh bridge, but he soon rode away again to business near Lincoln which was absorbing his attention.[3]

That following winter the Commissioners were told that he had been hurt by a fall from his horse and could not make the journey to Halesworth. There was a breach in the lock near Wenhaston water-mill about which Samuel Jones could only say that it was a cause of great surprise to him; Blyford bridge was in danger of falling. At a meeting in February the frustrated Commissioners resolved not to pay out any money to the unfortunate Jones till his master should come and if this was of no effect to publish Edwards' ill-treatment of them to the world. Although Edwards did then put in a fleeting appearance he very soon made tracks for the north again and in May indignant heads were put together at the Angel and an advertisement drawn up for publication requiring his attendance. Fortunately for Edwards he arrived, full of excuses, in the middle of this meeting and in time to prevent the proclamation of his neglect of Halesworth in the *London Chronicle* and the *General Evening Post*.[4] It was not till July 1761, four years after the first General Meeting, that the first keel laden with coals came up from Southwold into the basin at Halesworth. The Commissioners greeted it with much self-congratulation and now set about fixing the rates of the all-important tolls for using the Navigation on which their hopes were pinned. Dues were charged according to the goods landed or cleared at Halesworth quay – one shilling for a chaldron of coals, one shilling for a last of corn; wherries loading or unloading at Blyford must pay the same but for Blythburgh only half dues were required. Even now, however, the work on the river was not quite completed, while the land for the quay had not even been purchased.[5]

By now the money had run out. By June 1761, £3587 had been subscribed and the Commissioners, aware that this would not be sufficient, had opened a second subscription roll to which it was proposed every shareholder should subscribe an additional ten per cent. Not unnaturally many shareholders did not receive this idea with enthusiasm and despite repeated letters from the Clerk a good number of them never did subscribe their ten per cent so that the total subscription only reached £3822.[6] To add to their financial problems the Commissioners realized that it was essential to have a warehouse on the quay and in December it was agreed that another subscription roll would have to be opened to raise the £130 needed to build it. Despite sending out two of their members to 'canvass the Town' they could only raise £80 until eventually Samuel Rye, the surgeon, came to the rescue, took over the project and produced the capital required including an extra £10 for a crane. In anticipation of this warehouse the Commissioners drew up a notice in June 1762 for their Clerk to place in the *Ipswich Chronicle* as soon as it was built:

> *The Navigation of the River Blyth being now compleated and a commodious warehouse erected upon the Quay, corn and all kind of goods belonging to merchants, tradesmen, farmers and others may safely be deposited therein for any convenient time upon very easy terms. At the same place all persons may be supplied with the very best coals, cinders, lime, Bricks, Holland Tiles, Deals, wainscot, etc.*[7]

The sight of this small warehouse or granary on the quay seems to have kindled hopes and enthusiasm, for about two years later around £330 was subscribed to build a second warehouse and land south-west of the quay was bought 'to promote an undertaking so useful and beneficial to the publick'. This two-storeyed building of tarred weather-boarding, with massive oak beams, was so well built that it was removed in the 1970s and re-erected at Spexhall as a very attractive house.[8]

Despite their penurious condition the Commissioners agreed in September 1761 to appoint Samuel Jones as Collector of Tolls and manager of all the works at an annual salary of £45. The appointment highlights their dependence on paid professional help and it is noticeable that at this time Jones was also working on repairs to the pier and jetty at Southwold but that there he was working under the supervision of a Southwold merchant, John May, and that May signed his bills each week.[9] The appointment of Jones and the amount of his salary were symptomatic of the unrealistic optimism of the Navigation Commissioners who seem to have been expecting remarkable profits from the dues. By 1765, however, they had appreciated that they could not afford Jones and they appointed William Bickers, a labourer from Wenhaston, in his place, at a salary of £21 a year. Bickers was no surveyor and in 1776 and again in 1784 it was John Robinson, the Southwold timber merchant, who compiled for the Commission a list of the works needed to be done to keep the wherries sailing.[10]

For despite what can only be described as a catalogue of disappointments and financial difficulties, the wherries were sailing and goods were being landed and cleared at Halesworth staithe. Moreover, as we shall see, by the end of the eighteenth century the existence of the Navigation had materially affected the way of life in Halesworth. It was the transport for heavy goods provided by this penurious waterway which helped the town to change direction and move with the times (p.91).

Wenhaston Mill lock, early twentieth century. It was blown up in the Second World War to frustrate an invading enemy!

CHAPTER 5

The Commissioners at Work: Theory and Practice

THE NOMINAL ROLLS OF THE COMMISSIONERS for both the harbour and the Navigation were impressively long but totally unreal. In both cases the number of men who appeared at meetings was comparatively small and amongst these there were only a few who were prepared to attend actively to affairs. These few did, however, show a dogged determination to carry through the tasks initiated by the Acts of 1746 and 1757. Both sets of Commissioners were helped by the generally thriving condition of agriculture and by the growth of the East Anglian coastal trade, but for neither of them was the road easy.

The gentlemen who met at the sign of the Angel in Halesworth were always short of money. Until the end of the eighteenth century tolls on the river brought in on average less than £140 a year (Table 1). Yet somehow they had to keep the quay, the vulnerable brick and wooden bridges and the five locks with their wooden gates and posts in reasonable repair. They were also burdened with an impossible financial obligation to pay £190 a year to shareholders from whom £3822 had been raised at five per cent interest.[1] By 1777 it was clear that the financial situation was totally unrealistic and there was a move to relieve the situation by amalgamating with the Harbour Commission. In July of that year Sir Gerard Vanneck of Heveningham, Member of Parliament for Dunwich, was present at the Navigation meeting and it was agreed to try to obtain an Act of Parliament to incorporate the two sets of Commissioners and unite the funds. In hopes of persuading the Harbour Commissioners, the Halesworth men proposed that the Navigation shareholders should forgo all interest already due to them and also accept four per cent from now on; and as a further concession it was suggested that the Harbour dues on goods to be brought up the river should be at the same or higher rate, while for goods not brought up the river the dues should be reduced.[2]

The Navigation Commissioners got no further with these ideas than this hopeful proposal in their Minute Book. For a time they struggled on with payment of some back interest but in the mid eighties they eventually abandoned their obligations to shareholders. Already by this time the country gentlemen, disillusioned with the Navigation as a financial speculation and having no other obvious interest in it, were drifting away. Sir John Rous of Henham had always been a supporter and throughout his life he regularly attended meetings, but after his death in 1771 his son put in only one solitary appearance. Sir Gerard Vanneck did not continue to present himself and after

The Swan, Southwold, where the meetings of the Harbour Commissioners took place, as it looked in 1890.

The Angel, Halesworth, where the Navigation Commissioners met: a postcard of the 1930s. (The building on the right has long been demolished.)

1777 there were other defections. In consequence the Navigation Commissioners became little more than a Halesworth club. It was a club of those few men, mainly merchants and interested tradesmen, who were prepared to take an active interest in Navigation affairs and they depended heavily on the Halesworth attorney, Peter Jermyn, treasurer for over forty years, and who in the nineties often found himself taking the chair. There was, however, some support from the Church, particularly from the Reverend Isaac Avarne who was inducted as Rector of Halesworth in 1786 and who regularly attended the Angel meetings from the turn of the century. Halesworth was fortunate in its Rectors, who were also Lords of the small Manor of Halesworth Rectory. Avarne, a man of integrity, with a warm heart,[3] was prepared to shoulder responsibilities and give some of the leadership which might perhaps have been hoped for from the Lord of Halesworth Manor, the absentee William Plumer.

The company at the Southwold Swan was always more exalted. Miles Barne of Sotterley kept a careful watch on harbour affairs till his death in 1780. Subsequently his place was taken by the younger Sir John Rous (later Lord Rous and then Lord Stradbroke). Rous was well supported by Sir Thomas Gooch and they would usually find others of the 'quality' at the Southwold meetings – George Golding of Thorington Hall, Thomas Sheriffe of Uggeshall and in later years Sir Charles Blois and Barne Barne. Several private acts were passed renewing and amending the powers and duties of the Harbour Commissioners and appointing the Commissioners by name. The list of names in the Act of 1789 was impressive, containing, apart from the knights of the shire, four baronets, ten esquires, four clerks and only four plain commoners.[4]

With this support the Harbour Commissioners had much less cause for anxiety over finance than had their counterparts in Halesworth, always provided that physical conditions were reasonable. Too often at Southwold, they were not. In January 1779 the fierce winds and strong seas badly damaged the Haven House and the north pier gave way completely. Over £1800 had to be raised by a further subscription on mortgage of the dues.[5] In October, ten years later, on the Suffolk and Norfolk coasts:

> *One of the most violent squalls of wind from the North East came on that had ever been remembered . . . the whole coast exhibited a scene the most awful and distressing. Ships dismasted at anchor; others scudding before the wind without any canvas to set; and wrecks of ships that had been lost on the sands, floating in every direction. Between Southwold and Yarmouth, a space of only 25 miles, 40 ships were ashore.*[6]

Southwold harbour seems to have weathered these storms fairly well but it did not weather the stormy winter of 1795–6 and the winds which sent the Town Mill crashing to the ground. At the harbour the piles of the piers were 'mash'd by the high Tides' and the people assembled on the beaches night and day to try to salvage them.[7]

Generally over the years the takings of both the river and the harbour collectors reflected the overall national economic pattern. Both did well in the 1770s and both felt the decline of trade which resulted from the American War of Independence. Dues collected at Halesworth from 1780 to 1785 were only sixty per cent of those collected for the previous five years, and similarly the harbour dues were only seventy per cent. The long French wars of 1793–1815 had the opposite effect. National restrictions on imports brought a national demand for agricultural products, especially for corn, and in consequence enormous, though fluctuating, price rises.[8] Increased numbers of black-sailed wherries passed up and down the river and an increased number of ships fought their way in and out of Southwold harbour as merchants and farmers hastened to supply clamouring markets and make the large profits which now seemed to be within their grasp. On the river, tolls reached a peak of £1145 for the first five years of the nineteenth century and the harbour tolls for these years totalled £3929 (Table 1). Subsequently the income of both Commissions began to fall, but while the river takings continued to decline till 1820, the Harbour Commissioners in 1814 increased the rates on corn and coal by no less than fifty per cent and benefited accordingly.[9]

From the last decade of the eighteenth century there was increasing discontent over the conditions at Southwold harbour and the impediments to shipping caused both by the bar at the mouth and by the shoaling within. No doubt the increased number of ships plying in and out focused attention on the harbour, but the fact remains that between 1805 and 1818 it had to be dug out thirteen times.[10] This was also a time when the harbour administration was faltering as social upheavals in Southwold town brought irresponsible men into office. In 1799 the Commissioners for the first time appointed a professional engineer to supervise the harbour structures but after he left, in 1813, and until the welcome advent of the second Earl of Stradbroke in 1828, the Commission seems to have been half-paralysed by the problems and by the expensive remedies proposed (pp.97–8). Perhaps they did not care too much since the harbour income continued to rise, swollen by the heavy increases in dues they had imposed in 1814.

Admittedly the substantial income produced by these dues relieved the situation. It enabled the Commissioners to finance needed repairs and also to safeguard the annual mortgage interest due to themselves and their friends but it did so at the expense of merchants and shipowners. It was a serious blow to merchants using the Navigation, and by now their contribution to the harbour dues was not small. Although the corn floated down from Halesworth from 1810 to 1819 formed a very small proportion (only sixteen per cent) of the total corn shipped from Southwold harbour, the coal which was destined for the Halesworth wherries made up nearly half (forty-three per cent) of the total coal shipped in (see Table 2). There was, however, little sympathy between the two sets of Commissioners. After the death of the elder Sir John Rous in 1771 there was no one of stature to provide a liaison between them and, as we have seen, the landed gentry who dominated the Harbour Commission lost all interest in the Navigation. As the easy-going mid-eighteenth-century attitude to status gave way to increased snobbery the gulf in social class between the two bodies became more marked. The arrogance of the landed classes stiffened in the nineteenth century and the Harbour Commissioners were even less disposed to bother about Halesworth merchants. Yet the future of the harbour trade, and of the dues that trade brought in, lay with Halesworth. In the decade of the 1830s the Halesworth trade was nearly double all the trade using Southwold and Reydon quays. By that date, however, lack of liaison was developing into bitter enmity.

This briefly is the backcloth to the lives of the individual landowners, lawyers and merchants living in the Blyth valley, whose stories I have tried to tell in later pages. They are stories which I hope will illustrate in many cases the self-help and the drive, often in the face of formidable obstacles and hazards, which was so marked in the reign of George III, and not least in east Suffolk.

THE LANDOWNERS

CHAPTER 6

Rous of Henham: Portrait of a Landowner

ON SATURDAY, 8 MAY 1773, HENHAM HALL WAS burnt to the ground. Young Sir John Rous, approaching his twenty-third birthday, had only recently stepped into his father's shoes and he was away in Italy when the fire consumed the roof and the forty-eight rooms in the old house, leaving only a burnt-out shell formed by the great exterior walls which had been strong enough to resist the flames. The fire lit up imaginations in the Blyth valley and it was garrulously reported round Henham that Rous had been in Rome at the time and had committed some grievous fault against the Roman Catholic religion, as a consequence of which the Pope had ordered him to pay a fine of £30000 and to send home immediate directions to have his house destroyed by fire.

'Nothing is too absurd to be credited by the common people' wrote David Elisha Davy many years later, dismissing this fantastic rumour. But at least the gossip seems to have been right about the sum of £30000. It was generally accepted, and was reported in the Gentlemen's Magazine, that the house was not insured and that the loss amounted to this sum.[1]

Rous thus entered into his inheritance suffering from financial shock. He was, however, a young man of character who did not shy away from the unpleasant picture of his finances presented in the careful accounts which he kept. He faced the facts realistically, unpalatable as they often were, and unlike some of his contemporaries did not try to improve his position by heavy gambling, keeping his bets and cards under control. Combining the life of a bachelor-about-town – Boodles, the Jockey Club, Ranelagh, the Cocoa Tree, and much tennis – with sports and duties in east Suffolk, Rous and his agents, Richard and John Dresser, were hard put to it to manage on an income of under £5000 a year and Rous was usually in debt to the Dressers and to Peter Jermyn, his manorial steward.[2]

His first necessity was a country house. The obvious place was Darsham Hall which, however, had been occupied for about twenty years by the Reverend Robert Buxton subsequent to his marriage with Sir John's widowed grandmother, Dame Lydia, who had now been dead four years. Rous maintained that Buxton had repeatedly offered the house to him but Buxton in a letter written at the beginning of November 1773 protested that he and his present wife were shattered at the idea of moving and had 'not the prospect of even a cottage to hide our heads in . . . we cannot turn out at a moment's warning . . . we

The Old Hall, Henham. This illustration from Suckling's History and Antiquities *was copied from an early drawing but the artist has added her own contemporary figures.*

must provide ourselves with some place to receive ourselves and our furniture and that may take some time'. Rous replied indignantly but Buxton continued to protest that he could find no other house and capped his letter with an invitation for Christmas. Rous declined this invitation, 'doubting the sincerity of the intention for however strongly it may be professed I never give credit where I have been once deceived'.[3]

Rous was a forceful young man who expected and intended to get his own way and by March the following year he was established at Darsham Hall. Here his household, which included a butler and footman, comprised ten men and four maids which, including their expensive liveries, he reckoned cost him £493 a year. This, however, was not much more than half his outgoings to a Mrs. Digby who presumably ran his London establishment.[4]

At Henham the melancholy work of clearing up after the fire proceeded slowly as Thomas Wright, carpenter and reliable odd-job man, packed up the pewter and brass and took some surviving chairs and tables to Reydon quay for despatch to London. In March 1774 Wright sent in an account for several days spent salvaging among the ruins 'and sorthing the ould Iron that is Gathered together'. He also went to Southwold harbour to fetch the monument commemorating Rous's father which was put in Wangford Church, concluding his account as always with 'lowance for beer'. A year later Wright heaved out the Henham brewing copper and at the end of the following year he was rescuing the lead and lead pipes from the old walls.[5]

Some of the rescued stores, household goods and bricks were carried from Henham to Darsham and here Thomas Wright and the bricklayers were engaged on the more cheerful task of improving the stables and also building an imposing and capacious dog kennel to house spaniels and pointers. Rous's list of male servants included a 'dog feeder' who looked after his dogs and pups and a liveried keeper, Lionel Cottingham, who trained spaniels for him while despatching from the estate marauding dogs, house cats, 'martin and poll cats', stoats, hawks and owls. Rous was a great enthusiast for country sports but in these impecunious years he was not able to indulge his love of horses and racing to the extent that he was later able to do.[6]

Richard and John Dresser, Sir John's agents, paid all his country bills but despite his London activities Rous must have backed them in the two main improvements on which they embarked at this time: the Henham Park plantations of Scotch firs and oaks which stretched along the Beccles, Blythburgh and Southwold roads; and the river embankments and land drainage.

This latter work had started in 1747 under Sir John's father when a sluice was made at Wolsey Bridge in order to control the River Wang and reclaim the land on either side. A generation later Thomas Wright, carpenter, and Thomas Roe, bricklayer, were at work improving this sluice and subsequently walls were raised to protect the reclaimed marsh. In the mid seventies oak timber and slabs were sent to Bulcamp for a dam and sluice and there was marsh walling here also. A few years later, following purchase of land which increased his holdings at Bulcamp, Rous carried through the embankment of the Bulcamp marshes flanking both sides of the road from Blythburgh bridge to Henham. The undertaking was expensive. To buy the land he borrowed £500 from Dresser and found £110 from his own winnings at betting and cards but he then had to find £500 for marsh walling which did not include sluices and gates. Anxiously working it all out he reckoned that his rents would now be improved by £67 a year.[7]

This year of 1780 was full of extra expenditure. It was the year when Rous determined to follow his father as one of the two Members of Parliament for Suffolk and he reckoned the election, although it was uncontested, cost him nearly £400. Financial problems did not fade away and in 1785 and again in 1787 he compiled a formidable list of debts which would have to be met sooner or later and which were in the region of £17000; he included in this £5000 apiece due to his two sisters out of the estate.[8]

Like other eighteenth-century bucks Rous liked poetry and occasionally adorned

Nollekens' bust of John Rous, first Lord Stradbroke.

spare pages in his account books with his own or other people's verses, such as 'Ab omni Parte beatus' written by one W. L. Kingsman in 1783:

> *To blowsing Bess the new made Hay*
> *For wantoness affords pretence . . .*
>
> *Scintilla's lips of glowing red*
> *and heaving Breasts provoke new fire*
> *With her I press a servants Bed*
> *and satiate every keen desire*[9]

Perhaps he was growing inclined towards marriage and certainly he needed a bride with some fortune to help his finances. In 1786 he was corresponding frequently with that remarkable social climber, Eleazar Davy of the Grove, Yoxford (p.109) and in January 1788 he married Davy's step-daughter, Frances Wilson, heiress of Edward Warter-Wilson of Bilboa in Ireland, who brought with her Irish rents of over £1500 a year, and a complicated lawsuit in addition.

Despite the expectations from Ireland Rous continued to bemoan his poverty in his letters to Davy that year and he was keenly aware of the comparatively poor return on landed property:

> *I should be glad to sell every acre I have at 26 [years' purchase] and the Timber paid for. I consider Land as certain loss when it is not situated as an object to look at or to sport upon: £100,000 in money will produce in these days £4,500 a year and the same sum laid out in 26 years purchase after paying Taxes and repairs will bring in about £3,400.*[10]

In December he wrote to Davy that he would like to retire with credit. Parliament was a trouble and expense:

> *The only object to a Gentleman is an English Peerage, which I never have taken, nor ever shall take up the servile means and implicit way of voting to obtain. Besides I have certainly not an Income to support it, and probably shall not have an Heir to succeed to it.*[11]

Perhaps these letters were slanted for the consumption of his step-father-in-law. His depressed attitude to politics was probably due to his unpopularity with some of his fellow Tories caused by his decision to support Pitt in his opposition to the American war, a decision which earned him the name of 'Sir John Weathercock'. However that may be he threw himself behind the Tories in the election of 1790, declaring himself a supporter of the Tory opposition to repeal of the Test and Corporation Acts which pressed so heavily on dissenters. This was a bitterly fought election. Sir Charles Bunbury, the second candidate, agreed with Rous in opposing repeal but there was a third candidate – Sir Gerard Vanneck of Heveningham Hall – who championed the dissenters' cause. Sir Gerard's wealth was legendary and he used it lavishly.

> *The Report in Town is that Sir Gerard gains ground, that is I suppose that he makes all the People drunk wherever he is and they promise till their senses return to them*

wrote Thomas Holt of Redgrave Hall to Eleazar Davy on 13 May 1790. Holt was canvassing energetically for Rous but he was also anxious about the health of Frances Rous who ten days before had produced a daughter. His anxiety was sadly justified for Frances Rous died late in June. At the end of that month Rous and Bunbury won the election. Rumour was rife:

> *Such is the malice of our Opponents that now they are beaten out of the field they are endeavouring to make Sir John's friends unhappy by spreading lies about, one of which is that Sir John's Child is dead and the physicians expect his dissolution daily. . . . I came home from Woodleys last night where I met Stone, a firm Friend of Sir John's who had just heard Sir John was no more.*

Thus wrote Thomas Holt in another anxious letter to Davy and begged him to write and contradict the rumours.[12] Davy was able to reassure him. Rous was alive and so was his baby daughter, Frances, who was now to live with her grandmother, Mrs Eleazar Davy at the Grove, Yoxford.

Sir John continued to correspond with Eleazar and in December the following year he was writing enthusiastically about his interest in Miss W. – Charlotte Whittaker; 'her fortune is a good £25,000'. There was a marriage market in London at this time which was frankly recognized as a means of bolstering up the finances of the landed gentry. Mr Vernon, Mrs W's solicitor, seems to have been helpful in providing important information and may also have provided the introduction. The election had been an expensive one and now Rous was not only embarking on the rebuilding of Henham Hall but was also in process of acquiring more land, particularly in Sotherton, Henham and Bulcamp, to consolidate his estate. This is not to suggest, however, that Rous was not very taken with Charlotte.

> *At least one thing I am sure of, that there is no other woman in England whose conversation pleases me so much, or of whom I have an higher opinion; her person is elegant and her manners such as must engage the notice of any man of any age.*[13]

In a further letter in January 1792 Rous explained his plans to Davy. He had told Mrs Whittaker he would settle his Suffolk estate on an eldest son subject to jointures of £1400 a year to his wife and his mother and £10000 for the younger children. £10000 had already been settled on Frances. 'If all Parties be alive it will leave a slender Income for an Eldest Son, but...my Mother must be 84 before my son can come of age.' Charlotte would bring £18000 and some further expectations. He had written to hasten the journey to London of Peter Jermyn, his Halesworth attorney, 'as nothing can be done till he furnishes materials'. In February Rous took 'a charming house in Cumberland Place' for the season and that same month he and Charlotte were married.[14]

Cushioned by his wife's money and the Irish rents Rous was able to survey the financial return of his Suffolk estates with more equanimity. He had, however, as yet, no reason to anticipate the dramatic improvement to his income which these same Suffolk acres brought about in the next twenty years. It was in the 1790s that the great rise in rents in England began, a rise which rescued many landed families from their long accumulated debts and the unwelcome prospect of selling land. As the French wars and poor harvests pushed up grain prices, farming profits went up and rents went up with them while the real wages of farm workers probably did not.[15]

In 1799 the gross rent roll of Rous's Suffolk estates amounted to something over £5500; by 1809 it was over £8000 and by 1819 was nearly £11500. About fifteen per cent of this money was needed each year for taxes and tenants' repairs but on the credit side there were substantial receipts from manorial fines and quit rents and from the sale of wood. Sir John also, in company with many contemporary landowners, expanded his home farm and here, like his tenants, he reaped the benefit of the high prices not only for his corn but also for beasts, sheep and pigs. It is not surprising that when in 1807 he bought a boat for his own use he called it *The Revival of Trade*![16]

Rous had no need to wait for the generous years before rebuilding Henham Hall.

Construction work on the new Hall and also on the Gothic-style home farm with its dovecote and dairy proceeded apace from the early nineties.[17] James Wyatt was the architect but Sir John made his own contributions, telling Eleazar Davy in December 1791 that he had 'caught Wyatt on Tuesday morning and staid four hours in his office having his Plans all altered to mine which he has agreed to'. Rous himself made the drawings of the changes he proposed. 'I am much flattered by Mr. Wyatt's thinking he cannot make them better nor alter one Chimney Door or window from what I have marked.'[18] Both he and Wyatt probably thought themselves fortunate that so little was left of the old out-of-date house but inevitably this meant that a formidable quantity of bricks was needed. Already, before his marriage to Charlotte Whittaker, Rous's workmen were making a new brick kiln at Blumfield near Frostenden; and it was here and at Henham Clamps that clay was dug and the bricks for the new Hall were burnt. Sir John was enthusiastically interested in this work and his accounts record several visits and five-shilling tips to the claymen and brickmakers.[19]

To Rous and his contemporaries the setting of their houses and the layout of the park and grounds seem to have been as important as the building itself. Fashion dictated planned landscaping combined with some seclusion from the outside world and 'improvement' and 'improvers' were a favourite topic of conversation at dining tables. Jane Austen's family at Mansfield Park amused themselves delightfully in discussing Mr Rushworth's eager if confused ideas for the grounds of his house at Sotherton, inspired by the improvements made by his friend Smith. 'Smith's place is the admiration of all the country; and it was a mere nothing before Repton took it in hand. I think I shall have Repton.'[20] Sir John Rous certainly had Repton who came to view the premises as early as December 1790 and spent three years drawing up the plans for landscaping with carefully planted trees, walks, lawns and follies.[21]

Rous was also enlarging his estate outside the park and grounds. Some of his increased income from rents came from these acquisitions as he continued to buy up scattered holdings in Bulcamp, Henham, Sotherton, Wangford and other neighbouring parishes. It was accepted economics among landowners at this time to buy land and to consolidate estates which like Rous's were too fragmented. In addition Rous evidently had his eye on the land which encompassed his grounds. He wanted to know that when he rode or shot over the surrounding acres he was in no way dependent on the courtesy of some smaller landowner. He did not always buy land – sometimes an exchange was agreed. In 1795 some Rous land in Bramfield was exchanged with the parishioners of Sibton whereby Rous obtained the 8-acre ploughed field on the Blythburgh–Beccles road, the 2-acre Shott marsh and the turnpike meadow on the Blythburgh road.[22]

Rous family: members mentioned in the book

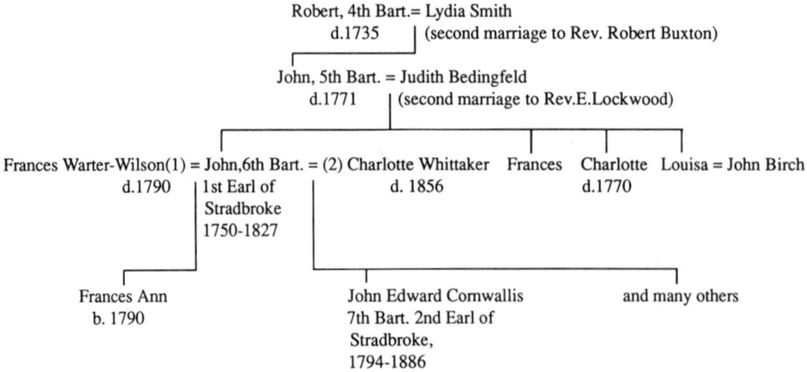

New Henham Hall, pulled down in 1953: engraving by Varrall from a sketch by T. Higham for Excursions through Suffolk, 1818.

CHAPTER 7

Rous and the River Blyth

THE COUNTRY ROUND HENHAM PARK WAS NOT ALL verdant pasture. The Bulcamp land which bounded Rous's estate on the south and which stretched along the river from Blyford to Wolsey Creek was mainly rough hilly ground, which fell down to river marshes, all of which up to Bulcamp lock were below the level of the spring tides. It was on these marshes especially that Sir John, his agent and his tenants focused so much energy, determined to change this habitat of salt-water plants – sea lavender, sea wormwood, sea aster – into grassland or even to make it fit for the plough.

As we have seen, despite his lack of ready cash, Sir John had already embanked some of the marsh directly below Henham park – on each side of the Blythburgh–Wangford road – and he had improved the banks and sluices at Wolsey Bridge. The work of building marsh walls and making new sluices and dikes continued unremittingly each year but the battle against the tidal river was not an easy one. Year after year there were breaches in the walls which had to be repaired; walls had to be raised higher, topped and sided; dikes had to be 'bottomfied'. Thomas Woods was in charge of this heavy work on the estate – work which seems to have reached a peak about 1806–1808. Woods' bills in 1807 exceeded £450. They included 6d. for manning Rous's new boat *The Revival of Trade* and taking Rous to the flats: no doubt Rous made this journey to survey Woods' efforts.[1]

Sir John's interest in the embankments spilled over into his account books at this time. He wrote himself notes on how to find the number of loads of earth in a marsh wall and how to calculate the square yards in a rod of marsh walling.[2] The cost of the embanking and draining must have been in his mind as he worked out these nasty arithmetical sums, but his rents were rising and he certainly hoped to recoup his money. More and more land was reclaimed – not all of it marsh. In 1794 Thomas Woods was 'levelling a hill fit for the Plough on Bulcamp Hills' and in the same year the hills by Southwold Road were newly ploughed for oats. Some reclaimed marsh was evidently put down for arable since in 1806 Thomas Freeman, the surveyor, submitted a bill for surveying the 'marsh that is plow'd at Bulcamp'. But the main value of the drained marshes lay in the summer grazing they provided, not only for sheep but also for Scotch beasts destined for Smithfield. Watering places were dug in the marshes; cartways and gangways were laid; and old walls were levelled.[3]

Rous found the lump sums to pay Woods and in some cases at least he charged his tenants interest on this expenditure. He also recovered his money by the rents he received, although these seem to have varied from year to year. In 1811 Samuel Crisp was paying £100 a year for new enclosed marshes at Bulcamp and in 1814, £150. In 1816 this rent was abated to £100 and in 1818 was £130.[4] Some of the enclosure, especially on the north-east side of Blythburgh bridge, could only have been marginally economic although the land was not returned to the flooding river till well into the twentieth century and even now the extensive green ribs of the old walls stand out.

Sir John Rous was not the only landowner to convert the lavish saltings and mud flats skirting the River Blyth into grassland. Towards the end of his life this conversion was held by some engineers to be responsible for the bar and the silting up which bedevilled Southwold harbour but there is no reason to think that this idea occurred to anyone when most of the work was done.

Rous's view of the river as it pursued its way through his estate was thus mainly in terms of the land to be rescued from its salty floods. He was quite uninterested in the Navigation up to Halesworth and in this he was very different from his father. The elder Sir John Rous headed the list of sixteen landowners who signed for making the river navigable in May 1753 and subsequently he headed the list of those who applied to Parliament for the Navigation Act; his subscription for shares (£220) was among the highest.[5] Rous's name and his support must have been of great value in lending credibility and respectability to the scheme. No doubt, lacking the financial means for expensive embankments himself, he saw the deepening and straightening by the River Commissioners as of substantial benefit. Moreover it was for landowners like himself that clauses were written into the Act of 1757 enabling owners and tenants of land within five miles of the river to carry straw, clay, marl and manure toll free; and safeguarding their rights to fish, shoot and sail their pleasure boats as they pleased.

The elder Sir John regularly attended the Navigation meetings at the Angel in Halesworth and was there in the summer of 1771, five months before his death. In contrast, his son, who was elected a River Commissioner in his place in June 1772, was only conspicuous by his absence from meetings and in 1785 he disgustedly wrote off the shares in the Navigation as a 'desperate debt'.[6]

Lack of interest in the Navigation was one thing; Southwold harbour with its quays at Blackshore, Walberswick and Reydon was a very different matter and the need to support it was probably appreciated even more by the younger Rous than by his father. A sophisticated man who spent much of his time in London, and who had absorbed the tastes of fashionable eighteenth-century society, he was constantly ordering goods from London shops and merchants – casks of wine, hampers of groceries, parcels of trees – and these all had to be somehow transported to Suffolk.

Up to a point Rous had some alternatives to shipping to Southwold. Certainly in the eighties when he was living at Darsham, the vessels of the Aldeburgh hoymen were entrusted to bring up hampers and kegs, tables and chairs; and in the following decade his baskets and parcels were frequently carried by road in William Frewer's Weekly Caravan, which left Aldgate on a Monday morning and after a stop in Ipswich reached Saxmundham on the Wednesday evening.[7]

But Frewer certainly could not have carried the twenty-four iron stoves which Captain David Carman brought to Southwold in 1796, together with plate glass and looking-glass for the windows and door panels of the new Hall at Henham. Freight of materials for the new Hall must have been of great financial benefit to Southwold masters and their crews as they sailed back from London with logs of mahogany, ironmongery and stone chimney ornaments.[8]

Rous also needed Southwold harbour for his coal supplies. He and his agent, John Dresser, watched the coal market and the competing merchants'prices very sharply since outgoings on coal were relatively heavy. By the mid nineties Rous's coal bills were exceeding £100 a year and by 1814 they totalled over £250 a year. Coal was needed not only for domestic burning but also for the blacksmith and the hothouse and, especially when the new Hall was being built, for the brick kilns. Over the years Rous and Dresser patronized coal merchants at a scattering of places from Westleton to Reydon and Halesworth to Southwold; sometimes they seem to have bought direct from ships. Some of the coal for Darsham was probably brought into Aldeburgh but for the most part, whoever might be the merchant, the coal for Henham was shipped into Southwold Haven and the collier brigs were unloaded at Walberswick or Blackshore or Reydon quays.[9]

But while Rous needed Southwold harbour as a port for provisions for his own mansion and farm, it was much more important to him in his capacity as a landowner whose tenants exported corn and farm produce and who certainly themselves needed coal as well as other heavy cargoes, particularly chalk and deals. His father had always recognized the key role of the harbour in the economics of the surrounding country and subscribed heavily towards the construction of the piers in the difficult early years. By 1758 he had a mortgage of £400 at four per cent.[10]

Sir John Rous the elder also faithfully attended the Harbour Commission meetings in Southwold but it was the businesslike Miles Barne of Sotterley who kept the sharpest eye on the harbour administration – working with the local merchants who were prepared to give a great deal of time and effort to the supervision of the constant repair work.

Barne died in 1780 and to a considerable extent the younger Rous took his place. His first serious attention to harbour affairs was in 1779, probably after he had made up his mind to stand for Parliament. In May that year he rode over to the Swan for the meeting. It had been a stormy winter and in January high tides and wind had damaged not only the piers but also the haven house. The gentlemen present were asked on the spot to subscribe for repairs and Miles Barne volunteered £250 and Sir Gerard Vanneck £100. Not to be outdone Rous volunteered £150. He was short of cash at the time but as he explained in his account book, he found the money from £310 he had won at betting and cards that year.[11]

As we have seen, after the turn of the century Rous no longer needed to turn out his pockets for cash. And as his wealth increased so too did his standing in society. In 1796 he became Baron Rous of Dennington and in 1821 Viscount Dunwich and Earl of Stradbroke. He moved in a much more prestigious social circle than his father had done and no doubt this was partly due to his enthusiasm for horses and racing. Horse-racing, and the Newmarket meetings in particular, were very much an aristocratic preserve.[12] Rous's horses were entered not only at Newmarket but at meetings all over the country – Lewes, Winchester, Salisbury. His long list of servants included two jockeys, and horses were bred and trained on his land.[13] This great interest in horses combined easily enough with his continued interest in his estate and in his home farm so that although, like his contemporaries, he always had a London house, he seems to have spent a considerable portion of his year in Suffolk. None the less it is probably true that he was to some extent distanced from local affairs in a way that his father had not been and this distancing cannot have been helped by the increasing deference shown to the local grandees at this time of growing class-consciousness and snobbery.

Judging by his attendance at meetings and his readiness to subscribe when required, Rous's attention to the affairs of the harbour is impressive. He did not confine his attendance to Annual General Meetings. In 1807 he was present as early as February and also attended in June, July and August to take part in earnest but not very fruitful discussions on how best to deal with the severe shoaling. In 1808 and 1809 he seems, in conjunction with the Clerk, to have been mainly responsible for drafting the new Act.[14]

Deference accorded Rous the Chair at the harbour meetings but while he was ready to attend meetings and to spend ten shillings on conviviality and dinner – as La Rochefoucauld observed: 'it is always at table that the English do business'[15] – he was not prepared to take a sharp look at the Commission's affairs or seriously to involve himself in problems that needed tackling.

There was an upheaval in Southwold town politics in the war years as new men, led by the arrogant Robert May, salt merchant, thrust their way to the top and established a firm hold on the Corporation. May and his allies, of whom we shall hear more (p.95), succeeded also in dominating the lower echelon of the Harbour Commission. Infected by the lack of economic and social stability which characterized the war years and with their minds fixed on the tantalizing opportunities for quick money and for new social importance, these men were not prepared to undertake the burdensome duties of supervision at the harbour which had been carried for so long by the merchant generations before them, so that from 1799 to 1813 the Commission found it necessary to employ an expensive professional engineer, John Druery from Gorleston.[16]

Druery ceased working for the Commission after 1813 and the following year Robert May was declared bankrupt and left the district. The landed gentry on the Commission, so comfortably placed at this time and absorbed in a life made pleasant by new wealth, now allowed things to drift on. In 1812 and 1814 they discussed two reports on the harbour's problems drawn up by a London engineer, William Smith. In 1820 they had an expensive report from John Rennie, C.E. But according to the revealing *Handbook to the Port and Shipping of Southwold* published in 1842 under the name of James Maggs, they 'allowed the report of Mr Rennie to be laid on the same shelf with that of Mr Smith'. For the first time no Southwold merchant came forward to supervise the repair work at the harbour and this task seems to have been left mainly in the hands of the Treasurer, James Jermyn, with some assistance from Walberswick men.[17]

James Jermyn was a thwarted academic, a wily manipulator and a clever barrackroom lawyer. He had a personal vendetta against the Customs officers and it is typical of his casuistic talents that in 1805 he persuaded Lord Rous and the other gentlemen on the Harbour Commission to sign a petition in favour of a fraudulent Coal Meter who was defying the Southwold Collector.[18] Jermyn held on to the Treasurership of the Harbour Commission until 1828. Especially in his last years expenditure increased heavily but with little benefit to the harbour, and given his persuasive abilities and the inertia of the Commission this is perhaps not surprising. It was not till the second Lord Stradbroke succeeded his father on the Commission that the badly needed leadership was given, reforms were put in hand and, as Maggs wrote, 'a new impulse was given to improvements' (p.115).

'Quiz', Lord Stradbroke's horse which won seventeen races including the 1801 St Leger. Portrait by Henry Bernard Chalon.

CHAPTER 8

Cockfield Hall, a Distracted Estate

THE LEADING LANDOWNERS TO THE SOUTH OF THE RIVER were in some disarray in the second half of the eighteenth century and in no position to devote much attention or money to the river and its marshes. As almost invariably happens at some point in the history of long-established families, the Blois family had struck a weak patch.

The family had their roots in Suffolk. In the sixteenth century four generations had traded as merchants in Ipswich, had been very successful, and had gradually built up for themselves an estate based on Grundisburgh. In the mid seventeenth century the head of the family, William Blois, abandoned trade and Ipswich and moved into the country gentry. A generation later the family acquired through marriage the estates of the Brookes in and around the Blyth valley: manors and land at Yoxford, Blythburgh, Walberswick and Westwood Lodge and in surrounding country places.

The Brooke estates were more lucrative and more prestigious than the Grundisburgh inheritance and Sir Charles Blois (created baronet in 1686) removed finally to Cockfield Hall at Yoxford towards the end of the century. It was following his death in 1738 that the difficult period for the Blois family began.[1]

When Sir Charles died he left as his heir his young grandson, Charles, who was then only seven years old and was severely afflicted with epilepsy. A long minority followed, troubled by family disagreements and much involvement with the Court of Chancery;[2] and the position was only exacerbated when in 1752 the invalid Charles reached the age of twenty-one.

Charles was incapacitated by his epilepsy and had to be pronounced a lunatic. His widowed mother, Jane Blois, was granted custody of her son and the estate was placed under the joint control of her brother, Sir John Kemp, and the Reverend Ralph Blois, Charles' youngest uncle. The result was nearly ten years of acrimonious divided rule. Jane, who under her marriage settlement had the benefit of a life interest in the extensive acres of the Westwood Lodge farm, lived at Cockfield Hall with her unfortunate son and his delicate sister, Mary. The Reverend Ralph lived at Kelsale Lodge and, since he was heir presumptive to his invalid nephew and also had at least a share in the control of the estate, he was generally regarded as *de facto* squire. Certainly he saw himself in that position and he seems to have adopted the expensive lifestyle necessary to sustain his prestige as a landowner. His frustrating position and his resentment towards Jane Blois,

Cockfield Hall, drawn and engraved by T. Higham for his Excursions through Suffolk, *1818.*

esconced in the family mansion of Cockfield Hall, must have been exacerbated when that remarkable fixer and shrewd operator Eleazar Davy moved in beside Jane as business adviser and close personal friend[3] (p.107).

Eventually in February 1760, Sir Charles Blois, the sad epileptic, died and at last Ralph was able to move into Cockfield Hall. But his inheritance came too late and even then was not satisfactorily complete since for most of the brief two years of his reign at Yoxford his sister-in-law, Jane, retained her life interest in part of the estate. When at last Jane died, in March 1762, Sir Ralph's health was failing. Leaving the business of the estate half completed, he was forced to set forth on a dreary, bone-shaking journey in the family coach to consult physicians in London. He never returned and he died on 8 May following.[4]

In his role as *de facto* squire the Reverend Ralph attended assiduously to local affairs in the Blyth valley. The incapacitated Sir Charles Blois was appointed a Harbour Commissioner under the first Harbour Act of 1746 and a Navigation Commissioner under the Navigation Act of 1757 but in both cases Ralph's name appeared as well. Ralph had a modest personal investment of £50 in the Navigation; he attended the inaugural meeting of Commissioners in June 1757 and occasionally attended meetings in the following years. He did what would be expected of the Blois family and he did not propose that they should be left out of a major local venture but he did not share the enthusiasm of Sir John Rous for the project.[5]

Ralph was, however, punctilious in his attendance at the Southwold harbour meetings despite the long drive from Kelsale Lodge; and he saw that his nephew's subscriptions to the harbour matched those of Sir John Rous so that in March 1758 each of these local landowners held mortgages for £400. It can only have added to Ralph's many frustrations that when Charles died these mortgages passed to his mother and sister and thence to Eleazar Davy, the sole heir of both. In consequence the Blois family remained with no financial investment in the harbour till the end of the century.[6]

The family, however, had other reasons for interest in the welfare of Southwold harbour. The Manor of Blythburgh with Walberswick which had come to them through marriage with the Brookes, carried entitlement both to 'wreck of the sea and groundage for all ships and goods cast on shore upon this Manor' and also to 'the Quay at Walberswick and Wharfage for all Goods Imported and Exported there'. By the eighteenth century the entitlement to wreck was probably of more value than the right to charge wharfage. The wharfage rents had to be collected in small sums from boat owners and the right must have been difficult to enforce. By 1762 the wharfage at Walberswick was being farmed out for £21 a year and ten years later Richard Burchett was paying £24 a year for wharfage rights combined with rent of the ferry. This rent was at least more substantial than the rent obtained for Blackshore quay which was farmed out by Southwold Corporation for about £10 a year till the end of the century. Clearly the rents of wharfage were not sources of great profit to their owners, nor can they be regarded as a guide to the amount of shipping using the quays.[7]

The real value of Walberswick quay to the Blois estate lay in the access for seaborne exports and imports which it provided for merchants and farmers in the neighbourhood, some of whom were Blois tenants. Certainly Walberswick was not full of ships in the first half of the eighteenth century so that the 1764 edition of Kirby's guide book could say: 'Walderswick, formerly a large place which traded considerably to Sea, but now is very mean'.[8] Yet even when this was written the situation was improving. Calver Wales, who owned land near the quay, had lime kilns and was supplying Sir John Blois with coal and lime in 1762. In 1755 Wales also sent shiploads of grain to London[9] but his mercantile activities were outclassed by those of Francis Robinson of Dunwich who was sending wheat and barley, cheeses, butter and other farm produce to London and to Rotterdam in the fifties and sixties and was also importing brandy and other strong drink. In the forties

Walberswick quay in 1903.

the administrators of the Blois estate had considered it worthwhile to acquire a warehouse on Walberswick quay and by 1759-60 Robinson was renting it from them. About the same time he took the tenancy of a Blois farm in Walberswick which no doubt had barns and sheds where he could store merchandise. We know that he also had a bin for storing coal on Walberswick quay and some of his coal must have been floated up in wherries to his coal bin on Halesworth quay[10] (p.84).

Two lanes converged in Walberswick and linked the little harbour town to the land behind and to the west. The northern lane gave access to Blythburgh and to the Ipswich – Yarmouth road. The lower one led directly to the great farm at Westwood Lodge from whence it struggled on to the hamlet of Hinton. Walberswick quay must always have been valuable to Westwood. Fifteenth-century household accounts record the despatch of large quantities of Westwood rabbits to London poulterers, but this scrap of evidence probably hides more than it reveals. Although the extensive acres of the Westwood estate included long stretches of sheep walks and warrens there was also good arable land and grazing for cows. Despite the fall-off in trade in the later seventeenth century, it seems probable that some Westwood produce – barley, corn, butter – was always shipped from Walberswick.[11]

It is not till the latter half of the eighteenth century that we have any direct evidence of ships leaving port laden with Westwood produce but there are indications that John Grimsby, the tenant in the mid eighteenth century, had trading interests. He did, for instance, as part of his tenancy agreement, supply Cockfield Hall with coal. Also, in contrast to his landlords, Grimsby was an active supporter of the Navigation. Not only did he invest £110, but also, unlike Francis Robinson, he served as a River Commissioner and was prepared to ride over to Halesworth regularly to discuss Navigation business.[12]

The natural and ancient link between Westwood Lodge and Walberswick did not extend to Cockfield Hall. The Blois family in the eighteenth and early nineteenth centuries did not find Walberswick quay a convenient journey from Yoxford and when they sent their chests and boxes by water carriage they generally preferred to use the port of Aldeburgh.[13] Aldeburgh, however, was of little use to farms near Blythburgh and Walberswick. For heavy loads of coal and agricultural grains, water transport had to be close at hand. As we shall see, Miles Barne, the go-ahead newcomer, was well aware of this as he battled to establish the rights of Reydon quay to the benefit of his tenants at Reydon and in the country behind (p.62). Miles also devoted time and attention to the recurring problems of Southwold harbour on which all the quays were dependent. A viable harbour at Southwold was as important to some of the Blois tenants as it was to tenants of other landowners in the Blyth valley. Unfortunately, for many years after Sir Ralph's death, the owner of Cockfield Hall was in no position to attend to harbour affairs.

The first half of the eighteenth century was not a prosperous time for landowners and the cumulative effect of the double households at Yoxford and Kelsale Lodge and the lack of co-ordinated management stretching back over many years was only too apparent in the inheritance which Sir Ralph passed on to his son John. A schedule of Ralph's debts and mortgages drawn up in January 1763 amounted to over £14000 and in addition there was a legacy of £5000 to be paid to John's sister Lucy.[14]

At the time of his father's death John Blois was in his early twenties and still at Emmanuel College, Cambridge. He was, however, contemplating marriage to Sarah Thornhill, whose sister, Mary, was married to Miles Barne of Sotterley (p.61). The Thornhill family was wealthy and Sarah would bring a very considerable fortune so that inevitably in face of the debts Sir John had inherited, the proposed marriage and the details of the marriage settlement which would be needed, were a matter of earnest debate. The Thornhills and the business-like Miles Barne would make every effort to safeguard Sarah's interests.

> *Sir John Blois came here the Friday after you went and stade till Sunday – the affair goes on, but nothing more settled than it was – we are to go tomorrow to Cockfield Hall and stay till Friday.*

wrote Mary Barne from Sotterley to her step-son, the younger Miles, at Cambridge in September 1762.[15]

The rents of Sir John's estates in 1762 amounted to around £2700 gross and about £1800 net. Sir John was considering selling off manors and land, mainly round Grundisburgh, to clear off all the debts. Miles Barne in contrast produced a scheme which involved very little selling of land but a severe retrenchment for four years and a new look at what he considered the very inadequate rent paid by the tenants of Westwood Lodge.[16]

The final decisions were left in the hands of Sir John and two trustees, Sarah's brother Thomas Thornhill and Francis Brooke of Ufford, a cousin of Sir John by marriage. Francis Brooke may have been brought in because his wife was a substantial creditor; her late father having lent Sir Ralph a considerable sum of money. Over the years, however, Francis came to take more and more responsibility for Sir John's affairs as financial problems mounted.

No doubt the Barne and Thornhill families hoped that John Blois would settle down to an unextravagant life in the country. The list of gaming debts which he produced in January 1763, amounting to over £7000, can hardly have lent them much encouragement and neither can the tailor's bill which he incurred, presumably in preparation for his wedding, and which included such items as a silver suit with twelve yards of rich silver ground flowered velvet (£49) and a suit embroidered in gold, with rich gold spangled embroidery (£36).[17]

But Sir John was young and perhaps he might have steadied down. He seems to have spent much of his time in Suffolk in 1763 and 1764 and to have played his part in local affairs. He attended meetings of the Harbour Commission in both years and in 1764 he was high sheriff. Very sadly, however, in May 1766 Sarah died, leaving him with a little daughter and a baby son, Charles; and in the years which followed the unhappy widower embarked on tours of France followed by more expensive ones in Italy so that his Yoxford attorney, John Ingham, found himself increasingly pursued by requests for cash (p.101).

The industrious Suffolk topographer, David Elisha Davy, is scathing about Sir John – 'very diminutive in person and equally so in mind' – and suggests that gaming debts were the source of most of his troubles.[18] David Elisha was brought up at Yoxford by his uncle Eleazar and was probably prejudiced by the enmity between Eleazar and Sir Ralph Blois, but whether or not there is truth in his stories about the gambling, it is certain that Sir John had little, if any, money sense. The remarkable fact about his long regime at Cockfield – he lived till 1810 – is that much of the estate survived.

The estate survived because Sir John followed the eighteenth-century cure for his malady, a cure which la Rochefoucauld described, observing that when embarrasssed by debts gentlemen set out with their wives in a carriage-and-pair and toured the counties till their economies had served to pay their creditors. François probably had Sir John in mind for his father was an old friend of 'Lady Blos'. He omitted to add that the estate was often also handed over to trustees empowered to use the rents to pay off debts while restricting the owner to a very limited allowance.

In 1772 Sir John married again. His bride was the seventeen-year-old Lucretia Ottley whose deceased father had been a West India Planter. In October of that year Sir John and Lucretia took this drastic course. The Grundisburgh estates were sold and Cockfield Hall and the rest of the estate were assigned to trustees of which Francis Brooke was one. Sir John and Lucretia set off to Dunkirk and thence to Switzerland.[19]

The trustees found a tenant for Cockfield Hall in Chaloner Arcedeckne, whose father had made a large fortune in Jamaica. Writing to a fellow-trustee, Osborne Fuller (who had married Sir Ralph's widow) expressed himself 'exceedingly rejoiced at Mr Archdeacon's arrival . . . Let Mr Archdeacon take a full View of Examination of the Hounds and Horses that They may not hang upon our Hands'. The hounds were sold for £52, the horses for £93 and the coach fetched £80.[20]

Chaloner Arcedeckne had the lease of Cockfield Hall till 1793 so that Lucretia was destined to have a wandering life with a variety of temporary residences. Perhaps we should not pity her on that account. Many a country gentleman's wife, confronting what could be a tedious and lonely existence, might have envied Lucretia. One of these bored victims sighed away her situation in the lines of a poem tucked among the Blois papers and possibly written to Sarah Blois, Sir John's first wife.

Fatigu'd, dear Sally, with these horrid shades,
These dull old walks and antiquated maids;
I've just this Moment wish'd them all good night
And half asleep, have set me down to write, . . .

The former scenes of pleasure I review
And waft my soul to Hill-street and to you.
Whene'er I see an Equipage pass by
I think of London, and bestow a sigh
Two months immur'd, how terrible and hard!
And three to come! O Lord! O Lord! O Lord![21]

If David Elisha Davy is to be believed, Sir John and Lucretia spent their first homeless years on the Continent. However, they were certainly in England by 1778 when they spent the autumn and winter in Bath where Lucretia managed to win £100 at cards. The following year they were in London and Ipswich and also stayed at Orwell Park. In the summer they were at Southampton, Tunbridge Wells and Brighton. In 1781 they took a house in Harley Street for three years and then from 1784 to 1791 they returned to Suffolk and resided at Melton. In the autumn of 1793 they returned to Cockfield Hall.

Lucretia did not share her husband's fecklessness and she bravely tackled her household finances. In October 1778 she opened an account book with a note on the first page, 'began housekeeping'; and from then on she wrestled with the expenses of their many journeys, rents of houses, bills for the clothes and education of her three children. In September 1793 she noted 'began at Cockfield'; and now her accounts start to reflect the usual bustle of country-house life: servants' wages (by 1803 they amounted to £195 a year, including the wages of gamekeeper and gardener); tradesmen's bills including the heavy outgoings on coal; receipts from the farm for sheep, wool and butter; profitable sales of timber.[22]

There must have been a further financial crisis about 1784 since trustees again took over the estate and ran it for about ten years. The central figure was now Francis Brooke of Ufford who supervised management of the estate and paid annuities to Sir John and Lucretia and also in later years to the heir, Charles Blois, the only son of Sir John's first marriage.[23]

Charles Blois celebrated his twenty-first birthday in 1787 and was then a Cornet in the Queen's Own Regiment of Dragoons. Two years later he married Clara Price, co-heiress of Jocelyn Price of Selby, Yorkshire. He followed an army career, commanded the Ouse Volunteers, and was twice wounded at the Battle of Waterloo, after which he left the army. Writing his frank and often highly critical memoirs, Henry Read, Charles' steward, described his employer as 'a good husband, an excellent father, a good Landlord and a good master'.[24] Fortune favoured Charles. The efforts of Francis Brooke followed by the great rise in agricultural prices and rents which took place during the French wars left him with a respectable inheritance. Sir John died in 1810 and Charles found in 1811 that the gross rent roll of the estate which he inherited was £4248.[25] A conscientious man who had a due regard to his public duties and great concern for his landed property, Charles' visits to London were limited and for the required change of scene and air he bought a house at nearby Southwold. Taking advantage of falling prices in the post-war years of agricultural depression he bought up land and farms. He acquired the Wales' estate in Walberswick, added to the Blois possessions in Blythburgh and bought up property at Hinton, and thus he consolidated his holdings on the south bank of the Blyth much as John Rous had consolidated his on the north side at an earlier period (p.38).

Blois family: members mentioned in the book

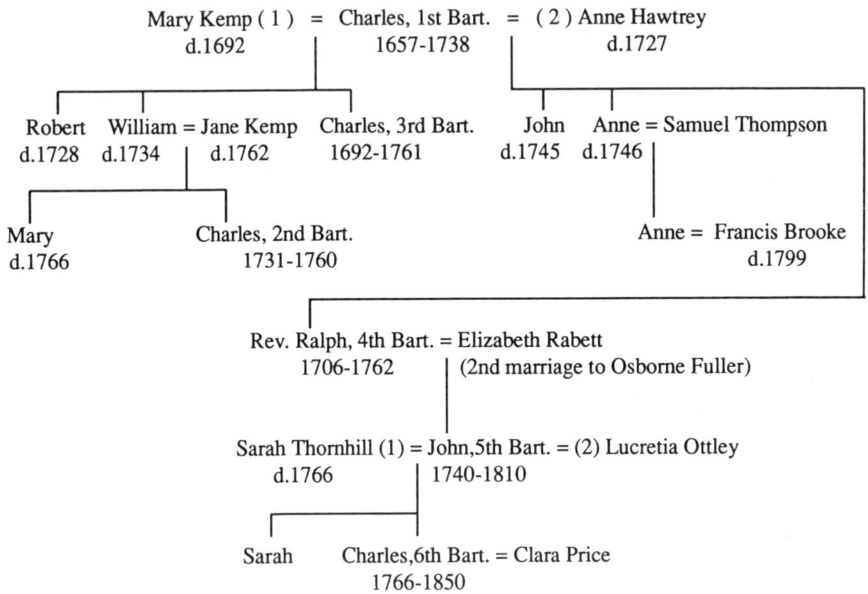

CHAPTER 9

Westwood Lodge

A shrewd observer in 1763 described Westwood Lodge farm as the cream of the Blois estate and about forty years later Arthur Young singled out this farm for praise – 'without exception the finest farm in the county'.[1] The Lodge and farm buildings stood amongst trees, two miles south-east of Blythburgh and two miles to the west of Walberswick, but the tenancy with its desirable mix of arable, heath and marsh had a spread of over 2500 acres in the eighteenth and early nineteenth centuries. For the most part the farm attracted very good tenants and there is no doubt that the rents which they paid played a principal part in the economic survival of the Blois estate.

The proximity of the River Blyth was a crucial factor in the success of Westwood Lodge and this was not only because its estuarial marshes were a component part of the farm's agricultural mix. Most important to the farm's well-being in the days before railways was the access to water transport and to the sea which the river and its mouth provided. Ships set sail from Southwold harbour and headed for the London market freighted with corn and farm produce, while other brigs and sloops arrived at the quays loaded with the coal, iron, chalk and foreign timber which were the raw materials needed for progressive farming.

Westwood Lodge was in many ways an estate within an estate – an independent entity complete in itself. Even to modern eyes and though stripped of its great farming acres, Westwood Lodge house is still redolent of past agricultural prosperity. Generously equipped with expansive yards and splendid barns – one timber-framed and a hundred feet in length, another brick-built with a crow-step gable – the Lodge stands astride high land and on the north looks towards the River Blyth. To the south and west it overlooks the marshes round the Dunwich river with a distant view of the sea. In the mid eighteenth century there were over 1500 acres of sheep walks on the sandy heaths and the Westwood Lodge lamb sales at the sign of the White Hart, Blythburgh, were always an important local event. But beside the heaths there were over 600 acres of enclosed and cultivated land where barley and turnips flourished on the sandy loam, enriched by loads of clay and manured by sheep folded on the arable. Contemporaries were somewhat vague about the total acreage of Westwood Lodge farm but there were over 2500 acres in 1769 and of these about 322 were marsh. Beside the River Blyth were Westwood Lodge marshes, the salt marshes opposite Reydon quay (now called Tinker's marshes). On the south

Westwood Lodge from the air showing the arable, heath and marsh in which the farm was set. Blythburgh is in the top left-hand corner, but the old lane from there to the farm has now been partly abandoned. The lane from Hinton to Walberswick passes in front of the house. (Private collection.)

side, bordering on Dingle, were fresh and salt marshes now called Westwood marshes.[2]

Jane Blois, mother of the invalid Charles, had been widowed in 1734 when Charles' father, William, died. Under her marriage settlement Jane had the benefit of a life interest in the Westwood Lodge estate; and when she died in 1762 her tenant, John Grimsby, was paying a rent of £400 a year together with a useful contribution to her housekeeping of six half firkins of the best butter. John Grimsby, who came from Leiston, was an educated, able man. He had taken the lease in 1752 for twenty-one years and he then set about improving the farm. He spread loads of clay on the sandy arable to the value of nearly £875; he bought cattle to graze the marshes; he built sheds; he made a seat in Blythburgh church.

When at last Jane died Sir Ralph Blois had already drawn up a draft agreement with John Grimsby. He had given it grave consideration and John Ingham, his attorney, noted that a whole day had been devoted to the final discussion between the landlord and his tenant. It is interesting to see that Ralph agreed to contribute £10 towards a parlour which Grimsby intended to make in the old Hall – farmers of Grimsby's calibre were no longer content to live only in their kitchens – but the main upshot was that the rent was fixed at £442 a year. Sir Ralph died before the agreement was engrossed but his heir promised to execute the lease and asked Ingham to erase his father's Christian name and substitute his own.

No doubt it was this moderate rent which Miles Barne had in mind when he proposed 'raising Walderswick' as part of his scheme for Sir John Blois's finances (p.49). The farm probably was undervalued and Sir John was roused to action by his friends. At his tenants' meeting on New Year's Day, 1763, he called Grimsby out of the company and told him he would not execute the lease unless Grimsby agreed to a rent of £600 a year. John Grimsby objected indignantly but Sir John pressed on and in April wrote to his tenant telling him either to quit the farm at Michaelmas 1764 or to agree to pay a rent now increased to £800. The affair escalated and Counsel were consulted by both sides. Finally landlord and tenant agreed to submit to the arbitration of Sir John Rous, George Golding of Thorington Hall and Eleazar Davy. These three duly held an inquiry at the Tuns in Yoxford as a result of which the rent was raised to £492 and the lease was reduced to seven years.[3]

There is a letter addressed to Sir John Blois among the Barne papers dated 2 October 1763. It is unsigned and was probably never sent but the writer was almost certainly Miles Barne and clearly he was writing with his tongue in his cheek to assist Sir John's case. He professed his willingness to buy Westwood Lodge farm; put its value at £20000; and put its acreage at the unlikely figure of 3460. Doubtless these were convenient exaggerations but behind them lay a shrewd appreciation of the farm. 'I should imagine that you would be advised to sell the Whole Estate together rather than part with the Cream from it.'[4]

In 1771 Nathaniel Howlett took the tenancy at a rent of £700 and when he died in 1790 he was followed by his son Robert. The Howletts farmed 2800 acres and enjoyed the benefits of that great rise in agricultural prices and farming profits which marked the last years of the eighteenth century and the early years of the nineteenth. As we have seen in the case of Lord Rous, the climb in prices was accompanied by a climb in rents, most welcome to landlords. I have not discovered how much rent was paid by Robert Howlett, but Thomas Taylor, the tenant who followed him in 1809, took a fourteen-year lease at a yearly rent of £2100 – three times the rent fixed in 1771 and almost half of the entire rent roll of the Blois estate.[5]

David Elisha Davy, from his intellectual heights, summed up Robert Howlett as a man who 'having been brought up as a farmer had very narrow views and through the whole of his life looked chiefly to the accumulation of wealth'. Sir John Rous, a practical man, found some words of approval for Nathaniel in 1785 when he scribbled in his old account book a song entitled 'Success to the Turnpike':

Little Blois! Little Blois!
Pray make no more noise
With your Wife go to Prayers, and get drunk with your son
The erecting of Gates
Will help your Estates
Ask Howlett! He has Sense and we think you have none.
Little Blois'[6]

Arthur Young, from yet another point of view, regarded the Howletts as leaders in agricultural improvements in a district where agriculture 'was carried on to great perfection' and as we have observed he singled out Westwood Lodge as the finest farm in the county. The Howletts obviously did very well by the farm but they also had the tenancy at a very fortunate time. Thomas Taylor took the lease at a time of agricultural bonanza but the good times did not last and he must have regretted his commitment to such a heavy rent. In 1818 Sir Charles Blois's agent complained of an incident when Taylor's conduct to Sir Charles was 'so unbecoming a tenant'.[7] Disgruntlement in face of the slump in prices which began towards the end of the French wars is not surprising. In 1816 Major Moor of Great Bealings described for the Board of Agriculture the situation as he then saw it:

> *As a magistrate for this county, heretofore so wealthy and happy, no day, scarcely no hour of any day passes, without some occurrence bringing before me some instance of agricultural distress. I see, however, your query is confined to the farmer . . . I could fill my sheet with a detail of their distresses.*[8]

In 1823 when Taylor's lease was up Sir Charles Blois was moved to give him a present of £500 'on his quitting the farm'. Taylor's rent must have played a large part in rebuilding the estate's finances.[9]

Taylor was followed by Rous John Cooper and his son James. James Cooper was an outstanding man who achieved fame in farming circles, particularly as a breeder of Down and half-bred Down and Leicester sheep and also as a cattle breeder for which he is named in the first volume of the Suffolk stud book. He weathered the difficult 1820s and 1830s mainly because he was a stock farmer on a considerable scale and was not like some of his unfortunate neighbours entirely dependent on corn and arable crops. In evidence to the Select Committee on Agricultural Distress, 1836, James maintained that farming was 'bordering on ruin' but admitted that he himself was getting by and able to find his rent which was then £970 yearly. The farm's acreage by this time had been much reduced but was still about 1630. With these expansive acres, a generous mixture of arable and pasture, James Cooper was thus able to weather the bad times better than many of his neighbours and subsequently he and his son were well-placed to enjoy the benefits of high farming which became possible again in the 1840s. Once again Westwood Lodge enjoyed the respect and admiration in the county which it had attained before the post-war depression.[10]

The River Blyth was an essential component in the economy of this great farm. Through its mouth came boats bringing Baltic timber and deals needed for farm sheds, bridges and sluices; but more important there came also collier brigs, laden with the cheap sea coal which was the essential tool behind progressive farmers. Coal and an occasional shipload of chalk, enabled Calver and Isaac Wales at Walberswick to burn the lime needed for building and also as a fertilizer. Coal was needed for iron work and needed by smiths such Mr Asbey of Blythburgh who amongst other things constructed two threshing mills for Westwood Lodge and was instigated by the Howletts to invent a machine which could be moved from stack to stack. Coal was needed for the brick kilns at nearby Hinton and was needed by the maltsters and brewers who bought Westwood barley.[11]

And the river also provided transport for the bountiful crops produced on a farm which in 1769 had perhaps 600 acres under plough and in 1836 about 780. Some of this produce may have gone by wherry to Halesworth as is suggested by John Grimsby's interest in the Navigation (p.48). Much of it must have been shipped from Southwold to London. James Cooper told the Select Committee on Railway Bills in 1846 that until recently he had always sent his corn from Southwold harbour and in the course of his evidence he also mentioned that he got artificial manures from London and Yarmouth by water.[12] It is reasonable to assume that Cooper's predecessors also sent much corn from Southwold and this is borne out by the appearance of Nathaniel Howlett in the Port Books in 1775. In January of that year he sent a ship in his own name with wheat, barley, oats, peas and beans to London from Southwold.[13] Unfortunately this is the last year in which merchants' names were recorded so there is no means of knowing whether this was an isolated venture. But in any case the Westwood corn must also have been shipped by other local merchants, such as Francis Robinson, with their regular contacts in London. Southwold harbour always had its problems but in the days before railways the facilities which the harbour and the River Blyth provided for carriage of heavy goods must have been of immeasurable value to Westwood Lodge.

Apart from this, the river also played its part as an integral factor in the farm management. As we have seen, much of the strength of Westwood Lodge lay in the mix of arable and stock which helped James Cooper to weather the depression years. Cooper told the Select Committee in 1836 that he had 527 acres of sheep walks, great stretches of sandy heath with turf and heather which had been grazed by sheep since the Middle Ages. He also told them that he had 272 acres of marsh and 20 acres of marsh walls, about one-sixth of his total acreage. This marsh, on which, in the summer months, the tenants of Westwood Lodge fed sheep and the black cattle for which Cooper was reputed, was generously provided by the river; and it was also by means of the river that much of the marsh was drained.

The draining of the marshes to the south-east, Westwood Marshes, began in 1742 when Jane Blois agreed with her tenant, Robert May, that she would make a creek from the marshes into the main river at Walberswick and make a timber sluice at Walberswick quay, provided May would keep the whole enterprise in good repair. She made the creek 12 feet wide at the top, 6 feet wide at the bottom and 4 feet deep and put down the sluice 'by which the water is now carried off the marshes to Robert May's great benefit'. Jane's horses were pastured on some of the marsh but subsequently John Grimsby bought cattle to graze them.[14]

Something in the region of 200 to 280 acres of fresh and salt marsh and reed beds to the south-east of Westwood Lodge were drained by ditches and drains flowing into the creek, and agreements for maintaining the creek and the sluice continued to be an important part of the tenancy arrangements, with the landlord agreeing to pay compensation if the walls should be breached and the works wiped out by 'inundation of the sea'. The marsh drainage was expensive for both landlord and tenant. Under the terms of his tenancy Nathaniel Howlett agreed to erect a mill to throw the fresh water out of the marshes at a cost of not less than £200 if the landlord should desire it. In 1774 the trustees allowed Howlett £100 towards walling the salts and remaking the sluice at Walberswick, and in 1779 when the sluice 'blew up' they paid a bill of £197 for a new sluice and cut into the river, known as Howlett's cut, to include repairs to the marsh walls and the wharf.[15]

On the Blythburgh side the farm tenancy also included both Micklefield marshes, 22 acres above Blythburgh bridge, and the salt marshes opposite Reydon quay, now all called Tinker's marshes. Here marsh walls were erected to check the flooding river in similar fashion to the embankments built on the Rous marshes: and the concession made to Thomas Taylor in 1809 permitting him to plough Tinker's marshes despite the danger of inundation by the river reflects again the greed for corn land at that date.[16]

Sir Charles Blois, who had inherited in 1810, devoted much time and trouble to his estate, assisted by his land steward, Henry Read, and Sir Charles was also a conscientious member of the Harbour Commission. When in 1819 he paid men for thirty-seven days walling at Tinker's marsh it is most unlikely that he thought his embankment might threaten the viability of the harbour.[17] Like Lord Rous he must have had little reason to think that the two interests might conflict. But this was the effect of the opinion delivered by the respected engineer John Rennie C.E. a year later when he pronounced that much of the shoaling in the harbour and the growth of the bar was due to lack of scour from the river during the ebb tide and that this lack of scour was in its turn due to the embankment of 1100 acres of ground over which the tides used to flow. It was an opinion which came to be frequently cited and which caused major argument in the first half of the nineteenth century.

Rennie's strictures, which were mainly focused on the embankments up the river and especially round Blythburgh, must have included the embanked Micklefield and Tinker's marshes. But although he was clear that to destroy the embankments and to 'allow the tide-water to flow into its ancient receptacles' would be the most obvious and effectual remedy, Rennie himself felt that this was really out of the question. As a palliative he recommended that to the south-east Dunwich and Howlett's creeks should be dammed to create reservoirs which could be opened at low tide. Nothing came of this and by this time indeed Sir Charles Blois had come to an arrangement for the drainage from the Barne lands at Dunwich to be turned into his creek and Barne Barne had built new sluices at considerable expense to both of them.[18]

Charles Blois, however, did subsequently make improvements at Walberswick. He followed the recommendations for alterations to the outlet of his creek, and more important, for the reconstruction of Walberswick quay – recommendations made by Lieutenant Ellis, the harbour surveyor, who hoped they would both help to clear away shoals and improve the bar at the harbour. Like his grandfather, Sir Ralph, Charles recognized his obligations to the harbour. He took his position as a Commissioner seriously and made his suitable contribution to the funds. At the same time he was a careful man, intent on restoring the fortunes of his estate. In the battles with the Navigation Commissioners which dominated the 1830s and 1840s he seems to have been happy to leave the leadership to Lord Stradbroke and, like the soldier that he was, to back his lordship loyally when required.

CHAPTER 10

Barne of Sotterley

IN THE MID-EIGHTEENTH CENTURY A NEW BREED of landlord appeared on the banks of the Blyth. Miles Barne, energetic and ambitious and with City of London wealth behind him, purchased the Sotterley estate from the Playter family in 1745 and he went on to purchase Sir John Playter's Reydon estate in 1746.[1]

Miles Barne's father, a director of the East India Company, had given him property in the City in 1741 for his advancement in life, and Miles threw himself whole-heartedly into that advancement, seeing it, like many contemporaries blessed with fortunes made in the east, as best achieved by establishing himself as a landed gentleman with a seat in Parliament. It was most probably the opportunity of a Parliamentary seat at Dunwich which attracted him to Suffolk although this did not work out as well as he might have hoped. Dunwich was a pocket borough under the control of Sir George Downing and in 1747 Sir George sold for £1200 one of the two Dunwich seats to Miles who sat in Parliament as one of the members for Dunwich until the election of 1754. Sir George, however, died in 1749 and his cousin and heir, Jacob, dropped Barne in 1754 so that Miles had to wait without a seat for ten years. Sir Jacob's death in 1764 at last gave Miles the chance to regain a Dunwich seat which with considerable astuteness he managed to achieve. He pooled resources with the Vannecks of Heveningham and each family took one of the Dunwich seats.[2]

In May 1745 Miles had married Elizabeth Elwick, daughter and heiress of the governor of Madras, who had brought with her a substantial dowry, and in the following years he continued to add to his Suffolk possessions, buying Willingham Hall from Robert Sparrow, a small estate at Dunwich from Charles Long and other land especially at Willingham, Weston, Uggeshall, Stoven, so that he could certainly feel that he had established himself among the more considerable landed gentry.[3]

For the Reydon estate Miles Barne paid Sir John Playter £2221; and in 1768 he also bought a farm with a malting beside Blythburgh marshes where he reserved the right to make malt at any time and take it away at his free will and pleasure. This farm was about 86 acres, so on both sides of the River Blyth below Blythburgh the Barne property was interwoven with the lands of the Rous and the Blois families, while to the east Miles owned the Dingle marshes which ran beside the large Blois estate at Westwood.[4]

In 1763 the Barne and the Blois families acquired a close link. Miles' first wife,

Sotterley Hall, rebuilt by Miles Barne about 1745 when his family replaced the Playters who had lived there since the fifteenth century. Drawing by H. Davy, engraved by J. Lambert, 1824.

Miles Barne, 1724–80.

Elizabeth, bore him an heir – Miles Barne the younger – but she died after only two years of marriage and in 1752 Miles had married his cousin, Mary Thornhill. Ten years later the financially embarrassed Sir John Blois proposed marriage to Mary's sister Sarah, and Miles Barne, as we have seen, was much involved in the negotiations over the marriage settlement and the arrangements for at least temporary retrenchment by the young couple. There was much coming and going between the two families and it was to the Blois home at Cockfield Hall that Miles drove in haste from London in February 1764 when he heard of the death of Jacob Downing.[5]

Mary Barne by this time was the mother of a large young family and she frequently had to leave them at Sotterley as she set off in the coach-and-four for a sojourn in the London house in Berkeley Square. She worried about them in her absence and eventually came to rely considerably on her step-son. Miles Barne the younger, who went up to Cambridge in 1760, seems from her letters to have been a shy young man and she tried to encourage him to be more forthcoming and social.

> *The Saxmundham Concerts is likely to go very [well]. Mr Barne intends to be very constant at them, we expect you will be greatly Improved in your Musick and will cut quite a figure amongst them*

she wrote hopefully to him in the autumn of 1762. Miles kept her letters and liked them. 'I have an opportunity of sending you a letter full of nothing but as you desired it I have done it . . .' she wrote to him and later in the same term she wrote again, delighted with a cheerful letter from Miles about Cambridge and telling him that Sir John Blois 'says he never lived so happy anywhere as there'. Many of her letters contained messages from his father about his estates and legal matters; she was also greatly concerned to find young Miles a suitable manservant and to equip him with the family livery; she sent Miles silk and worsted stockings by the Beccles coach. And as he grew older she relied on him to keep an eye on the children left at Sotterley. She wrote in February 1768 from Berkeley Square, pleased to hear that Elizabeth and Ann 'had performed better' and had promised to mend for the future. 'I flatter myself they will behave themselves so well that we shall have no occasion to send them to an Ipswich schooll, but I hope you will let us hear how they go on in every letter.' A few years later she was writing:

> *I received your very friendly letter and am greatly obliged to you for acquainting us with the accident that happened to Cesia's neck . . . it is a great comfort to have one one may depend upon if anything happens of that sort when one is away from home.*

Miles Barne senior had his London solicitor and he also employed a steward, Arthur Watling, who lived in a substantial house in Sotterley. In the early days, however, he seems to have relied on John Sayer of Thurlton, near Beccles, and it was Sayer who arranged the purchase of the Reydon estate. 'I hope you will have a good bargain of Reydon Estate' he wrote to Miles in November 1746. 'It will not be proper in my Opinion to set about repairing the Banks of the Marshes before Spring but then to fall on with a good number of hands.' The two farms at Reydon and the 120 acres called Pecks marsh had possibilities of improvement and there were shooting and fishing attractions for which 'a Little Building or Summer house' beside the river was provided.[7] But the main asset must have been the quay built about 1737 by Sir John Playter, mainly at the instigation of William Lenney of Reydon, a yeoman farmer and a merchant (p.76).

Ships arriving at Southwold haven could find enough water to bring them to this new quay and thus farmers and merchants from Reydon and Wangford and beyond would be saved four miles or more of the lumbering wagon journey to Blackshore. Lenney had land of his own but he also rented a farm from Playter together with the new quay where he had warehouses, granaries and a timber yard. Here he ran his merchant business and as part of his tenancy agreement wagons fetching coal from the collier brigs and bringing grain and other country produce for export to London were allowed to use paths and tracks over the fields to the staithe.[8]

Not surprisingly Southwold town which owned the Blackshore wharfage regarded the new quay as a dangerous menace. The wharfage dues were small beer but the benefits to Southwold of having the only recognized quay on the north side of the river were substantial. The Southwold Customs officers, local men themselves, were on the side of the town and from the beginning they had been hostile to the shipping of goods and corn at Reydon.[9] The Collector of Customs at this time was Samuel Nunn, an independent-minded member of an old Southwold merchant family (p.72). In February 1747 Barne received a letter from the Custom House:

> *Sir we have this day considered the nature of your Demand . . . it has appeared clearer than ever that Reyden key is not within the limits of any legal Port whatever. As to Walberswick key it is to demonstration within the Port of Southwold who of consequence can in no degree make in your favour.*[10]

Undeterred by this, Barne continued to fight for the rights of his new acquisition and eventually, after much consideration, the Board in London wrote to Southwold telling them that while shipping or landing of foreign goods was not to be permitted, they were to allow coast goods to be landed and shipped at Reydon quay 'and you are to take care accordingly'. Coastal shipments, coal from the north-east coming in, and corn bound for London going out, must have been the main trade expected at Reydon quay but Barne was not content with this. He wanted the 'Special Suffrance' from the Customs needed to bring in foreign goods – timber, deal board, stones, flax. In July 1752 he took Counsel's opinion, only to hear from Sir Thomas Bootle that the Board was not compelled to grant this concession.[11]

A few months earlier, for reasons unrevealed, Miles Barne had written to resign from the Harbour Commission. But although no longer himself a Commissioner, it must surely have been he who was behind a petition in 1754 from the Harbour Commissioners to His Majesty's Commissioners of Customs asking them to make Reydon a free quay. This sent waves of alarm through Southwold. The Grand Assembly meeting in December 1754 proclaimed their horror at the idea 'which if suffered will in Time be the ruin of this Town'. Samuel Nunn, who as we have seen was Collector of the Customs, was elected one of the two town bailiffs by this meeting and the Grand Assembly, headed by Nunn, then proceeded to arrange a counter-petition to prevent 'so pernicious a scheme' and moreover included a request to His Majesty's Commissioners 'totally to hinder Corn or any Merchandise to be shipt Coastwise at Reydon key'.[12]

This was unwise for in so doing they ran headlong into a formidable man, skilled in strategy, with whom they were already at odds over the harbour finances. Miles Barne was always the highest subscriber to the harbour and by October 1751 he had lent the Commission £550 on mortgage of the harbour dues. In May 1754 the Commissioners were unpleasantly aware that 'unexpected ravages from the Sea Worms destroying the piles' would mean further heavy expenditure and they called a general Meeting at the Swan to induce the creditors to agree to a reduction in the interest on their mortgages from five per cent to four per cent. They also sent an anxious message to Miles Barne asking him to let them choose him as a Commissioner again. Miles had very different ideas. He alone of all the creditors refused to accept the reduction of interest and a 'friendly visit' by the Reverend Mr Smear and Mr Baylie to 'engage him to consent' was of no avail.[13]

During this difficult year Samuel Nunn, merchant of Southwold, was leading the desperate efforts to keep the haven in repair without adequate funds; yet as Bailiff of the town and Collector of the Customs he was prepared to further antagonize Barne by the petition against Reydon quay. Miles Barne now sprang into the attack and in May 1755 he served a label of subpoena in Chancery on the Commissioners. At the same time he was continuing to increase his financial grip on the Commission by snapping up other mortgages as they became available. By May 1757 he was owed over £950.[14]

Annoyance over the opposition of Southwold to his plans for Reydon quay no doubt reinforced Barne's determination; but beyond that he had strong objections to the sloppy provisions of the original Southwold Harbour Act and to the way he saw it being administered: the very inadequate controls on finance and accounting and the undoubted fact that the dues as laid down under the Act would never be enough to safeguard the capital invested or to meet the interest on it. He allowed the case in Chancery to rumble on, costing the Commission a good deal of money, until eventually he got what he wanted. A new Harbour Act was passed in 1757 which increased the dues and laid down stringent controls of finance and safeguards for creditors.[15]

At an amicable harbour meeting at the end of May 1757 Barne agreed that the case should be brought to a halt and dismissed out of court. Now he was prepared at last to agree to the reduction of interest to four per cent. An important part of the deal must have been a satisfactory agreement over the status of Reydon quay. The quay and the alehouse nearby, where thirsty seamen and carters could refresh themselves, continued to render valuable service to the neighbourhood for more than a century.[16]

Lenney, who played such an important part in the early work on the harbour piers, had died in 1753 and Miles then leased the wharf and the alehouse to Samuel Farra, another farmer merchant of Reydon. Farra, as we shall see (p.78), built up a large export-and-import business and his success and the success of other village merchants suggest that Samuel Nunn and the Grand Assembly of Southwold were right in their forebodings about the effect of the new quay. The story, often told, of the 300 or 400 tubs of liquor smuggled into Reydon quay in 1821 suggests that the customs officers were also right to have misgivings about the staithe. They arrived too late, the smugglers' boat was gone and was later found on Blythburgh flats.[17]

After the passing of the new Act, Miles Barne took his place again as a Commissioner and from this time onwards he drove over from Sotterley to the meetings at the Swan with clockwork regularity. Nor did he let his resumption of the Dunwich seat in 1764 interfere with his active interest in the harbour's affairs, although like his fellow mortgagees he gradually reduced his financial interest.

With his commerical background and his energetic approach Miles Barne was a new experience for Southwold. He forced the town and their bailiff, Samuel Nunn, to realize that the old days had gone; the gentry were no easy touch and the harbour no longer belonged to the town but to the Harbour Commission. None the less Southwold still had merchants prepared to give their time and skills to supervision of the constant repair work needed to keep the harbour viable. Samuel Nunn had worked hard for the harbour in the early days and now his place was taken by John May and John Robinson, merchants with more specialized interests, but both substantial men. For the twenty-three years that Miles served as a Commissioner these two wrestled with the damage caused to the fragile harbour structure by winds, high seas and voracious worms; they assessed the problems, procured the timber and nails needed, and inspected the work.

Barne was backed up at the Swan meetings by other landowners but, with the exception of Sir John Rous (faithful till his death in 1771), their attendance was irregular. The regularity of Miles Barne and the authority and the financial expertise he could bring to bear must have provided great support to the Southwold merchants and a very valuable and necessary financial discipline. Shortly before his death he again answered a call for money. The stormy winter of 1778 coincided with the falling-off of harbour dues and in the following summer Miles headed a new subscription list with £250 and followed this up with a further £62 in December 1780, the month of his death.

The younger Miles Barne who now succeeded his father was very comfortably placed. He had inherited an estate in Kent and a large personal estate from his maternal grandfather and he entered on his Suffolk inheritance at a time of rising agricultural prosperity which culminated in the highly profitable years of the French wars. By the early nineteenth century the income from the Suffolk rents had more than doubled and in 1818 he was receiving well over £4000 from the Sotterley and Reydon estates. The rents from the Reydon estate alone were put at about £700 a year in 1810 and this included rents of £14 and £10 from two Southwold merchants – Crisp, maltster, and Peregrine Edwards, miller – for the granaries at Reydon quay. The maltings and mill and about 90 acres at Blythburgh, for which the tenant had paid £30 a year in 1771, were bringing in a rent of £111 a year in 1818.[18]

The Watling family continued to manage the estate for Miles who seems always to have been of a retiring disposition, perhaps because he did not enjoy good health. He did not play a great part in public life and when his father resigned the Dunwich seat in 1777 it was taken by his eldest half-brother, Barne Barne; and although, following Barne's appointment as Commissioner of Taxes in 1791, he did himself occupy the seat for five years, he was soon content to pass it on to his younger half-brothers.[19]

Miles was unanimously elected a Harbour Commissioner in 1781 in the place of his father but he did not share his father's interest in the harbour and after a courtesy appearance at the Swan meetings he did not attend again. Barne Barne, however, following his election as a Commissioner in 1810, presented himself quite frequently, and his interest in harbour affairs is not surprising since he had property at Westleton and Dunwich, including the Dingle marshes.[20]

Barne Barne was a zealous property improver with a reckless disregard of capital costs. In 1808 when the creek which drained the Dingle marshes was choked and blocked by a high sea he had reached an agreement with Sir Charles Blois to drain his marshes into the Westwood creek, and as a part of the agreement Barne put down a new sluice at Walberswick. In 1813 he impressed the neighbourhood by replacing this with a new type of brick sluice, crowned by a bridge adorned with the initials 'B.B.'. This cost him £1100 and within a year the sluice was blown up by a high tide and the bridge collapsed. He was little more successful with the bridge which he built in 1809 across Buss Creek near Southwold harbour, later christened Waterloo Bridge. He built it, according to James Maggs, the Southwold diarist, 'entirely at his own expense for the accomodation of Trade from Blackshore Quay to New Quay [Reydon Quay] And repairs to be done at his *Cost*'. The bridge was taken down in 1828, the year of Barne's death.[21]

In an undated letter to Miles, Barne claimed that his improvements to the Dunwich farms had increased the rents from £556 to £2384 a year and the capital value from £16680 to £71520. He told Miles that the increase of produce from 'the Marshes' was 'so great that they cannot fail of being very valuable in themselves and contributing to the value of the neighbouring uplands'. In this letter he went on to defend his expenditure in Kent, for his improving activities were not confined to the Dunwich property and in 1784 he had purchased from Miles an annuity on Miles' Kent property.[22]

Barne Barne claimed that his figures for the Kent property were a 'sufficient answer to those who say that the money has been injudiciously laid out', but the fact is that his capital expenditure on development in Kent, together with that at Dunwich, built up a mountain of debts. He was not the only landowner to be dazzled by the dramatic increase of prices and rents at the time of the French wars. Other landowners over-extended themselves and were caught by the subsequent slump, but Barne Barne whose debts reached over £150000 is a very sobering example.[23]

LOCAL ADVENTURERS: THE MERCHANTS

CHAPTER 11

The Role of the Middleman

Yon is our Quay! those smaller Hoys from Town,
Its various Wares, for Country Use, bring down;
Those laden Waggons, in return impart
The Country-Produce to the City Mart:
Hark! to the Clamour in that miry Road,
Bounded and narrow'd by yon Vessels' Load;
The lumbering Wealth she empties round the place,
Package and Parcel, Hogshead, Chest and Case:
While the loud Seaman and the angry Hind,
Mingling in Business, bellow to the Wind.

George Crabbe, *The Borough*, Letter 1.

THE BUSTLING BUSINESS AT THE QUAYS was the life-blood of most merchants in the Blyth valley. These local men were not glamorous figures like the London merchants and financiers who traded with the Indies, amassed large fortunes and established landed families in Suffolk – the Barnes, the Arcedecknes, the Vannecks – but on a smaller scale they valiantly encountered the same risks and hazards. Winds came on to blow hard and heavy seas built up and they might wait up all night for the *Belle* returning with ballast from London or the *Johns Adventure* overdue from Sunderland. They might have to watch a brig which had made safe passage from Rotterdam go aground near the harbour. Less dramatic but none the less expensive were delays faced by those merchants whose cargoes were piled into wherries bound for Halesworth. On a windless day the wherry sails drooped and only by laboriously quanting the craft upstream with a pole could the wherrymen make any sort of progress. Even downstream the journey had its hazards since broken bridges and decayed locks were an ever-recurring problem on the Navigation.

Poring over their order books and daybooks these country entrepreneurs wrestled with fickle markets and fickle harvests, lack of coinage, bad debts and poor communications.

They were self-reliant men with some education; several were members of the Independent Church and often they were the offspring of yeoman families, who could somehow find the capital which was essential to their business. As a rule they had a second occupation. They were also maltsters, millers, farmers, and the most successful were often also brewers. For the most part they traded in the heavy bulky goods which could be transported so much more cheaply by water: grain, timber, lime, fish, spirits – anything which might bring in some profit; but the cheap 'sea' coal brought in by collier brigs was the mainstay of most businesses.

The coal trade was not a new phenomenon. Shipmasters based at Dunwich, Walberswick and Southwold had been fetching coal from Newcastle since the Middle Ages; and although they mainly carried it to London and foreign ports they were certainly discharging some locally in Tudor times. By the mid eighteenth century, as timber grew increasingly hard to come by in sparsely wooded Suffolk, it is not surprising to find that the tenancy agreement for Westwood Lodge specifically required the carting of six chaldrons of coal to Cockfield Hall, nor to see the sharp eye that Rous of Henham kept on his coal bills (pp.41–2).[1]

Home fires were consuming increased tons of coal but more significant were the growing needs of local industries. Salt-making, a source of prosperity in Southwold in the second half of the century, required many chaldrons to fire the iron pans in which sea water and brine were evaporated. Brewing was one of the early rural industries to use coal and coke, which were needed not only to heat the brewer's copper but also, and on a substantial scale, to kiln the malt. And as prices rose and farmers and farming flourished and expanded, coal and coke were wanted for the many brick kilns in this part of Suffolk and by the blacksmiths who were working iron not only into horse shoes but into hoops and bands for wheels and into new farm implements.[2]

Most of these general merchants themselves coked coal in mounds or cinder ovens lying on rough ground within easy distance of the staithes. And nearby they had limekilns where imported chalk was burnt to make lime. Lime was in great demand, not only for agriculture, but also for making mortar and cement and for the plaster and lime-wash used inside and outside Suffolk timber-framed buildings. There were coke ovens and limekilns grouped on both sides of Southwold harbour and near staithes further up river. They were noisy, grimy places belching fumes and creating miniature black countries. Crabbe's observations at Aldeburgh apply equally to parts of the Blyth valley:

Behold the wealth that lies in public view
Those far-extended heaps of coal and coke
Where fresh-fill'd lime-kilns breathe their stifling smoke.[3]

Coal, coke and lime; soft-wood timber and deals from the Baltic; foreign wine and spirits: these were the main products which the local merchants provided for their neighbours; and at the same time they were the middlemen through whom these same neighbours found a way to the London market for their barley, wheat and malt, beans and peas, and to Holland for their smoked herrings and red sprats.

Most of the merchants who figure in the chapters that follow achieved considerable success for inevitably most of the failures make little appearance in contemporary records. Yet even those who achieved success sometimes ended up with little to show for their endeavours. Great skill and application were needed to judge the risks involved and to juggle with the capital resources; and on top of this there was the important matter of luck:

Yet let us own that Trade has much of Chance
Not all the Careful by their Care advance.[4]

'Collier Discharging' by E. W. Cooke.

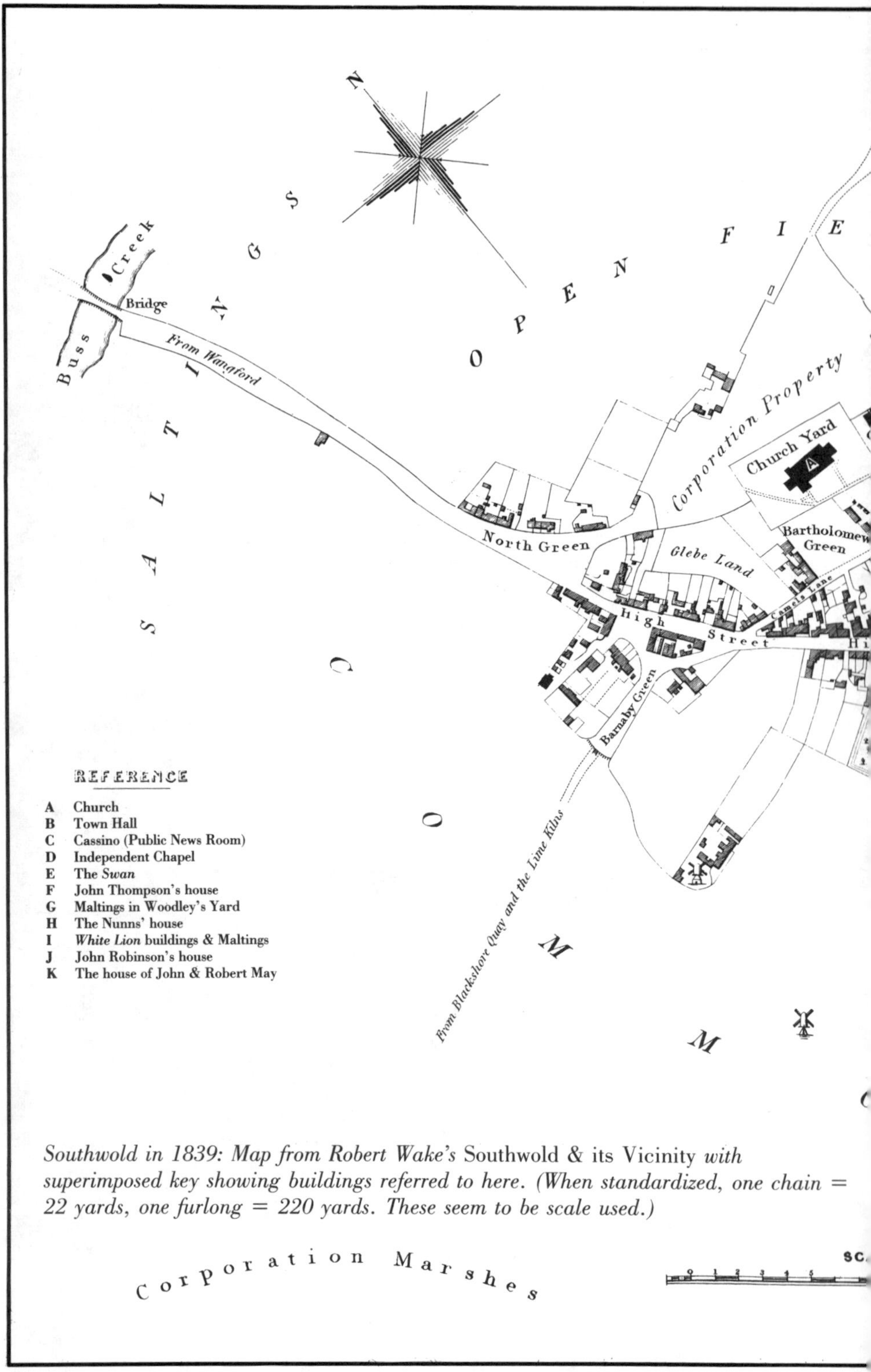

Southwold in 1839: Map from Robert Wake's Southwold & its Vicinity *with superimposed key showing buildings referred to here. (When standardized, one chain = 22 yards, one furlong = 220 yards. These seem to be scale used.)*

SOUTHWOLD.
Latitude 52° 20' North. Longitude 1° 40' East.
Drawn & Engraved, expressly for Mr. Wake's History of Southwold, and its Vicinity.
GERMAN OCEAN
BEACH
Beach
St. James Street
St. James Terrace
North Green
East
East Lane
North Cliff
Long Island
Green Lane
East Street
Market Place
Centre Cliff
Cliff Houses
Pinkney's Lane
Queen Street
New York Cliff
Mill Lane
South Green
Tamarisk Villa
Acton Place
South Green House
Meeting House Lane
Park Lane
Park Villa
Marine Villa
Low Water Mark
High Water Mark
Centre Villa
Skilmans Hill
Gun Hill
The Lodge
C
South End
Salt Works
Saint Edmunds Hill
Stone House
N
Wall
Path to Walberswick (abt. 5 Furs.)
Salt Marshes
To the Pier about 5 Furlongs
Jetty Road
HAINS
15
20

CHAPTER 12

The Caretakers of the Harbour: Southwold Merchants

THE HANDSOME MERCHANTS' HOUSES WHICH GRACE Southwold High Street indicate that some merchants did very well indeed. Perhaps the most impressive is Buckenhams, the mansion in which the Thompson family lived from the beginning of the eighteenth century and which they embellished with a Georgian facade. Close to Buckenhams was their brewery with its maltings (now occupied by Barclays Bank and the Club and houses behind) and this together with the Swan brewery was the basis of the Thompson family's prosperity, reinforced in the usual brewer's fashion by a bevy of public houses of which the Swan itself was the crown jewel.[1]

But the Thompsons also owned ships and in an early surviving Port Book (1720) we find John and William Thompson, masters of their own boats, sailing coastwise: south to London with herrings and malt and north to Sunderland to bring back coal; and sailing also across to Rotterdam with barrels of red herrings. Twenty years later the name of Thompson still frequently recurs in the Port Books. Robert and William Thompson both sent many boats with barley and malt to London in 1741 and William carried on this trade till his death in 1752.[2]

William's son John (1736–1806) was the only Thompson male heir and on the death of his uncle, Robert, in 1755, he inherited most of the amassed wealth and property and carried on the brewing business which Robert had been running. John sent barley and a little malt to London in 1755 but after that he ceased the export of corn and fish from Southwold harbour.[3] We have no means of knowing whether he abandoned also the family interest in the coal trade but he would need coal for malting and brewing and the very active interest which he took in the Navigation suggests that he dealt in it as well. The waterway was welcomed by Southwold coal merchants as a route to valuable new customers and John Thompson both subscribed the substantial sum of £110 for Navigation shares and also in 1760 volunteered himself as a river Commissioner.[4]

Registering John Thompson's death in 1806 at the age of sixty-nine, the curate evidently felt constrained to embellish the usual bleak entry and added 'an old and most respectable inhabitant of this town'. He was describing probably the wealthiest man in Southwold, but John Thompson was not a man of vaulting ambition. Like other rich townsfolk he had money invested in land and he owned farms at Uggeshall and Stoven but he did not aspire to become a country gentleman and he was first and foremost a good

Southwold, 1820: engraved from a drawing by H. Davy. The salt works look like a tall wigwam, John Thompson's octagonal Casino is conspicuous.

Buckenhams in Southwold High Street, once the residence of John Thompson.

citizen of Southwold.[5] He made efforts to improve the town's attractions and add fashionable pleasures which could be patronized by neighbouring gentry and affluent visitors. In 1766 he constructed the bathing house near the harbour which came to be known as Thompson's folly; and more successfully, in 1801 he erected the Casino on Gunhill to be used as a subscription reading room. Already in these early days he was encouraging Southwold's change of direction towards the role of seaside resort which brought so much profitable trade to the town in succeeding years, and not least to the town's brewers.[6]

John Thompson served Southwold faithfully as chamberlain or bailiff nearly every year from 1759 to 1802 and after his election as a Harbour Commissioner in 1760 he walked across the road to the Commission meetings at the Swan with an equally conscientious regularity. To us who know so little about him he seems rather a pale figure, an inoffensive man who generally side-stepped the heated controversies which so quickly blew up in the small community; and in this he was very different from the surviving member of the other long-established Southwold brewing and malting family, Samuel Nunn.

The gentlemanly Thompson is conspicuously commemorated in Southwold church both on the chancel wall and on the stone floor, but Samuel Nunn who died in 1770, was buried in Walpole churchyard where a table monument proclaims his 'benevolent social disposition and constant charity to the Poor'. He was buried close to John Crompton, the well-loved minister of Walpole Chapel. The Nunns were members of the Independent Church and Samuel had the robust individualism which was sometimes characteristic of its members.[7]

The Nunns owned the White Lion in Victoria Street and here, between Victoria Street and Church Green, they had a range of buildings including a malting with capacity for about 2000 quarters of malt a year. Their spacious house, burnt down in 1928, fronted the High Street on the corner of Church Street.[8] Like the Thompsons the Nunn family had a sea-going mercantile tradition and although they are not prominent in the Southwold Port Books in the first half of the eighteenth century, in 1755 and 1759 Samuel's father, Thomas, was sending quantities of wheat and barley to London and he also sent barrels of red sprats to Rotterdam: it seems the Dutch Christmas was never complete without these delicacies from Southwold. Thomas Nunn died in 1762 and Samuel, although he added to the family warehouses at Blackshore in 1760, seems like John Thompson to have ceased shipping grain and fish from Southwold. Probably, however, he continued to trade in coal and he, like Thompson, certainly welcomed the construction of the Navigation, writing to Thomas Knights that he looked forward to the benefits of craft carrying coals up the river.[9]

Samuel was a public-spirited citizen and a man of integrity who served the town for many years as bailiff or chamberlain and who, from the 1740s until his death, was Collector of Customs at the Port of Southwold. A true man of Southwold, he tried to do his best for the town and its haven and as we have seen (p.62) he fought against Miles Barne and the supporters of the new quay at Reydon which he felt was bound to harm Southwold trade. With the Commission under the cloud of Barne's hostility and very short of money, Samuel directed the work of bolstering up the worm-eaten harbour piers in 1754 and 1755 and arrested 'the Destruction of the haven committed to our care and trust'. He supported the move for a new Act in 1757 and it was he who produced the Yarmouth Act as a model. But soon after the passage of the Act and the general reconciliation with Miles Barne which followed, Samuel withdrew his investment in the harbour and although he continued as a Commissioner he left the supervision of the work there to others.[10]

John Thompson and Samuel Nunn were the last direct members of two wealthy brewing and trading families of a kind never quite seen again in Southwold. During their lifetime the coastal trade in grain and farm produce from Southwold harbour was moving into

Thomas Nunn, 1686–1762.

Bank House, John Robinson's house in Southwold Market Place.

outside hands. By the end of the 1750s this trade to London was dominated by merchants from villages outside – Samuel Farra of Reydon, John Crisp of Wangford and Francis Robinson of Dunwich. How much these outsiders dominated the coal trade the records we have do not reveal.

Was it the status which Miles Barne procured for Reydon quay which enabled village merchants to establish themselves at the expense of the Southwold merchants who had earlier done so well from this general coastal trade? Samuel Nunn was surely right in his foreboding about Reydon quay. The quay was all-important to Farra who had the tenancy; it must have been very convenient for John Crisp and also for Robert Barfoot, another Reydon merchant, who took over Lenney's lime kilns near Wolsey Bridge. Certainly this general trade in agricultural produce gradually moved away from Southwold and the two merchants who flourished in the town from the 1760s both owed their success to one specialized lucrative product. John May's prosperity was built on salt. John Robinson imported foreign timber and deals. Like the Nunns and the Thompsons, May and Robinson both had houses in the centre of Southwold, elegant houses which still reflect eighteenth-century comfortable living. Bank House, overlooking the market place, was built early in the century for the Thompsons but passed by marriage into the capable hands of John Robinson. About mid century John May built the 'Manor House', standing then in nearly two acres of ground.[11]

Miles Barne, besides establishing the position of Reydon quay, also helped merchants in outside villages by making sure that the Harbour Commissioners kept a firm hand on the administration of the harbour and ensured that it did not again become a perquisite of Southwold town. None the less it was still Southwold merchants, the same John May and John Robinson, who came forward to wrestle with the recurring havoc wrought by wind and high seas; to watch, assess damage and supervise repairs. Without these men in the front line the Harbour Commission would have been lost.

John May sent some agricultural produce to London in the fifties but towards the end of the sixties he was instead sending boat loads of white salt to Yarmouth.[12] Exactly when he became a major salt producer is not clear but his business probably sprang from the needs of the Free British Fisheries, established in Southwold in 1750. In 1754 he became a Harbour Commissioner and for twenty or more years, usually in combination with John Robinson, he supervised the 'surveyors' and carpenters and saw to the purchase of oak and fir timber and the broad-headed nails used to strengthen the piles. His death deprived the Commissioners of an irreplaceable lieutenant. His thrusting son, Robert, who took his place as a Commissioner in 1787 had grandiose ideas and was by no means prepared to go down to the harbour and supervise repair work. Robert, captain of the local Volunteers, formed to resist French invasion, gave his attention to Southwold politics and focused a formidable attack on John Robinson who had so often worked with his father on the harbour structures. Robert succeeded in ousting Robinson from a long pre-eminence in the town government and stripping him of the lease of the Town Farm. He provoked the Robinsons to such an extent that John Robinson, when approaching seventy years of age and nearly at the end of his life, found himself at the Bury Assizes charged with assault on Robert May.[13]

John Robinson was not just a small town figure. The timber and deals which he imported from Norway and the Baltic found customers over a wide area and he supplied both the Rous and Blois estates.[14] He was a formidable man who dominated Southwold town politics for nearly forty years and to a very great degree he also came to dominate the Harbour Commission. In May 1770 the Commission agreed that while oak timbering was rapidly eaten by sea worms, imported fir timber nailed with broad-headed nails was far less vulnerable. From then on John Robinson became the monopoly supplier of the loads of timber which were needed each year to repair the damage wrought by the winter seas. In addition, by the end of the sixties he was relied on more and more to help supervise the work and from 1776 till his death in 1802 he was Collector of the dues, a heavy proportion of which went to pay for his timber. But he was no armchair book keeper. He was a familiar figure at the harbour directing the carpenter's repairs to the timber structures that he knew so well; and in his last years his son James came to his aid and watched and worked with the men at the piers when the winter high seas rose dangerously. In the dreadful gales of 1795–96 James was 'with the people sundry times in the night and day saving the piles etc. mash'd by the high Tides'.[15]

John Robinson, whose father had been a Halesworth attorney, also devoted time and energy to the Navigation. In 1760 he offered his services as a River Commissioner and the following year he agreed to be a trustee of Halesworth quay. He supplied deals and timber for the Navigation and the River Commissioners, like their fellows at the Harbour, relied on him to survey the works – the locks and bridges – and to tell them what repairs were wanted. It was also John Robinson who was deputed in 1770 to confront the intransigent widow Ball over the ever-recurring problem of Wenhaston Mill and who at last got agreement for its conversion to a breast-mill.[16]

The degree of trust thus reposed by both sets of Commissioners in their timber merchant must seem to us very remarkable. The Harbour Commissioners especially did not find his position incongruous. He could supply timber and he understood the piers and for many years they were glad for him to carry the administration of the harbour on his shoulders. To the eighteenth-century mind this was the more acceptable in that the harbour was vital to Robinson's business. He imported shiploads of fir timber from Russia, Prussia and Norway and often these cargoes came in foreign boats whose captains would be less familiar with the vagaries of Southwold winds and sandbanks.[17] Captains from Christiania and Riga bringing deals, fir quarters, boards and palings into Southwold had to have a reasonable passage up to Blackshore and John Robinson made it his concern to keep the harbour viable. Self-help was essential in the eighteenth century and no one was going to be nice about the division of economic interests.

The head of Salt Creek, Southwold. From here the sea water was pumped by a cloth-sail windmill across the lane to the saltpans. A Woodburytype print of the late nineteenth century.

CHAPTER 13

The Village Merchants: Reydon and Wangford; Walberswick and Dunwich

THE YARDS AND WORKPLACES OF COUNTRY MERCHANTS must have been conspicuous landmarks in the eighteenth century; yet for the most part they have left few traces behind them. Their weather-boarded granaries and warehouses, their sawpits, their lime kilns and their coal sheds, misleadingly known as bins, even their small solidly built maltings and kilns have mostly disappeared. What is there left now to mark the activities of William Lenney on ground stretching from Reydon quay to Wolsey bridge? Lenney, a yeoman farmer from Sotherton, bought the land to the west in the early 1740s. It was a mixture of rough heath and marsh but close to the surface ran a ridge of chalk which had long been used for lime burning and where the caves from which the chalk was dug can still be found. Lenney's acquisitions included lime kilns and sheds and also a haven near Wolsey bridge where he could unload extra chalk imported through Southwold harbour. To the east he leased a farm from Sir John Playter together with the new staithe at Reydon where there were two granaries or warehouses and a timber yard.[1]

Sir John Playter built Reydon quay about 1740. Gardner, who gives the date of its construction as 1737, attributes the idea to Lenney, explaining that Lenney was infused with the notion when a sailing ship, the *Bell*, made its way to a place up river with a load of chalk, only to find on arrival that the cargo could not be discharged except by a makeshift arrangement using planks of wood as a stage for the carts awaiting it. Since ships could find enough water to reach this point, which was much further inland than Blackshore quay and so much more accessible to traffic from Reydon and the villages behind, the New Key (as Reydon quay was first called) was the obvious answer. It did, as Gardner observed, save 'considerable charges of Land-Carriage'. Indeed, writing in 1754, he reckoned that for some parts of the country the quay was 'above four miles nearer than Black-shore so that the major Part of Business except in Salt and Fish, is already transferred there'.[2]

Lenney was a general merchant who apart from his lime-burning sent barley and oats to London and timber and agricultural produce to Yarmouth.[3] His business at the quay drove him on to play a very positive part in the rehabilitation of Southwold harbour to which he subscribed £80. Miles Barne who bought the quay from Playter in 1746 shared his tenant's interest in the harbour and it may well have been Barne who insisted that

The Blyth from the air, showing towards the top the lane leading to Reydon quay which cut down the long journey to Blackshore (bottom left).

Lenney should be entrusted with so much responsibility when the new construction began: the appointment of a surveyor and assessment of his proposals; the purchase of loads of oak timber and alder wood; the supervision of the labourers. Lenney dealt in timber and understood it and so in these first years his experience was relied on just as Robinson's was in later years.[4]

Samuel Farra, who succeeded to the tenancy of the quay when Lenney died in 1753, did not devote a similar attention to harbour affairs and the task of overseer reverted once again to Southwold merchants. Farra rented two farmhouses at Reydon from Miles Barne together with the two granaries, a gravelled gangway leading to the quay and also a cottage used as an alehouse. This alehouse, although in recent years it has ceased to sell beer, is the only memorial of a once busy centre up-river and of a staithe which is conspicuous only by its entire absence on the grass bank.[5] Farra, however, has a gravestone in Reydon churchyard. It stands alongside other worn-down Farra slabs but his is more obtrusive than the rest and despite the crusts of lichen proclaims him still as Samuel Farra, 'Merchant'. Samuel had every right to the title. He was exporting grain to London from the early 1750s and in the sixties he built up his connections and became the largest exporter from Southwold harbour. He sent some wheat, rye and barley across to Rotterdam but his ships usually cleared the harbour to head for London. Barley was his main shipment down the coast but he also sent considerable quantities of wheat, peas and oats as well as white salt, candles, tubs of red herrings and even a little Suffolk cheese, despite its reputation, 'too big to swallow and too hard to bite'.[6]

About the time that Farra became tenant of Reydon quay, Knights was airing his plans for the Blyth and Samuel Farra was very quick to see the commercial opportunities of the Navigation and to seize them. His were among the first boatloads of coals to sail up the river to Halesworth – in July and August 1761. The following June he was granted land on Halesworth quay to enclose for coal bins and five years later he asked for more land there to erect a lime kiln and to 'lodge coals and chalk'. In 1763 Farra widened his field and bought the Nag's Head (now the Harbour Inn) at Blackshore together with some land on the quay. Keels and wherries plying up and down to Halesworth with his cargoes must now have met sea-going ships both at Blackshore and at Reydon, and Farra must have owned ships or shares in ships himself since soon after his death in 1769 there were complaints made that a sloop or vessel of his had sunk near Reydon quay.[7]

There is a lane leading from the Reydon–Wangford road which is still marked 'Quay Lane'; and early maps show three other lanes leading from Wangford and Henham to the quay marshes. Up these lanes lumbered heavy wagons with coal for Henham Hall, for the comfortable dwellings of well-to-do farmers and tradesmen; for blacksmiths' forges and brickmakers' kilns. They made the return journey loaded with farm produce – wheat, peas, beans, but above all with barley. Barley which grew so well on the light soils in this part of Suffolk was always the main export of the village entrepreneurs who organized the coastal trade from Southwold harbour. In the later years of the eighteenth century, London brewers, Trumans, Whitbreads, Barclays, were turning increasingly to pale malt in place of the Hertfordshire brown, so much favoured in earlier years; and for the best pale malt the brewers wanted the short plump thin-skinned barley from Norfolk and Suffolk.[8]

Robert Barfoot, who by the seventies was both working Lenney's lime kilns and selling coals to his neighbours, shipped 9800 quarters of grain to London in 1775 and nearly half of this was barley or malt. Barfoot lived at Lime Kiln Farm, Reydon, only a short distance from Reydon quay and linked by roads and tracks with farms in Reydon, Henham and Wangford. He was well-placed to ship his neighbours' corn and the Barfoot family also profited from lime-burning. The farm where they lived is still called Lime Kiln Farm and the trade in lime continued there till the mid nineteenth century.[9]

The outstanding Wangford merchant in the second half of the eighteenth century was John Crisp, a maltster and a yeoman farmer with land in Reydon as well as in

The site of Reydon quay: no trace of former activities is left.

The alehouse by Reydon quay, now converted to a dwelling house.

Wangford.[10] John Crisp, like Samuel Nunn, was a dissenter, a member of the Independent Church (later Congregational) which was so strongly supported in this part of Suffolk. He is remarkable not only for his own achievements as a merchant but also for the achievements of his large family of merchant sons and grandsons who faced the difficult post-war years of depression with resilience and some of whose descendants went on to achieve great commercial and social success.

John and his brother, William, both married daughters of the Rector of Wrentham, the Reverend John Steffe, a devout man who was more concerned with godliness than orthodoxy. On his death bed in the summer of 1737 he advised his wife and daughters to look for Christian guidance in the Meeting House, warning them that the man who he knew was to succeed him in the Wrentham living was a man who did not know the truth. From then on until her death, old Mrs Steffe attended the Independent chapel at Wrentham together with her daughter Martha and Martha's husband, John Crisp. Here they would meet each Sunday many other Crisp relations and other like-minded friends. Social and public avenues open to conforming contemporaries were closed to nonconformists at this time and in consequence of this and of their religious principles they developed their own way of life and supported each other not only in personal and religious practice but also in business activities. It was a way of life which seems often to have resulted in an unusual degree of enterprise especially in the commercial field. Nationally, families like the Barclays and the Darbys spring to mind. Locally, the Crisp family in east Suffolk is an outstanding example.[11]

The founder of the family, John Crisp of Wangford, exported barley on a substantial scale. In 1752 he sent nearly 3000 quarters of barley to London and in 1775 nearly 4500. But while barley was always his main concern he also sent quantities of wheat, oats, peas and beans and sometimes made up a shipload with salt or candles or the odd bag of rags. The records do not show us whether he owned any of the boats, the *Farmers' Adventure*, the *Henham of Southwold*, the *Farmer's Liberty*, which carried his corn. He may well have owned shares in ships but there is no mention of them in his will. His will, however, does show that he had prospered. When he died in 1778 he left his house, his maltings and his farm lands to his youngest son Steffe together with £120; Martha, his wife, and his deaf and dumb son, Thomas, were to have £800 each; up to £500 was to be invested for his daughter; and his four other sons were to have £600 each.[12]

These four sons set themselves up either in Southwold or in Beccles, both small ports where they must have reckoned they had the best prospects for trade. Samuel and James moved to Southwold, William and John to Beccles. Although their father was a maltster he had never sent large quantities of malt to London. The London brewers in these early days usually bought in barley and malted it themselves. This, however, changed and the brewers began increasingly to look to East Anglian maltsters to do the malting for them. John Crisp's sons took with them the malting skills which they had learnt at home and James Crisp at Southwold and John at Beccles were both maltsters as well as merchants.

James Crisp moved to Southwold about 1786 and built up a mercantile business first with his eldest brother Samuel and later with his own son Downing. Following the usual pattern the Southwold Crisps dealt in coal and eventually Downing established himself as Lord Rous's main coal merchant. As maltsters James and Downing were able to take advantage of the gaps left in Southwold by the eclipse of the Thompson and Nunn families. They worked John Thompson's maltings in Woodleys Yard off the High Street and eventually bought it. They also rented Samuel Nunn's maltings near Church Green although they lost this tenancy when Messrs Prest, corn factors of London, thrust their way into Southwold in 1809 (p.93).[13] Writing in 1812 George Crabbe pinpointed the frequent connection between dissent and mercantile trade. His dissenter, Jonas Kindred, was

> *vendor of hops and malt, of coal and corn*
> *And like his father he was merchant born*[14]

Apart from deaf and dumb Thomas all the sons of John Crisp of Wangford were merchants and the family ties between them were very close. When James Crisp's son and business partner, Downing, died prematurely in 1809, still in his early thirties, it was his first cousin, William, son of James's brother William (respected merchant and soap boiler of Beccles), who came to Southwold and took his place. William moved into the High Street house (where Barclays Bank now stands) and took over the maltings in Woodleys Yard. In 1814 with another dissenter as his partner he bought the Church Green maltings, which by now had been much enlarged, for £1200. William also rented the maltings at the Reydon Bear and maltings at Yoxford. He had the granaries at Reydon quay and a granary at Blackshore and he owned shares in ships. [15]

The prospects for a maltster must have looked rosy in 1814. The price of malt had soared during the French wars and reached 96 shillings a quarter in 1813, almost three times the price in 1788.[16] But the end of the war brought prolonged depression and low prices. The twenties and thirties were gloomy years for the malting trade and William Crisp was driven to diversify. In 1825 he bought the brewery at the back of the Swan and he gradually fell back on brewing 'Crisp's Ale' and importing London porter. When he died his big maltings by Church Green were bought by the John Crisps of Beccles.[17] The Crisp business at Beccles had proved to be the stronger, it weathered the depression and in the prosperous years which eventually followed, it blossomed. By the late nineteenth century the firm of John Crisp and Son of Beccles was a famous name which dominated the malting trade in the country north of Ipswich. There is no doubt that in one respect the John Crisps had a great advantage over their Southwold cousins, an advantage which must have helped them to survive the depression years. They sent their malt by wherry from Beccles to Yarmouth from whence it was shipped to London. They did not have to endure the delays and mishaps suffered by merchants shipping from Southwold harbour.

John Crisp of Wangford, the stem of this notable family, lived at Elms Farm situated north of Reydon Wood and here his maltings still survive close to the splendid farmhouse. John died in 1778 and left his property to his youngest son, Steffe, but in 1813 Steffe, who was perhaps the least successful of John's able-bodied sons, sold the maltings and farm to Lord Rous.[18] Some years later they were tenanted by Benjamin Reeve, a member of another Wangford family with a mercantile tradition.

The Reeve family, like the Crisps, seem to have been brought up to the malting business and the trade in heavy goods which so easily combined with it. Robert Reeve moved to Halesworth in the 1750s and, as we shall see, achieved remarkable success there as a maltster, merchant and brewer. His bachelor brother, Benjamin, remained in Wangford as a farmer and merchant and when he died in 1790 his business was taken over by Robert's son, another Benjamin.[19]

During the French wars the younger Benjamin Reeve (1765-1853) must have done very well in association with his brothers, Robert Reeve's other sons, James of Halesworth and young Robert, who had set up as a corn factor in London. Benjamin was able to establish himself in a gentlemanly fashion at the Elms and weathered the post-war depression. When he died he was farming about 250 acres and was well-known as a maltster.[20]

The stories of these rural entrepreneurs are difficult to piece together for they left no records. Their accounts, their order books and bundles of receipts have not survived them. Moreover this was a time when commercial activities were considered beneath the notice of most contemporary writers and when local topographers were only prepared to be distracted from absorption in pedigrees and antiquities by supernatural or violent events. The busy lives of these village merchants and their hard-working wives did not invite the glare of publicity. They lived comfortably enough but they had little time for anything outside a routine which demanded industrious application to business and on top of which they had family commitments, inescapable local duties and in some cases also religious duties.

William Crisp of Southwold, 1784–1844, maltster and brewer. Photograph of a water-colour believed to be in the possession of the Crisp family.

John Crisp's Maltings at Elms Farm, Wangford, photographed in 1989.

There was, however, one village Hampden amongst them who indirectly played his part on the national stage. Francis Robinson was the acknowledged leader of the 'little freemen' of Dunwich in whose hands lay the power to elect two members of Parliament. The story of his battles and bargaining with the landlords who owned this rotten borough will be told by the historian of Dunwich. Here we need only observe that without the independent income which his merchant business gave him, Robinson would have been much less strongly placed to stand up to the would-be patrons of Dunwich, the Downings, the Barnes and the Vannecks.

Francis Robinson had followed his father as tenant of a farm in Dunwich but his mercantile activities were based on Walberswick quay where, as we have seen, he was renting a warehouse from the Blois family at the beginning of the 1760s and at much the same time he also took the tenancy of a Blois farm at Walberswick. He was well-placed to act as middleman for the substantial farmers who worked the land to the south and west of Walberswick – not only for the tenants of Westwood Lodge but also for other wealthy neighbours like Henry Coates, farmer and brick-maker of Hinton Hall, William Woods, farmer of Hinton, and Alex Woods, farmer and maltster of Westleton Grange. These men cultivated the flat fields of light sandy loam which skirted the heath fringes of Dunwich forest; good land for barley, like the fields at Reydon, so that for Francis Robinson as for Farra and Crisp, barley was the main grain shipped to London though he also sent much other local farm produce.[21]

Besides this coastal trade to London, Francis Robinson had a variety of other interests. Lime-burning he seems to have left to the Wales family who for many years pursued this trade in Walberswick, but he sent coal by wherry to Halesworth and by wagon to Darsham Hall and no doubt he supplied neighbouring brick kilns and maltings; he sent ships to Rotterdam and he was also a wine merchant who imported brandy and gin from the continent. In 1775 we find him sending the *Prince of Wales* to Oporto to bring back port wine and also sheet cork for his bottling activities. Robinson probably owned several ships and we certainly know that he was the owner of the sloop *Dunwich* which was registered at Southwold in 1786.[22]

When he died in 1790 his son, also Francis, must have carried on his trade at least for some time and it was probably for him that another *Dunwich* was built at Walberswick in 1803.[23] In contrast to his father, the younger Robinson was very active in the affairs of the harbour. Appointed a Commissioner in 1810 he was among the few who in the uneasy post-war period attended meetings with reasonable regularity. He was one of the five Commissioners who subscribed £100 each in 1814 to rescue the harbour finances (the others were either peers or baronets) and in 1824 he agreed to help supervise the work of repairing the south pier.[24] There is no evidence that he continued his mercantile activities for long and he probably abandoned them in the post-war slump. He continued, however, as an active Harbour Commissioner till two years before his death in 1843 and was a warm supporter of Lord Stradbroke in the violent controversies over the harbour in the 1830s and 1840s.

Descendants of John Crisp of Wangford: mentioned in the book

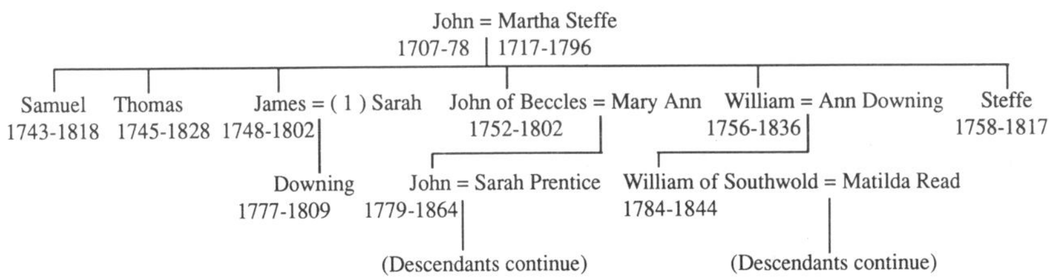

CHAPTER 14

Halesworth: A New Economy and a Changing Society

THE ARRIVAL AT HALESWORTH IN 1761 OF THE first keel laden with coals was 'attended from the Town Lock up to the great Bason by a numerous Concourse of People, assembled not more to satisfy their Curiosity at the Novelty of the Sight, than to join in the general Joy and Triumph on the Occasion'.[1] It is difficult for us to appreciate the extent to which the Navigation was indeed a novelty for the Halesworth townsfolk and, as we have seen, it was a novelty which was regarded by some with considerable mistrust (p.21). A little market town where many were still absorbed in the crafts related to the surrounding farming families – leather trades, wood trades, the making and selling of hempen yarn and cloth – was not sure what to make of the Navigation and it is perhaps hardly surprising that it was not a Halesworth man but Samuel Farra from Reydon whose name is the first recorded as sending a vessel laden with coals up the river.

Other entrepreneurs from villages outside – Francis Robinson of Dunwich and Samuel Badeley of Walpole – were quick to apply for room on Halesworth quay to enclose for sheds to house the heavy loads of coal and chalk which could now be floated up the river. Two men in a wherry could comfortably transport nine or more chaldrons of coal from Blackshore to Halesworth in a day – a burden which on the rutted roads would need four heavy wagons each pulled by four sweating horses.[2]

This was a business which was unlikely to appeal to Halesworth drapers, grocers and small craftsmen – men accustomed to calculate in stones and yards rather than chaldrons and coombs, men who had for the most part little capital and had besides little understanding of mercantile business. Moreover the misgivings of Halesworth townsfolk must have been powerfully reinforced by the conspicuous collapse of the ambitious projects of the main instigator of the Navigation scheme – Thomas Knights himself.

Following the death of his father in 1735 Tom Knights had been acquiring property in Halesworth on a lavish scale and had built up a typical brewer's conglomerate of brewing and malting property and local public houses. Amongst other property, he acquired the prestigious Angel tavern, the bowling green and bowling green house nearby, and a large acreage of land behind and to the south of the Angel, which stretched down to the river and on part of which he built a commodious brewery with a malthouse and store house.[3]

By 1750 Knights was in financial trouble. Perhaps he had hoped for a larger inheritance from his Uncle Philip who died in 1747; perhaps he had persuaded his creditors to this effect. In April 1750, however, London distillers, headed by Sir Robert Ladbroke, obtained a release of most of Knights' property on trust to sell it for the benefit of his creditors, and included were three public houses in Halesworth: the Black Swan, the Green Man with adjoining brewing offices, situated by the river, and the Angel with 16 acres of meadow behind.[4]

Somehow Knights managed to emerge from this crisis. The property he lost was mainly outside Halesworth. He managed to retain the Angel and the land behind, and also the two other Halesworth public houses but he did so only by mortgaging most (if not all) of his Halesworth property to Henry Coates of Blythburgh. By 1757 he owed Coates £1450 with £72 outstanding interest.

In April 1757, the month when the Navigation Act at last received Royal Assent, Knights found himself in urgent need of a further £647 and this Coates refused to lend under the existing mortgage. Tom Knights now pinned his hopes on a dubious scheme which centred on a wealthy but sickly young man in his late twenties. John Colston of Walpole was cared for by Knights' sister, Mary, and in his last days moved to Halesworth to live in Knights' house. Knights induced Colston to join with him in a bond which Knights and his very sharp solicitor (not a local man) hoped would throw Knights' debt on to Colston's estate. The signing of the bond certainly persuaded Henry Coates to advance to Knights the £647 he so desperately needed and thereby Tom Knights gained a little respite. But the respite was brief. In June 1757 Colston died, leaving all his property to Mary, and the Court of Chancery in 1759 upheld Mary Knights' claim that all Knights' mortgaged property must be forfeited to Coates before any of Colston's property was touched. In August 1764 Henry Coates was advertising Knights' brewing empire for sale: the Angel, the Green Man, the Ship, the White Lion; the commodious brewing and malting offices which Knights had lately built; the land by the river; two half-built houses 'with materials on the spot for finishing the same'.[5]

In June 1762 Knights attended a Navigation meeting for the last time. Desperately needing money, he had been trying to claim that he had personally expended £229 in his journeys and efforts to obtain the Navigation Act but the Commissioners considered his claim 'very unreasonable and Exorbitant'. In June 1765 he sent a message to the Angel asking for at least some money towards these supposed expenses and in response to this appeal the Commissioners, hard put to it for money themselves, sent him ten guineas. Less than a year later he was dead.[6]

Tom Knights' ambitious projects far outran his means; and as he juggled with debts it seems that the Navigation scheme must have been part of his gamble with the realities of economic life in Halesworth. He had meadows and property by the river and he had breweries and maltings at a convenient distance. He was well-placed to benefit and he must have convinced not only himself but his creditors that the Navigation would transform his situation. In pinning unrealistically extravagant hopes on the scheme he was not alone; but in any case for Knights the completion of the works came too late. He was actively engaged in plans for the Navigation early in 1753 and probably before then, but nine years had passed before the Commissioners could say that the Navigation was complete. By then Knights' time had run out.

Knights was floundering in schemes as unfamiliar to himself as to most of his fellow citizens. Amongst these Halesworth townsfolk, however, there was at least one man who launched himself on a successful mercantile career at this time and had the enterprise and the wealth to take advantage of the Navigation. The curiously christened Alderman Skoulding was the hard-headed son of Thomas Skoulding, a wealthy draper, who had been among the few Halesworth tradesmen actively to support the Navigation. Although he bought no shares, Thomas Skoulding was elected a Commissioner and was most constant in his attendance at meetings. Perhaps he had read the warning signs in the declining Halesworth hemp trade; certainly his son, Alderman, deployed his capital in other directions. Alderman usually called himself a liquor merchant but like other successful merchants he was ready to deal in any profitable commodity. In 1772 he erected a coal shelter on the quay and took shares in a wherry and in this same year he followed his father as a River Commissioner. A thrusting man, whose violent rudeness drove Peter Jermyn to tender his resignation as Treasurer of the Navigation, Alderman had his finger in many pies and when he died his property included two granaries or warehouses on the quay together with yards for coal; and he also owned the malthouse, kiln and barley chamber through the Angel yard.[7]

But Skoulding seems to have been unusual. For the most part it was not the Halesworth tradespeople but merchants in the surrounding neighbourhood who were excited by the possibilities opened up by the Navigation and in some cases their expectations led them to move into Halesworth bringing with them not only new drive but also very necessary capital resources.

Robert Reeve of Wangford was prominent among these new arrivals. He was the son of a Wangford yeoman farmer who may well have been himself a maltster and dealer. Robert's bachelor brother, Benjamin, stayed in Wangford as a merchant and farmer (p.81) but Robert was assisted by his father-in-law to launch himself in Halesworth. In 1757 he had married the daughter of Richard Smith, an affluent timber merchant at Sotherton, who had always warmly supported Knights' plans and had acquired land and buildings close to the quay basin together with a thatched house appropriately christened the Wherry Inn. As soon as Knights' vision became a reality Robert Reeve was shipping coal up to Halesworth and obtained permission to make a cut of water from the quay basin to a lime kiln erected on Smith's land.[8]

Both Reeve and Smith moved to Halesworth and Smith helped to launch his son-in-law on a mercantile career which combined effectively with malting and brewing. Robert began in Halesworth as a maltster and acquired the Pound pightle (enclosure) with a malthouse in 1758. Six years later he was describing himself as a beer brewer and it was probably at this time that he acquired the tenancy of the Three Tuns in the Market Place with its brewery, stables and bowling green and the Tavern meadows behind.[9]

Reeve never bought the brewery which he worked although he bought much other property in Halesworth and outside. Like all enterprising brewers he bought up public houses, including the White Hart and the Castle in Halesworth, and in 1778 he bought the property on the south-west side of the Market Place close to the Three Tuns and the brewery – a conglomeration of buildings, into which he moved his large family. After his death in 1793 his son James moved into this house and took over the brewing business. Between them, father and son eventually bought up about thirty public houses in Halesworth and the villages around.[10]

Robert and James were both River Commissioners and James became Treasurer of the Navigation in 1810. The wherries which brought up coals and liquors and carried down heavy barrels of beer rendered an important service to brewers and publicans but the Reeve family were always merchants as well as brewers and maltsters. Apart from the lime kiln and cinder oven near the quay which he inherited from his father-in-law, Robert also had a sawpit and timber business there. In the 1790s the Reeve family were well-placed to take advantage of the rising corn prices and strong enough to withstand the alarming price fluctuations. When Robert died in 1793 he had established his eldest son (also Robert) as a corn factor in the City of London and, as we have seen, his son Benjamin was following in the footsteps of his uncle Benjamin as a farmer and merchant in Wangford, where he also became well-known as a maltster. Sir John Rous was selling large quantities of corn, beans and peas to the Reeves in the nineties and in 1796 they paid him over £1200 for grains. They must have been sending this corn to London and it would probably have gone by wagon from Henham to Reydon quay or Blackshore quay. But Rous can hardly have been their only supplier and they probably also sent corn down to Southwold harbour in wherries.[11]

We know that Robert Reeve was interested in wherries. In 1772 he asked the

The Wherry Inn, Halesworth quay, about 1890.

Halesworth Market Place; a postcard about 1890. The Three Tuns is on the right with the brewery chimneys behind. On the left is the main part of the Reeve family house.

Navigation Commissioners to sally forth from their meeting at the Angel to inspect a wherry which he had 'lately erected' in combination with Brame Oxford, the miller of Holton, and Alderman Skoulding of Halesworth. The three complained that several bridges were too low for their new wherry and requested permission to raise them at their own expense. The request, somewhat reminiscent of the curious logic of the dotty wise men of Gotham, was turned down and they were persuaded that it would be more practicable to alter the wherry. This wherry was probably the *Halesworth*, possibly the only wherry ever built in the town but which eventually sailed successfully on the Blyth Navigation till 1818.[12]

In 1799 society in Halesworth and the surrounding district was shaken by news of the bankruptcy of two affluent merchants. This was no ordinary little affair for Samuel Badeley and John Woodcock both stood high in the Blyth valley. Neither was a native of Halesworth. The Badeleys were very well-to-do yeoman farmers who lived in a large mansion in neighbouring Walpole where they had considerable property; the Woodcocks had moved to Halesworth from Norfolk.

Four generations of Badeleys were baptized in Walpole Chapel and like their friend, Samuel Nunn of Southwold, the Badeleys had the independent outlook and self-reliance which is often associated with members of the Independent Church. The elder Samuel Badeley (1709–80) was enthusiastic about the Navigation from the first and was included in Knights' preliminary list of 'Gentlemen, Proprietors of real estate in the neighbourhood of Halesworth' who testified approbation of the Navigation proposal. He was one of the original Commissioners, subscribed £100 for shares and in 1757 was appointed Treasurer; and although he held this office for only two years he continued faithful in his attendance at the meetings and in 1769 he was joined on the Commission by his son.[13]

Samuel Badeley the younger (1741–1823) evidently shared his father's belief in the propects opened up by the Navigation and he decided to base his business in Halesworth. He subscribed to both the warehouses built for merchants using the quay; he rented meadows adjoining the river and as early as 1762 he applied for room on the quay to enclose for coal sheds.[14] By the mid fifties the Badeleys were exporting barley, wheat and malt from Southwold harbour to London and although their name disappears from the Port Books in the late sixties and seventies, Samuel Badeley the younger was claiming a debenture from the Customs on exported wheat in 1785. But he also described himself as a wholesale brewer and in this enterprise he went into partnership with John Woodcock.[15]

The Woodcocks were wealthy drapers from Harleston who seem to have decided, like the Skouldings, that the time had come to deploy their accumulated capital in other directions. Presumably they were attracted to Halesworth by the new Navigation for John Woodcock and his well-heeled father both moved into the town some time in the sixties. The younger John Woodcock also moved into brewing and acquired the brewery and maltings in Bridge Street, Halesworth, later operated by William Hooker, the world-famous botanist. The brewery property which included granaries, stables and a wine-vault was well-placed between the Bungay–Ipswich road and the river; and John Woodcock also acquired meadows adjoining the quay where he had brick-yards and the inevitable coal sheds.[16] He bought up property and public houses – the Hawk and the King's Head at Halesworth, the White Lion at Heveningham and the Bell at Middleton and no doubt many others in neighbouring villages. In 1770 John Woodcock also bought the Bear Inn at Reydon with its adjacent maltings and proceeded to accumulate public houses in nearby Southwold – the Crown, the White Lion, the Red Lion and the Nag's Head (now the Harbour Inn) on Blackshore quay. River transport must have been very useful to this widely spread enterprise and John Woodcock was a conscientious River Commissioner.[17]

John married the daughter of John Garneys, surgeon and man midwife at Yoxford. She was her father's heiress and eventually inherited from him the Lordship of the Manor of Westleton-Cleves. John and Elizabeth and their twelve children lived in a large brick mansion off the old Bungay road and away from the brewery smoke. Surrounded by paddocks and rich land, their spacious garden contained not only the 'summer house' beloved by eighteenth-century town dwellers but also a greenhouse and a melon ground.[18]

The calamity which overtook Woodcock and Badeley sprang from their decision to set up as bankers. Exactly when they took this step is not certain but in 1791 Woodcock procured a draft for over £300 to help Rous pay his election expenses; the following year we find them lending Brame Oxford, the Holton miller, £800; and in 1794 they were listed as bankers in *The Universal Directory*. In adding banking to brewing they were but following in the same path as other provincial brewers like the Cobbolds of Ipswich and the Lacons of Yarmouth, but they can hardly have had the same financial resources as these two families and the risks in the small, economically unstable town of Halesworth were great. By 1799 they had over-extended themselves and a Commission of Bankruptcy was issued against them. Woodcock, backed by his father and fortunate in the wealth of his wife, came out of the bankruptcy relatively unscathed but Badeley saw his property dismantled.[19]

Samuel Badeley was one of those independent yeoman landowners whose numbers were gradually decreasing. He was educated at Woodbridge Grammar School and he sent his sons, Joseph and Samuel junior, to Norwich Grammar School. The value of his estate was some £400 a year and his house in Walpole, situated on high ground with a pleasing prospect, outclassed many a small gentleman's seat. Probably though, like Crabbe's great-uncle at Parham and other Suffolk yeoman farmers, the family lived in the large kitchen along with their servants, leaving the drawing-room and dining-parlour for social occasions or visits from distinguished neighbours such as Sir Gerard Vanneck whose candidature for the County seat in 1790 Badeley warmly supported.[20]

Badeley's farms and property in Walpole, including the impropriate Rectory which he owned (and with which went the right to nominate the Curate of the church), were put up for auction at the Three Tuns in Halesworth in the late summer of 1799, together with his mansion house – 'extremely well adapted to be the residence of a large genteel family'. In September his neighbours pored over his solid old-fashioned household goods, four-post bedsteads furnished with damask and moreen, three-hundred ounces of plate. The house in Walpole belonging to his son Joseph was also sold and then similarly invaded for three days for the sale of Joseph's very modern and fashionable furniture, bedsteads with printed cotton and dimity, fashionable mahogany articles and elegant tea equipage of Wedgwood ware.[21]

The Badeleys were not reduced to penury. The two sons, Joseph and Samuel, who had been baptized in Walpole Chapel now hastily established themselves in the Church of England and were publicly baptized at Wrentham Church in the week before the auction. They then both took holy orders and in due course became vicars of Ubbeston and Blewbury respectively. Joseph eventually became Rector of Halesworth cum Chediston in 1831. David Elisha Davy, a great friend of the third Samuel Badeley, states that all the creditors were paid and a surplus remained. The elder Samuel Badeley retired to Yarmouth where he lived to be over eighty.[22]

In October 1790, at the request of Sir Gerard Vanneck of Heveningham Hall, *She Stoops to Conquer* was presented at Halesworth theatre. The company was 'as genteel as it was numerous' and 'the dresses were almost new'. No doubt the occasional presence of the Vannecks at nearby Heveningham enlivened life in Halesworth but it is also true to say that by the last decade of the century Halesworth had been well shaken out of its early-eighteenth-century mould. It is significant that in 1782 Gurneys and Turner decided to open a branch of their Yarmouth bank at Halesworth and that they made the Halesworth bank the headquarters of most of their Suffolk banks. From the mid eighties a turnpike road from Bungay to Ipswich ran through the town and there were frequent coaches and post to London. In June 1790 a Halesworth shopkeeper announced in the Ipswich Journal that he had just returned from London where he had informed himself of every dress in the present fashion and that he had ordered from London a variety of clothes, fancy waistcoats and Manchester goods.[23]

Some of the social change in Halesworth must be attributed to the lifestyle of the new affluent families like the Reeves and the Woodcocks who would patronize the subscription Assemblies and the concerts of instrumental music at the Three Tuns. It was a social change which may have widened the gulf between rich and poor, between those in the genteel sashed dwellings and capital mansion houses and those in the run-down tenements. It reflected the fact that Halesworth was ceasing to be a town of small traders and craftsmen and a market for dairy farmers from surrounding villages who supplemented their income by growing and weaving hemp.

How much did the Navigation contribute to the economic and social changes in Halesworth? Even before the digging began the idea of the new river route had caught the imagination of entrepreneurs in the surrounding neighbourhood; and when at last the work was completed some were very quick to establish trading yards at Halesworth quay while others, as we have seen, moved themselves and their families to Halesworth and made the town their base. The main attraction of the Navigation, at least in the earlier years, lay in the cheap transport for coal which the keels and wherries provided. Coal and coke were the basic commodities in which most merchants dealt and which they needed besides for other undertakings – lime-burning, malting, brewing. A great deal of the activity at Halesworth quay was concerned with coal.

In the 1770s trade was good and this was a hopeful time when tolls on the river brought in on average £146 a year which would mean 300 to 400 journeys a year by craft carrying full cargoes on the two-day trips to and from Southwold harbour. Halesworth quay and the surrounding meadow must have been noisy, bustling, grimy places in these years and the Wherry Inn which abutted on the quay must have provided much-needed refreshment for dusty throats. Besides the original warehouse built by the Commissioners and the much more 'commmodious' one built in 1765 (p.27), there were open coal grounds and sheds owned by individual merchants; coke ovens and lime kilns belching smoke; and piled up heaps of bricks, stones and timber unloaded from the wherries. In 1774 Messrs Tolver, iron merchants of Yarmouth, were given permission to lay coals on the quay and to build a warehouse for lodging iron floated up the river; and the following year a new granary was erected for corn brought up to Halesworth.[24] In the eighties, however, when trade over the whole country was half-paralysed by the effects of the American War of Independence, tolls on the Navigation fell off. This was a parsimonious time for the Navigation and its finances did not recover till nearly the end of the century despite the abandonment of interest payments to shareholders and the welcome increase of income from tolls in the nineties.

The decline of trade in the eighties was too much for Messrs Tolver of Yarmouth who went bankrupt, leaving as a memorial at Halesworth the great 'iron warehouse' which Alderman Skoulding acquired to store coal and which continued to brood over the meadow for about a hundred years.[25] None the less the arrival of these iron merchants at Halesworth quay is symptomatic of the possibilities opened up by the Navigation and it foreshadowed the establishment of an iron foundry in Halesworth by Messrs Easterson and Seaman early in the next century. This iron foundry, situated east of the Thoroughfare and close to the river, is a late example of the shift of commercial life in Halesworth towards the river, a shift which must have caused the small tradesmen on Soap Hill and in Chediston Street to lament the old days.

The old days, however, were passing. The prosperous dairy farmers whose custom had been the life-blood of early-eighteenth-century Halesworth were turning from cows to corn, while Lancashire cotton goods were replacing hempen threads and cloth. The distant rumble of the industrial revolution can be heard behind these changes. Most important for bucolic east Suffolk was the growing need for more bread and beer to feed the rapidly increasing populations in crowded industrial towns. It was this which caused the gradual revolution in agricultural practice and the switching from pasture to arable as demand drove up the price of corn in the second half of the eighteenth century. The great contribution of the Navigation to Halesworth was that it enabled the town to adjust to this change from green to brown, from cows to corn which was taking place in the surrounding country and which rapidly accelerated when prices rose to dizzy heights during the French wars. An enterprising maker of hemp cloth like James Aldred of Chediston Street and well-established tanners and workers in leather like the Hugman family[26] could still make a good living in Halesworth, but the men attracted by the Navigation built up commercial businesses in coal together with industries based on coal and other heavy raw materials which could be floated up the river. They were men with capital who could accumulate brewing and malting empires and they were gradually sending more corn and farm produce down the river to be shipped from Southwold harbour. It was an adjustment which, as we shall see, became increasingly apparent in the nineteenth century and which brought prosperity and work to many in Halesworth. It has to be admitted that in the eighteenth century and still more in the years which followed, the Navigation never quite lived up to expectations and that for some merchants it proved but a glittering siren, but none the less without it Halesworth would have been left marooned.

East view of Halesworth from Castle Hill, engraved in 1847 by W. J. Gilbert, a local painter living in Pound Street.

CHAPTER 15

The French Wars and Shadows of Post-war Slump

ONE OF THE OBJECTIONS TO VOLUNTEER CORPS, Lord Rous complained in 1804, is 'that it makes some persons feel so much consequence that they never afterwards get into their proper places'. For the Blything Volunteers Rous had appointed three field officers from what he considered an appropriate stratum of local society – David Elisha Davy, Henry Jermyn and Richard Gooch – only to find that the six captains he designated to serve under them objected strongly. These presumptuous captains included James Reeve, brewer and merchant of Halesworth, and his brother Benjamin, farmer and merchant of Wangford, and also the younger Francis Robinson of Scots Hall, Westleton. The Napoleonic wars were the first of the great wars to shake up the set patterns of society. In Southwold Robert May, captain of the local Volunteers and Edward Killwick, captain of the Marine Fencibles, 'obtruded' themselves, ousted the Robinsons and for about twelve years were cocks of the midden. They exercised power with a reckless arrogance which included a high-handed argument with the vice-admiral commanding at Yarmouth.[1]

The social assertiveness which irrritated Rous was not merely a matter of temporary sashes and feathered helmets. Perhaps he had not grasped that the expanding food market and the dramatic rise in corn prices which enabled him to raise his tenants' rents had also brought increased prosperity to farmers and to local merchants. He certainly was not prepared to recognize their consequent aspirations to gentility.

For the merchants the accumulation of wealth which made these aspirations possible became increasingly risky and something of a gamble during the wars. There was a get-rich-quick atmosphere and a lack of stability. Rapid inflation and the demand for food resulted in a dramatic and alluring rise in corn prices. Wheat which was 47s. a quarter on average in the decade before 1793, averaged 77s. from 1793 to 1801, 92s. between 1803 and 1813 and reached 126s. a quarter in 1812. Coal prices though more moderate followed the same trend. Crisps had supplied coal to Henham in 1793 at 27s. a chaldron; in 1798 they asked 30s. and in 1807 39s. Yet at the same time there were potentially disastrous fluctuations in prices year by year, due as much to the state of the harvests as to the vagaries of diplomacy and war. In February 1797 Parson Woodforde sent his man, Ben, to Norwich with ten coombs of barley but found he could get 'little or nothing' for it: 'The Corn Merchants said that it was at present such a glut that they had almost as soon not have it as have it.' The parson got only 12s. a quarter for this barley, yet in 1801 barley reached over 90s. a quarter. It fell to below 26s. in the next years but was over 50s. in 1809–10 and fetched nearly twice as much in 1812. During the next two years grain prices began the long trend of descent which brought with it prolonged agricultural depression but even before this a heavy toll had been taken of merchants who had been tempted to over-reach themselves.[2]

In September 1799 William Benstead of Halesworth 'informed his friends' by means of the *Ipswich Journal* that he had large stocks of Cognac brandy and rum together with fir balks and timber. However, in the same issue of the *Journal* he was constrained to warn customers that he could not in future give credit for coals purchased. By 1808 Benstead and his partner, John Clark, now described as maltsters and corn merchants were bankrupt. Stephen Self, corn merchant of Chediston Street, who had joined Benstead in the warning about credit for coals, survived longer but was also bankrupt by 1811. In June 1808 poverty-stricken cottages in Chediston Street, most of them divided into tenements, were auctioned at the Angel following the bankruptcy of Samuel King, who in the 1790s had been the carpenter employed to repair bridges and locks on the Navigation but who now also called himself 'merchant'.[3] These hopeful men who jumped on the corn band wagon depended also on the coal coming up from Southwold harbour to keep their trade going and competition in the coal market was intense. Lord Rous and the other local gentry could make or break a small opportunist like Stephen Self, who after supplying coal to Rous for five years was dropped completely. Rous and his agent were very sharp and were quite prepared to bring up coal themselves from Aldeburgh or to send wagons to Walberswick or Reydon quays and deal directly with the Masters of the *Halesworth Trader* or the *Fountain*, with a tip to the sailors for drinks.[4]

For the small men with inadequate capital, mercantile business was a gamble and they often went under, at least for a time. In contrast the Reeves with their powerful brewing and merchant business accumulated property and wealth and on the strength of it developed ambitions to enter the ranks of the landed gentry – a social jump which seems always to have been easier for brewers. In 1810 James Reeve purchased the Manor of Westleton-Cleves. In the 1830s Davy noted that the Reeves drove a carriage with arms on the side.[5]

Through most of the nineties the Navigation was in debt to the carpenters and bricklayers who worked on the locks and bridges, but in June 1799 the Commissioners noted with satisfaction 'the increase of Trade upon the River, the additional number of crafts employed' and in the five peak years which followed over £1100 was collected in tolls. More grain was going down the river and *Holden's Directory* for 1811 informed its readers that barges from Halesworth passed down the Navigation three or four times a week 'with corn etc. for the London market'.[6]

Barley and malt were the grains which London most wanted from east Suffolk. The big London brewers were stepping up their use of pale malt made from East Anglian barley and now rather than malting the barley themselves they were increasingly looking to local maltsters to malt the barley for them. Early in the new century Messrs Prest, City of London corn factors of Laurence Pountney Lane, descended on Halesworth and established themselves in granaries and maltings with wharves beside the Navigation. They bought up property and installed Mr Hammond Ringwood, their agent and manager, in a solid house in Quay Street beside the maltings. Prests did not stop there. They also thrust into Southwold. In 1809 they financed George Lloyd, a small maltster in Church Street, Southwold, and enabled him to purchase the old Nunn malting on Church Green for £400. Lloyd went on to buy the rest of this complex of buildings in 1811 when the White Lion and its surroundings were knocked down to him for £110. His rise to these giddy heights, however, was short-lived for in this same year he was found to owe over £1200 in malt tax and the King's writ was levied on all his property.[7]

The Prests and their shrewd agent, Hammond Ringwood, must have benefited the

Navigation but they added to the pressures and disruptions of this hectic period. Ringwood also sold malt locally and wrested business from maltsters like Steffe Crisp of Wangford who in 1813 decided to sell up his malt office and the farm where John Crisp had brought up his family. Then in 1819 the Prests, ships that pass in the night, themselves went bankrupt.[8] As so often happened in these cases, however, the agent seems to have feathered his nest and Hammond Ringwood emerged possessed of wherries, a lime kiln yard, coal sheds, granaries and the maltings with two kilns beside the quay. He also owned cottages in Quay Street and he himself continued to live in the house on the turnpike road beside the maltings and counting house.[9]

Ringwood may not have worked the maltings himself and in fact he always called himself a coal merchant and perhaps he decided that coal and lime were safer commodities to deal in as the slump set in. Coal at this time was still the mainstay of the Navigation. Between 1810 and 1819 out of 230000 quarters of corn which were shipped from Southwold harbour only about 40000 quarters were credited to the Halesworth trade (Table 2). The main corn trade must have continued in the hands of men who shipped from Blackshore, Walberswick and Reydon – men like the younger Francis Robinson and the Crisps. We have a very scanty picture but we do know of one successful merchant, Jacob Mealing of Reydon, who eventually went into partnership with Robert Mills. Mealing shipped corn extensively from Southwold but about 1811 he decided he could tolerate Southwold harbour no longer. Mealing and Mills moved to Norwich where at one time theirs was the largest firm of corn merchants in the city.[10]

Mealing's decision to move highlights the fact that on top of the general commercial risks, the merchants in the Blyth valley were confronted by an additional hazard. Southwold harbour was in all sorts of trouble during the war and immediate post-war years. Few fully loaded ships could cross the bar and in 1790 the masters and owners were forced to spend £200 on a lighter, the *Good Intent*, to help get the heavy cargoes across. Weary seamen bringing coal from Sunderland arrived in sight of the skeleton pier heads only to find they must wait in the breaking seas till their turn came to use the *Old Drop* as they derisively nicknamed the lighter.

A petition complaining about the pool of Southwold in 1803 was followed by the extension of the south pier in 1806. This seems to have temporarily improved the bar but did not solve problems caused by accumulated shingle within the harbour which choked the entrance so that in 1810 and 1811 it had to be dug out six times.[11]

Despite these hazards and frustrations merchants and farmers were still eager to ship from Southwold harbour and cash in on the exciting profits to be made in the London market. Benjamin Whitney, valuing a farm in Dunwich in 1810, stressed that 'being so near the Port of Walberswick is a great advantage on account of the Shipping Corn there'; and another valuer looking over a farm in Henham in 1801 pointed out the advantage of 'being so near the port to ship corn'.[12] A great corn bonanza was on and dues collected from ships using Southwold harbour which had fallen off in the eighties rose in the following three decades by more than seventy per cent (Table 1).

The increase in revenue seems to have lulled the landowners and gentry of which the Harbour Commission was largely composed into complacency and neglect and meetings were often adjourned for lack of attendance. Lord Rous attended more assiduously than most but meetings were on several occasions chaired by the few Southwold merchants who were on the Commission. The situation in fact was far from deserving complacency. On top of the physical problems at the harbour, Southwold was suffering from social upheavals and an instability which was soon to affect the harbour administration.

The French wars themselves had a destabilizing effect and brought new problems and an increase in old ones. There was a feeling of disorder which is reflected in the letters despatched by the Collector of Customs in Southwold to the Board in London in the late 1790s and early 1800s. He repeatedly asked for dragoons and cutters to be stationed at Southwold to help the Revenue Officers combat the large gangs of smugglers, sometimes armed with muskets and cutlasses, who were landing goods at Benacre and on the open plain and marshes round Dunwich. In 1798 he welcomed the arrival of the *Wasp* gun boat with four heavy guns on board and fourteen men, and hoped that Lord Rous was writing to the Admiralty to ask them to station the *Wasp* at Southwold. Soldiers were despatched and then withdrawn but without their assistance 'it is impossible for the Revenue Officers to prevent the illicit trade now carried upon this part of the coast'. In June 1802 the Customs boatmen while on duty were attacked by the crew of a smuggling vessel all armed with muskets and cutlasses who detained them as prisoners the whole day while they ran in casks of liquor and bags of tobacco. Unfortunately military quartered in the town had left it six days before and there were no soldiers either at Yoxford or Saxmundham. 'We cannot omit stating to your Honours the necessity of some Horse Soldiers being immediately quartered in this town and neighbourhood.'[13]

But if Southwold welcomed the regular dragoons and sailors who must often have thronged the streets and public houses they suffered from the voluntary corps which were formed at this time and from their arrogant officers. The Fencibles, formed in 1798 and consisting of 203 fishermen, were commanded by Captain Edward Killwick and the Customs Officers did not particularly relish their assistance. The Collector informed the Board in October 1798 that Captain Edward Killwick of the Fencibles at this Port 'having received a Deputation from your Honors and sworn into this Office on 19 June last' had heard about some run goods in Benacre and without consulting the Customs Officers had sent a party of his men to seize them. He had then lodged four kegs containing ten gallons of geneva in the Customs office. He did not accompany his men himself and 'we beg leave to inform your Honour that amongst the Fencibles here are some very suspicious Characters that would rather assist Smugglers than render the Revenue the least service'.[14]

Killwick was the ally of Captain Robert May who commanded the Volunteers. Between them they succeeded in pushing out John Robinson from the position of unrivalled authority he had held in the town for nearly forty years and they then themselves established a firm hold on municipal office. May had two other associates both of whom were disliked and mistrusted by William Revans who had been appointed Collector of the Southwold Customs in January 1803; one was Francis Wayth, a dealer in timber, who may well have grudged the Robinsons their large timber business; the other was James Jermyn the erudite and devious nephew of Peter Jermyn who was attorney to Lord Rous and also Town Clerk of Southwold. Revans wrote of Wayth in August 1806:

> *we admit Mr Wayth have been chosen one of the Bailiffs of this Town but Truth oblige us to confess that we do not consider that choice to have been in consequence of any respectability attached to him either from situation, circumstances, Abilities or Integrity of Character.*

He explained to the Board that Wayth had been chosen bailiff 'for the wish of the parties thro' whose influence he was chosen to have a pliant man' and added that he had been earlier committed to prison but had escaped. James Jermyn was a recurring thorn in the flesh of the Southwold Customs officers and this Revans attributed to James' disappointment at the decision not to appoint him to succeed his drunken father as Collector at Southwold. Revans wrote to the Board over one incident:

> *Mr Jermyn . . . made use of all the Interest in his power to have succeeded to the Collectorship of the Customs at this Port on the dismissal of his Father. We have reason to suppose from his Conduct on the present occasion as well as some other that have occurred that disappointment has urged him to catch at every opportunity to give trouble and to create difficulty in the business of the Customs at this Port.*[15]

In 1799 May and his friends, who were already successfully ousting John Robinson from his position in the town, turned their attention to the Harbour Commission. Robinson, as we have seen (p. 74), had for many years been the backbone of the harbour administration, the 'non-commissioned officer' on whom his social superiors in the Commission entirely relied. May did not intend this situation to continue and took advantage of the fact that he had himself been elected a Commissioner in 1787 in place of his very different father, John, who had for so long worked for the harbour beside John Robinson.

In April 1799 after a long absence from the harbour meetings Robert May appeared at the Swan accompanied by his confederate, Killwick, who was qualified to attend following his election as town bailiff. The meeting, which was chaired by the mild John Thompson, proceeded to appoint a professional engineer, John Druery from Gorleston, to survey the harbour and at the meeting in June which followed Druery was told to go ahead with repairs to the south pier and to contract for timber and find a head workman. In August it was agreed that Druery should obtain 58 loads of timber for repairs to the north pier.[16]

Robinson was present at these meetings but in face of May his authority seems to have gone. The decisions were a slap in his eye both as supervisor of the harbour and also as supplier of timber, but they also mark an important new development in the harbour administration. Never before had the Commissioners employed a paid professional to look after the harbour structures; but from this date they employed Druery, who introduced a pile-driving engine driven by horses, for nearly fourteen years. The amiable eighteenth-century understanding between the Harbour Commissioners and local merchants was over. Lenney, Samuel Nunn, John May and John Robinson had certainly looked after the harbour piers from self-interest, but their efforts were voluntary. Druery was paid for his services.

Robert May had not finished with the Robinson family. John Robinson died less than three years later and May determined that John's son James should not succeed his father as Collector of the harbour dues. He contrived to have David Burwood, 'a very weak timid man' appointed as temporary Collector but in the meantime James had already obtained Lord Rous's backing and he complained accordingly to Rous. Peter Jermyn, Town Clerk of Southwold but also Rous's most devoted attorney, had unfortunately, or more probably designedly, become involved in May's machinations. Now Peter hastily arranged for Burwood to waive his appointment, writing a long letter of exculpation to Rous:

> *I assure you I haven't seen anything in the Conduct of the Bailiffs that could possibly be construed into any disrespect of your Lordship . . . The moment they knew of your wishes they waived their own Sentiments and did everything in their power to adhere to yours.*

Peter Jermyn was furious with James Robinson for approaching Rous. He dismissed James Robinson's complaints about Burwood's behaviour to him:

> *With respect to any insolent Behaviour of Burwood, I do not believe a Syllable of it, as he is a poor wretched animal as much afraid of a Robinson as a Boy of the Rod.*

And Jermyn went on to blacken James Robinson and his brother:

> *Indeed my Dr Sir! I am sorry to say the young ones are much more full of malice and resentment than the Old Man – the general opinion always was that they urged him on – and I am inclined to believe it from some Expressions of James; that he had got Hold of May and would never quit him till he was avenged.*[17]

James Robinson by his appeal to Rous had succeeded in obtaining the temporary appointment, but at the Annual Meeting which followed in June it was James Jermyn, Peter's nephew, who was appointed Treasurer and Collector.[18] The animosity of Robert May and the deviousness of the Jermyns had defeated the Robinson brothers as far as any further participation in harbour affairs was concerned. James Robinson was never appointed a Commissioner and he did not supply timber for the piers. It may be indeed that he did not continue his father's timber import business. He was vice-consul and agent for the Dutch, Swedish, Prussian and Norwegian governments and probably found this sufficient business. He settled down to enjoy his great wealth, spent money generously and was always popular with the poor folk in Southwold. Twenty years later a Southwold poet wrote:

Who e'er goes to Southwold that beautiful place
To take the Sea air, or to visit the Race;
With glee and good humour will certainly hear,
of Robinson's feast and his Old English cheer.
Down down hey derry down

Whilst making the hearts of his wealthy friends glad,
He did not o'erlook those, whose faces were sad;
He fed all the poor with Beef and good Beer,
So Hurra! to James Robinson's Old English cheer
Down down hey derry down.[19]

Druery was purchasing the timber for harbour repairs from a Yarmouth merchant and in 1806 Francis Wayth was in trouble with the Customs for attempting to smuggle in amongst the harbour timber some laths for his own business. Despite this he was successful in the election of the bailiffs in 1807 as he continued to be every other year till 1813. The following year, however, he and Killwick lost their leader. The flamboyant Robert May finally saw his triumphs turn to disaster. After over-spending both the town's money and his own he was declared bankrupt and his stylish 'Manor House' was auctioned to help pay his creditors.[20]

In 1813 John Druery ceased to work at Southwold harbour and from that time on the Commissioners seem to have drifted uncertainly. Lord Rous, the accepted head of the Commission, gave more time to its business than most and in 1809 had given personal attention to the drafting of a new bill for the harbour and, following its passing, to the licensing of twenty-two pilots and the appointment of two Harbour Masters. Yet for the all-important structures the Commission, after Druery's departure (largely disregarding expensive reports from two professional engineers), fell back on a local joiner, Richard Bonniwell, while with remarkable complacency they usually left both the purchase of timber and the supervision of the work to the Treasurer and Collector whom they had appointed in 1802 – the plausible James Jermyn, whose great concern was the enormous dictionary of synonyms and epithets which he was compiling.[21]

By the 1820s money poured out on timber for the piers and on digging out shoals with the aid of a dredger was averaging over £1200 a year, although this was masked by an increase in revenue – an increase, however, which was partly a result of the raising of the harbour dues in 1814 (p.31). Despite the expenditure, following the winter gales in February 1827 the harbour was blocked and on 24 February 'Carriages went to and from Walberswick during the day beyond the piers, being from 30 to 40 feet dry beach'.[22]

This was the situation which John Edward Cornwallis Rous, second Earl of Stradbroke, confronted at the Commissioners' meeting on 25 September 1828. Stradbroke, who had succeeded to the title on his father's death in August 1827, was an experienced man. As an officer in the Coldstream Guards he had served under

Wellington in the classical battles of the late Peninsular War. Now he did not like what he saw. He proposed immediately that a salaried inspector of works be appointed. He also objected to the way contracts for materials were handled. Suspicion was focused on Jermyn's accounts and the following spring James Jermyn resigned from the positions of Treasurer and Collector. Berry Edwards was appointed Treasurer in Jermyn's place, but the major change in the harbour administration was the appointment in June 1829 of Lieutenant Francis Wilson Ellis R.N. as Collector and Surveyor of Works. The do-it-yourself regime was finally over.[23]

Crowded shipping in Southwold harbour in the 1800s: a contemporary water-colour on wallpaper by an unknown artist.

MEN OF AFFAIRS

CHAPTER 16

Pullyn of Halesworth; Ingham of Yoxford

POWER AND RESPONSIBILITY WERE DECENTRALIZED in eighteenth-century England. After 1688 the grip of the state was loosened and the reins of government were left in the hands of landowners and corporations. It was these local men who ran everyday affairs in the counties and towns and it also fell to them to initiate new economic corporate enterprises. In the country the upper echelons – the Lords Lieutenant and the Justices of the Peace – were in charge not only of much of the administration of justice but also of a wide variety of governmental functions and not suprisingly most of these landed gentlemen were always looking for willing horses with sufficient status and probity to carry some if not all of the burden for them. This applied also to new enterprises, to the trusts and commissions which were set up to carry out desirable local improvements, particularly in the field of transport. For these bodies too there was a need to find men of probity and education who would take an active share in the work.

Landowners recruited among themselves and were the more inclined to welcome newcomers to their social class because aspiring entrants were often prepared, for the sake of the prestige, to shoulder more than their fair share of duties as magistrates and could also be persuaded to serve on wearisome boards and committees. But for the main workhorses the landowners looked to men in the rank immediately below them. They drew a line separating themselves and the gentlemen clergy from a second class who might be regarded as the NCOs of the period. In the Blyth valley this is well illustrated by the line-up of the Directors and Guardians of the new House of Industry at Bulcamp who held their first meeting in June 1764 at the Angel, Halesworth. The Directors, headed by Sir John Rous, Bart, included Sir John Blois, Bart., Sir Thomas Gooch, Bart., and Miles Barne Esq., with six other country gentlemen entitled Esquire; the last of these named being Eleazar Davy who had somehow managed to squeeze himself into this category and whose remarkable career is discussed further below. In addition there were eight gentlemen parsons headed by the Reverend John Leman J.P. The Acting Guardians listed in the second column of the minutes were headed by John Ingham, attorney and steward to the Blois and Plumer families, and included three Halesworth attorneys, James Jermyn, John Woods and Peter Pullyn the younger; two prominent Southwold merchants, John Thompson and John Robinson; small freeholders like Samuel Badeley of Walpole and Martin Meadows of Mells; John Grimsby, tenant of the great farm at Westwood Lodge, and some others of similar rank and substance.[1]

Between them these officers and N.C.O.s held patriarchal sway. But at the same time they moved in a law-encrusted society and there were many attorneys in the ranks of the N.C.O.s. Attorneys had the legal and financial expertise needed to thread the way through the elaborate contemporary procedures for purchase and sale of land, mortgages, wills, marriage and other settlements, on behalf of private clients, and needed also to run the new economic corporate enterprises: bridge and turnpike trusts, canal companies, enclosure commissions. Many of these enterprises were based on privately sponsored legislation and here again local communities frequently looked to attorneys for assistance. The Acts were steered through Parliament by local members but the groundwork was left to the lower rank of society.[2]

Thus the Southwold Corporate Assembly in August 1745 turned to their Town Clerk, Mr Peter Pullyn, a Halesworth attorney, to obtain an Act for opening and improving the haven; and in 1747 the newly appointed Harbour Commissioners, who seem to have automatically adopted Pullyn as their Clerk also, borrowed £200 to pay him for the expenditure incurred. A year later they elected him a Harbour Commissioner but Pullyn was now sixty years old and in October 1748 he failed, perhaps deliberately, to make the journey to Southwold for his clerkly duties and the meeting appointed in his place an energetic Southwold attorney, Robert Jenney, who had already replaced him as Town Clerk. It was not till Jenney died in 1764 that Halesworth attorneys once more became prominent in Southwold, providing again both the Clerk to the Corporation and the Clerk to the Harbour Commission.[3]

Peter Pullyn had a large and varied practice but his eminence in the Blyth Valley and neighbouring villages was due to his stewardship of the many manors of which the Rous family held the lordship. This happy position he probably owed to his wife Sarah whose sister, Lydia, was married to Sir Robert Rous. Pullyn was already holding the Rous manor courts in the late twenties and Sir Robert, who died in 1735, expressly stipulated in his will that Peter Pullyn should continue as steward of all his manor courts.[4] Probably Pullyn drew up the will. He certainly did other legal work for the Rous family.

The profession of attorney was subject to general abuse in the first half of the eighteenth century and was constantly vilified in contemporary plays, pamphlets and novels. Tom Clarke in Smollett's novel *Sir Lancelot Greaves* 'never owned himself an attorney without blushing'. Dr Johnson observed that 'he did not care to speak ill of any man behind his back but he believed the gentleman was an *attorney*'.[5] At the same time the position of steward to a substantial landowner gave the holder considerable local power and prestige as well as opportunities for personal gain, such as those evidently taken by John Norman, steward to the Adairs of St Margaret's, South Elmham, who, according to David Elisha Davy, 'feathered his nest so well that Sir Robert thought he died too rich to have been honest'.[6] The position also often gave the steward an intimacy with the lord and their family which to say the least could be very helpful. Robert Buxton, whose father was steward of the Rous manors before Peter Pullyn, married Sir Robert Rous' widow, Lydia, and lived the life of an affluent gentleman parson, occupying the desirable Darsham Hall for many years (p.32).

Functions were not clearly differentiated in the early part of the eighteenth century and 'steward' was an ancient title which was casually used. The manorial steward might also be his lord's land steward (later termed land agent) but equally well he might not. The manorial steward was usually an attorney but again he might or might not be the family lawyer. However, at this time in east Suffolk copyhold was still an important tenure. Peter Pullyn as manorial steward held the Manor Courts, admitted new tenants, collected the substantial fines on admittance and on occasion arranged the eviction of undesirable tenants and to some extent the mantle of his lord's prestige and power was cast upon him.

A similar mantle was cast on John Ingham of Yoxford who as we have seen played a leading part in the construction of the Blyth Navigation. The Ingham family came from

Theberton: 'that acquisitive race', the chronicler of Theberton called them and certainly John Ingham had a rich inheritance which included Lordship of the Manor of Theberton. His main advantage, however, lay in the fact that he stepped into the shoes of his uncle, William Ingham, attorney of Halesworth and Yoxford. When William Ingham died in 1734 he left John the Rookery estate in Yoxford together with a flourishing business in which the chief prizes were the positions of manorial steward to the Plumers of Halesworth and to the Blois family.[7]

William Ingham may well have hoped he was laying the foundations of a county family. The scorn poured out on attorneys in the early decades of the eighteenth century made many of them anxious to escape from the ranks of the 'pettifoggers' and to claw their way into the landed gentry. John Ingham, however, had no family and indeed he never married. When he died in 1776 he left his practice, his house and all his estate to his partner, Richard Crowfoot. By this time the position of attorneys had changed for the better and many of them had a professional pride. The aim of many country lawyers towards the end of the century was not to become landed gentlemen but to found a professional family or a respected firm and John Ingham may well have seen his practice in this light.[8] Certainly great responsibilities descended on the little Yoxford firm and the careers of Ingham and Crowfoot illustrate the important roles which country attorneys could be called on to play.

As steward of the Manor of Halesworth John Ingham had a position of authority in the town since the Lord of the Manor, William Plumer, was living in Hertfordshire–in those days a considerable journey away. Both Plumer and Ingham backed the Navigation project and once the Navigation Act was on the statute book it was Ingham who took the lead over the practical side of the construction. It was he who contacted Langley Edwards and made the arrangements for him to survey the river and in the following months Ingham was prominent in the arrangements for purchase of land, the reconstruction of Blythburgh bridge and the unsuccessful efforts to prevent the occupier of Wenhaston mill from running off the water. There is no doubt that Plumer was in favour of the Navigation. He invested £500 in shares and he was amenable both to the digging of a new cut across his meadow near Halesworth and to the construction of a lock thereon. As Lord of the Manor he also had Manorial rights over the land chosen for Halesworth quay so that it fell to Ingham to make the arrangements with the new trustees. It is clear that Ingham was determined to see the project properly launched since he personally was among the few subscribers to the first warehouse and in 1764 he also subscribed promptly and generously to the second one.[9]

By the late sixties, however, both John Ingham and his partner, Richard Crowfoot, were growing less constant in their attendance at the Halesworth meetings and it seems reasonable to assume that Ingham was distracted from Halesworth by affairs at Yoxford and that his duties as attorney and steward to the Blois family were beginning to crowd his life.

Ingham was steward of the Blois manors both round Blythburgh and Yoxford and also at Grundisburgh and in addition he covered most of the routine legal work for the family. Both Jane Blois and Ralph Blois, however, did have other shoulders to lean on. Jane Blois, as we shall see, had Eleazar Davy at her elbow; the Reverend Ralph who was greatly addicted to legal argument and action, had an old friend and lawyer in Woodbridge, John Wilson, and also corresponded at length with a London solicitor. The deaths early in 1762 of both Jane and Ralph changed this. It left Ingham with much more responsibility for running the estate and with complicated legal matters to handle: the prolonged negotiations over Sir John's elaborate marriage settlement; the help and advice needed by the trustees who were trying to deal with Sir Ralph's creditors.

A few years later the weight of Blois problems was pressing increasingly on Ingham's shoulders. In October 1767 Sir John wrote to him from Florence explaining that travelling in Italy was more expensive than in France and that he had been obliged 'to buy several

Gala suits as they call them'. He asked Ingham to procure £500 and send the money through Mr Child. Ingham procured the money on his own security and the following year he procured a further £2000 to send to Venice where Sir John was finding that the Italian tour 'has made me quite fond of Pictures, so much so, that I have made a Collection which has cost me several hundred pounds'. Ingham raised the money by journeying round and finding four people whom he persuaded to make small loans at 4½ per cent and again he did this on his own bond. Six months later he was summoned to London where he had to hang about for twenty-five days before Sir John arrived to receive a futher £4000 which he had requested. This time the attorney obtained the money from William Plumer by drawing an additional mortgage.[10]

Ingham and Crowfoot were now also managing the Blois estates both at Grundisburgh and at Yoxford and Blythburgh. Sir John authorized Ingham by Special Letters of Attorney to receive his rents and manage his affairs. An extant Special Letter of 27 January 1770 gave Ingham powers to administer the Manors and estate, collect the rents and with the money to pay all outgoings including the annuity to Sir Ralph's widow and 4½ per cent interest to William Plumer on a £10000 mortgage, 'Paying me residue'.[11]

Eventually Sir John's mounting financial difficulties, as we have seen, grew beyond anything which John Ingham and Richard Crowfoot could resolve. The estate was put in the hands of trustees and in 1772 Sir John and his new bride set off on their travels, leaving Cockfield to their wealthy tenant, Chaloner Arcedeckne. Ingham was one of the trustees but more important was the fact that between them he and Richard Crowfoot ran the estate and gradually paid off the creditors. When Ingham died in 1776 Crowfoot manfully carried on and in 1779 he arranged the reconveyance of the estate to Sir John.[12]

Crowfoot was blessed with a son who attended little to the business and he was also unfortunate in his partner. John Barmby, who had been a clerk in the Yoxford office for many years and who according to David Elisha Davy was 'a man of mean abilities and low manners',[13] was not capable of matching up to the tasks confronting the practice. By 1784 Richard Crowfoot was sixty-five and the burden of administering the estate was taken over by Francis Brooke of Ufford (p.50).

Their absorption in Blois affairs must have helped to deflect the attention of the Yoxford lawyers from Halesworth and the Navigation but it is probable also that as the years progressed they shared the growing disillusionment with the unprofitable waterway. Ingham, who was always more interested than his partner, ceased to attend the Angel meetings after June 1771 and Richard Crowfoot very rarely appeared after that date. Their defection, however, left no vacuum since the Navigation Commissioners were now able to rely on the attendance of a remarkably able Halesworth attorney, Peter Jermyn.

CHAPTER 17

Peter Jermyn of Halesworth; Eleazar Davy of the Grove, Yoxford

PETER JERMYN WAS ELECTED TREASURER OF THE Navigation in 1771 and held the post for forty years, dying in office in 1810 at the age of seventy-three. As a young man in Halesworth his ears must have rung with the talk about the Navigation since both his father, James, to whom he was articled, and his eventual father-in-law, the surgeon Samuel Rye, were strong supporters of Thomas Knights' project. Rye, who had some private fortune, was very much involved in the fortunes of the waterway. He bought £100 in shares and in 1762 when the plan for the first warehouse on the quay was faltering for lack of funds he stepped in to advance the money needed and erected the warehouse and crane himself. He also did some business in coal on the quay. James Jermyn, a circumspect attorney, was never prominent as a River Commissioner, but none the less in 1765 he acquired meadows along the river bank close to the quay, and including the piece of land on which the second warehouse was built.[1] (See family tree p.109.)

Peter Jermyn therefore had every reason to support the Navigation Commission and he did so through good times and bad, of which the latter certainly predominated. For the first ten years of his Treasurership business at Halesworth quay was encouraging but, as we have seen, trade fell off in the eighties and interest outside Halesworth also dropped off so that the townsfolk were very much left to themselves. In this claustrophobic atmosphere the arrival in Halesworth of Peter's unreliable elder brother, Robert, who had been commanding a ship in the West India trade seems to have brought embarrassment. Robert went into partnership as a liquor merchant with Alderman Skoulding but the partnership was abruptly terminated at the end of 1790. At their meeting in June 1792 the Navigation Commissioners were alarmed to find that Peter Jermyn was absent and had resigned as Treasurer as a result of the 'ill-treatment' he had received from Skoulding at the Annual Meeting in the previous year. They anxiously sent Jermyn a letter 'expressive of their ideas of the gross impropriety of Mr Skoulding's conduct'. Exactly how Skoulding had conducted himself remains a mystery.[2]

Jermyn was mollified by the letter and turned up at the next year's Annual Meeting when he took the Chair. In the following years when most of the other Commissioners showed a marked lack of enthusiasm for attending meetings he plodded doggedly on, often acting as Chairman at the poorly attended gatherings. By now his son Peter and Robert Gostlin White (also in his office) had been appointed Clerks[3] and with them he wrestled with increasing debts for bricklaying and carpenter's work as every year the locks decayed and the bridges needed attention, until gradually towards the turn of the century trade looked up, there were more craft on the river and the position temporarily eased.

Peter Jermyn's faithful attendance to the affairs of the river was certainly not due to lack of other business. Like other country attorneys in the eighteenth century he was in the thick of local life, dealing with land purchase and sale, wills, marriage settlements and mortgages. He acted for merchants like the Crisps of Wangford and John Woodcock of Halesworth; further afield he sold property for Dudley North at Glemham and he was appointed Clerk to the Ipswich to Southtown Turnpike Trust. He was a clever, competent man who must also have had considerable physical stamina. He took the journey from Halesworth to Southwold in his stride.

> *The procession from the Swan at Southwold to the Guild Hall on Church Green yesterday was very badly calculated with a north east wind for my tender lungs; and has made them so musical that I must defer seeing you till Wednesday or Thursday morning*

he wrote to Eleazar Davy in December 1788.[4] Southwold Corporation was given to slow-moving processions in the east wind (as indeed it still is!) but this did not deter Jermyn from being sworn as their Town Clerk in 1774 at a salary of four guineas a year and holding the office for more than thiry years. With more financial reward he acted as solicitor to the Harbour Commissioners, drawing up mortgages for them in 1781 and soliciting the Harbour Act of 1789 for which service he received £344. Under this Act there were only four men named as Commissioners who were not given at least the title of 'Esquire'. Peter Jermyn was one of these four and it was as a Commissioner that he subsequently attended the meetings at the Swan. No doubt he was content to see the Clerkship go to his son, Peter, and on young Peter's untimely death to Robert Gostlin White who at this time was working with him.[5]

Over Southwold harbour affairs Peter found himself in his last years again placed in an embarrassing position by his brother Robert's family, this time in the person of Robert's son James. James involved Peter in his intrigues to oust James Robinson from the office of Collector and Treasurer to the Harbour Commission and obtain it for himself (p.00).

Peter Jermyn's great concern was that Lord Rous who had been appealed to by Robinson should not think ill of him or of his nephew James: 'And I also flatter myself you will not see anything in the conduct of either me or my nephew which you could have wished not to have seen.' His concern is understandable for by far the most important and prestigious part of his business lay in the position he held with the Rous family and by this time he had built up an intimate relationship with the future Lord Stradbroke which caused him to finish up his letter of exculpation: 'I am my Dear Sir yours most affectionately'.[6]

Peter's father, James, had been a respected attorney in Halesworth, sufficiently well-known for Gertrude Vanneck to mention his death in a letter to Eleazar Davy in January 1778: 'Nothing new here except old Jermyn's death who quitted this earthly scene suddenly on Tuesday morning'.[7] James was Steward of ten manors round Glemham pertaining to Dudley North but he was never the chief Steward of the Rous manors. It was John Granger, another Halesworth attorney, who succeeded Peter Pullyn in this position and it was Granger who passed on to James's son Peter not only the treasurership of the Navigation but also the stewardship of the Rous manors. Peter Jermyn held the position from 1776 and he was also acting as Sir John's attorney. Rous was hard-pressed for liquid money in the seventies and eighties and perhaps it was for this reason that it was not till 1799 that he settled Jermyn's bills for 'Law Business & Conveyancing done from 3 October 1777 to 25 December 1798', totalling £1766. The bill for 1799 to 1804 was £160 and from then to March 1810 it totalled £198.[8]

The heavier bills in the early years must have included Sir John's two marriage settlements which were both carefully discussed with Jermyn and then drawn up by him, and they must also have included Jermyn's efforts in the disputes over the Cullen estate in Ireland brought to Rous by his first marriage. Rous employed John Dresser of Blyford Hall as his land agent but it was on Jermyn's advice that he relied in the difficult years when there was not quite enough money to do as he wanted. 'As Peter Jermyn says very truly nothing but the most regular keeping down of interest money etc, has saved me from being absolutely ruined' he wrote to Eleazar Davy in December 1790.

As his correspondence with Davy also shows, Rous admired Peter Jermyn's skill as a lawyer. The Cullen estate dispute came before arbitrators in 1789. Peter 'has been our great support, not only in drawing the last Case so clearly and satisfactorily to the arbitrators, but in being ready at the Meeting to answer every objection of Ryder's'. Ryder was the opposing lawyer. 'Ryder was a child in the hands of Jermyn.' The arbitrators then dallied and failed to make any decision. 'Mr Jermyn whom I saw at the Southwold Meeting is out of all patience.' Nearly two years later; 'My patience with Lawyers is quite exhausted . . . No meeting of Arbitrators has taken place.' Even Jermyn 'begins to despair'. Rous's willingness to rely on a local small-town lawyer seems to have been reinforced by various experiences in the metropolis. 'London lawyers', he wrote to Davy in 1792, 'do little in a long time and allways make as much unnecessary business as they can.'[9]

As was not unusual at this period Sir John also turned to his attorney to perform the duties of his political agent. For his trouble and attendance in the course of three elections for Suffolk – 1780, 1784 and 1790 – Jermyn received a gratuity of £450. The election of 1790 was heavily contested by the Vanneck interest and Jermyn's bill for payments and disbursements at this election was £3224.[10]

Peter Jermyn dined frequently with Rous in the course of their many business discussions but their relations, though friendly, were always professional. Rous was certainly clear himself about the social gulf between his family and solicitors. He described as a very unpleasant event the day when his sister Louisa walked out of the house in Portman Square and threw herself into the arms of a younger son of Mr Birch, the Prince's solicitor.[11] Clearly Jermyn appreciated this position. His whole approach to life was that of a professional man with a pride in the practice he was building up and with no desire to elevate his family into the ranks of the landed gentry. He brought up his elder son Peter to understudy him but in 1797, when just over thirty years of age, Peter the younger died. Six years earlier Peter Jermyn senior had been bitterly disappointed by the marriage of his younger son Henry to the Widow Douglas who was already blessed with two sons and four daughters. Henry had been called to the bar and his father had hopes for him.

> *Poor Peter is much discomposed by his son Harry/his favourite/having played the fool and married a Widow with six children aged 32 without giving him any notice of his intention*

Rous told Eleazar Davy in 1791. And he went on: 'He looks upon it as a fatal Clog to his getting forward in his profession just at a Time when he entertained great hopes of his doing well'.[12] Peter Jermyn did not get over his anger at this disastrous marriage and he and Henry were permanently estranged.

After the untimely death of his elder son, Jermyn was understudied by the husband of his niece Elizabeth, Robert Crabtree. Crabtree acted as deputy steward for the Rous manorial courts and in the later years sometimes settled the final accounts with Lord Rous. Crabtree also occasionally took Jermyn's place as Clerk to Southwold Corporation when Jermyn could not face the windy journey. Peter Jermyn gave his confidence to Robert Crabtree and saw him as a man to whom he could entrust the business which he had so successfully nurtured.

But Crabtree was deeply resented by Henry Jermyn who since his injudicious marriage had been treated by his father with unremitting coldness. In June 1810 Peter Jermyn died and Henry was on tenterhooks. He poured out his problems in daily letters to his friend David Elisha Davy: his reluctance to attend the funeral because he was 'loath to justify by my conduct the very unjust and harsh usage I have experienced'; his anxiety over the will; his own desire to have the stewardship of the manorial courts.

When he heard the contents of his father's will Henry admitted it to be fair and equitable in that the property was to be divided among the four children, but–

> *Mr Crabtree is there received as the person who for twelve years has been privy to all his Transactions and therefore best able to settle all his affairs, to him he leaves all Lawbooks and nothing more – He is also to have the use of the Offices for one year – . . . Crabtree not named as an Executor but merely to settle his affairs . . . Crabtree's legacy of Books and the etc. etc. is the most splendid and solid Bequest of the whole will – Business and Connection in every Event exceeding £1200 per annum. The great and large Injustice of which I have been uniformly complaining, now complain and must now continue to complain of the exclusive powers given to Crabtree are I consider materially detrimental to my interest.*

Henry's resentment fixed on the stewardship of the manorial courts. Lord Rous was Lord of most of these manors but the Jermyns had also the stewardship of some others including those of Charles Long, Dudley North and Sir Thomas Gooch.

> *The fact is I have no doubt my father's Introduction of him will be a good 1,000 or 1,200 for him – independent of the Courts of which Ld R, Mr L and Mr N have about 30 – these I suppose would not average more than £5 p.a. each which is only £150 – Surely he ought to concede this pittance to me.*

The solution proposed by Rous and Long and Crabtree himself was a joint appointment. Apart from the consideration that 'Crabtree and myself are oil and vinegar', Henry Jermyn as a barrister considered he must refuse a joint appointment with an attorney. 'This' he told Davy, 'would I have no doubt send me to Coventry by the Bar and I do not feel I ought to lose sight of my own profession.' Jermyn himself proposed that he should take all the courts and make Crabtree his deputy steward with half the profits for his assistance.[13]

Whatever may have been the outcome and the temporary arrangement, Robert Crabtree did in effect take over the Rous manorial courts as well as taking Peter Jermyn's place as Rous's attorney. Building on Peter Jermyn's practice Robert and his son John established themselves as the leading solicitors to the gentry in north-east Suffolk. In 1846 when John Crabtree was giving evidence before the Select Committee on Railway Bills he was respectfully asked: 'You are professionally concerned I believe for a great number of noblemen and gentlemen about your part of the country are you not?'[14]

Peter Jermyn's well-built house and office fronted Halesworth Thoroughfare, with gardens and the river-lined meadow behind. He also owned farms at Holton and Chediston, but Henry's off-the-cuff valuation of his father's estate in June 1810 totalled only something over £10000, a modest estate. On the other hand, Henry, as we have seen, valued the goodwill of Peter's practice at £1000 to £1200 a year. Peter Jermyn's ambitions were concentrated on his practice and the eminence it achieved under the Crabtrees would have brought him great satisfaction. He did not aspire to move into the class of the landed gentry and in this his attitude contrasts with that of his slightly younger contemporary, Rous's land agent, John Dresser of Blyford Hall. Dresser bought up land and also bought not only the manor of Blyford in 1785 but also the manors of Thorington Hall and Wenhaston Grange in 1800. He achieved the expensive but socially desirable honour of being pricked as sheriff in 1809.[15]

The rise in the social scale achieved by the Dressers pales into insignificance beside the remarkable feat of social elevation achieved by Eleazar Davy of the Grove, Yoxford. Although Eleazar was undoubtedly a prominent and an unusually persevering member of the Navigation Commission and also played his part as a Harbour Commissioner, his services to the two bodies perhaps hardly warrant his inclusion in this book. He was, however, a ubiquitous gentleman, here, there and everywhere in the district round the Blyth, so that his life touches my story at many points and in any case his successful rise to local eminence deserves to be chronicled.

Eleazar was not an attorney and indeed his nephew and chosen heir, David Elisha Davy, was probably reflecting his uncle's dislike and distrust of lawyers when he described a Bungay attorney whom he had found to be surprisingly honest as 'very like a black swan'. The Davy family were yeoman farmers at Rumburgh and they may have been of some substance although the early acquistions of Eleazar, a younger son, quite baffled R. T. L. Parr, the historian of Yoxford:

> *Eleazar Davy had begun to acquire landed estate in Cratfield, Rumburgh and Wissett as early as 1748 when only 24 years old, where he got the money from does not appear.*

His nephew David described him as 'a man of very polished manners and highly popular in the neighbourhood'.[16] He must have been a man of great charm which he combined with perfect manners and both financial and legal acumen. He knew his way around and made himself exceedingly useful to local landowners of which the first to value his services seem to have been the Kemps at Ubbeston Hall. Sir John Kemp who inherited in 1752 when he was over fifty was a London merchant who lived in Tooting and he must have come to rely on Eleazar to run his Ubbeston affairs. In his will (1761) he left ten guineas to Eleazar's elder brother, David, described as his bailiff, but he left £500 to Eleazar and made him the trustee of his complicated will with an additional 200 guineas 'for his trouble'. He also died in debt to Davy.[17]

Eleazar also won the complete confidence of Sir John's sister, Jane Blois, widow of William and mother and guardian of the unfortunate epileptic, Charles, and of his sister Mary. Some time in the late 1750s Davy moved into Cockfield Hall and he was now Jane's close adviser and confidant. He evidently had consideration for his family for his elder brother David acted as bailiff to some degree and he also persuaded Jane to be godmother to his niece, Jane Harvey, and bequeath her a handsome legacy. When Jane Blois had to move from Cockfield to Ubbeston Hall Davy moved with her and when she died in 1762 she had appointed Davy her sole executor, left him a considerable property in Yoxford and made him her residuary legatee. Her daughter Mary had also succumbed to Eleazar's charms. She also made him her sole executor and residuary legatee, but more significantly there is also in Davy's papers a draft marriage settlement between Mary and Eleazar.[18]

It was probably Mary's ill-health – she died in 1766 – which thwarted this plan but the polished Eleazar moved on to better things, a successful wooing of the widowed daughter of George Evans, second Baron Carbery of Cork. Davy's marriage to the Hon. Frances Warter-Wilson took place towards the end of the sixties and in 1770 his position among the landed gentry was triumphantly recognized when he was pricked as sheriff for the county. Two years later he bought the Grove estate at Yoxford and proceeded gradually to build himself a fine house there while at the same time he added to the estate.

I take it for granted the Park will be well stocked with Deer and the lakes abound with noble fish so that venison and fish you will be able to command at all times

George Golding of Thorington Hall wrote to him in March 1777.[19] An imposing house with a park was a recognized status symbol among the landed gentry. Even more so was a London house. In London Eleazar and his new wife resided at 33 St James Street, Westminster.

'We quit this *lively* place next Thursday', Gertrude Vanneck wrote to them sarcastically from Heveningham Hall in January 1778, 'to dine in Town on Friday. Saturday evening I shall *know* in what part of St James Street No. 33 is to be found. Do breakfast with us that morning.' Eleazar and Frances had not finally left Ubbeston Hall for the new house at Yoxford and the proximity of Ubbeston to Heveningham was very welcome to Sir Gerard Vanneck's sister Gertrude, lately lady-in-waiting to the Princess of Wales, who found the occasional sojourns at Heveningham Hall extremely boring.

Why will you be such an Eve and lead us into temptations before we are awake . . . Mr Davy's note arrives. We want not humble applications. You supply our only want. Who can resist? Not your sincere and affectionate, Gertrude Vanneck.

wrote Gertrude to Frances in a letter she forgot to date.[20] Frances, the honourable Mrs Davy, who moved easily in grand circles was just the wife that Eleazar needed.

Eleazar Davy took great pains to cultivate the right people and contrived to bring himself to their notice. Rowland Holt of Redgrave Hall was the County Member from 1771 till 1780 and in the seventies Davy produced for him Southwold pencils ('being very famous') and five brace of goldfish which were transported in a 'tin machine'. Holt later reciprocated with a couple of Chinese pigs. Davy also built up a friendship with Rowland's brother Thomas who inherited Redgrave Hall when Rowland died in 1786. Davy entertained Thomas and his wife at the Grove, corresponded with him about politics, and in 1790 asked him to be godfather to his step-grand-daughter, Frances Rous.[21]

Eleazar's successful social climbing was due in a large part to his willingness and ability to make himself so very useful. He gladly embraced duties which while they usually carried prestige were at the same time wearisome to many landed gentlemen and unwelcome interruptions to London life or sporting amusements in the country. To a considerable extent this applied to the office of sheriff and it also applied to the magistrate's bench on which Eleazar served for many years.[22]Although he despised attorneys he enjoyed legal complexities and argument and anyone who was capable of threading his way through the intricacies of the eighteenth-century legal web must have been a valuable colleague.

He seems always to have been regarded as a man of influence so that in 1756 Tom Knights wrote him a personal letter asking him for his support for the Navigation project. Eleazar was in fact fully prepared to interest himself in the scheme. He subscribed £100 and Jane Blois did the same, no doubt on his advice. He was obviously an excellent choice as one of the trustees of Halesworth quay and was duly admitted to the copyhold with Sir John Rous and three other gentlemen in October, 1761. He subscribed to both the warehouses and he was most regular in his attendance at the meetings until nearly the end of the seventies. After that he ceased to attend either because of his move to Yoxford or more probably because he shared the disillusionment of other landed gentry.[23]

Inevitably he soon found his way on to the Harbour Commission. Although he had not made his mark in the neighbourhood by 1746 and was not named as a Commissioner under the Harbour Act of that year he was none the less appointed a Commissioner as early as 1755, despite the fact that he was not himself a subscriber. The invalid Sir Charles Blois, however, did subscribe and Eleazar eventually inherited mortgages to the value of £400 through Charles' mother and sister. Although he reduced this holding, Davy at one time held the biggest mortgage on the dues.[24]

Eleazar's encyclopaedic knowledge of local affairs combined with his polished manners and good sense no doubt commended him to the young Sir John Rous who when he succeeded his father in 1771 had much to learn about his estate and local responsibilities. Davy's final social triumph was the marriage in January 1788 of his step-daughter, Frances Juliana Warter-Wilson, to Sir John. Rous wrote frequent confiding letters to Eleazar in the years before and after the wedding, often discussing cases about to come before the magistrates or arrangements in the neighbourhood such as those for the provision and dressing of a turtle for the Free and Easy at Yoxford; but also pouring out worries about his health and, no doubt in the context of proposals for the marriage settlement, worries about the inadequacy of his income. Frances brought with her Irish estates of over 9000 acres which, when she died in childbirth two years after the wedding, involved Rous in long and acrimonious legal struggles about which he kept Davy up to date. Frances's death must have been a sad blow to Davy as well as to Sir John. Her baby daughter, another Frances, was taken to live at the Grove with her grandmother and Eleazar. Rous continued to write to Davy for some time, regaling him with his plans for the new Hall at Henham and for his second marriage.[25]

Davy's desire to found a county family led him to provide in his will that anyone taking his property should use the name and arms of Davy only. But his chosen heir, David Elisha, found when his uncle died in January 1803 that he had over-reached himself. Then, hit by the post-war slump, David was eventually forced to put the Grove into the hands of Gurney's Bank and to retire from county society.[26] He concentrated instead on antiquarian pursuits (which included an intense interest in pedigrees perhaps inculcated by his uncle). We owe him a great debt for his work, but Eleazar might have thought him a failure. Like that of many other aspiring entrants to the ranks of the country gentlemen the rise of the Davy family was ephemeral.

Jermyn family: members mentioned in the book

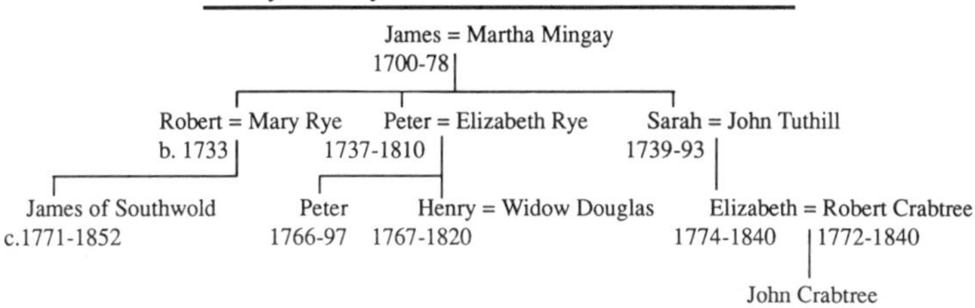

The Grove, Yoxford, the seat of D. E. Davy, Esq., Eleazar's heir. Drawn and engraved by T. Higham for Excursions through Suffolk, *published 1818.*

CHAPTER 18

The Clergy: a Postscript

Any attempt to look at the role of those whom I have called men of affairs must include at least a glance at the clergy. The eighteenth century devolution of so many functions to local effort resulted in considerable reliance on clergymen, educated men from whom probity might be expected. They were involved in most administrative and governmental concerns, including the magistrate's bench, and as might be expected there were always parsons on both the Navigation and the Harbour Commissions. Although I have not studied their lives in any detail it would be unbalanced not to mention briefly the valuable contributions which some of them made.

Thomas Forster, Rector of Halesworth, and Robert Buxton, Vicar of Darsham, were two parsons who in their very different ways supported and assisted the Navigation project. Both of them were counselling Knights when he was struggling to get the Navigation Act on the statute book. Buxton, self-important and excitable, shrilled out advice as early as November 1753, urging Tom Knights to get the bill promoted before the election due the following year. In 1756 he frightened Knights' Club in Halesworth with his alarming report that Knights was about to deceive them and have the dues assigned to himself. Robert Buxton was intensely interested in the project and he also himself contacted Firebrace of Long Melford Hall, the County Member, with his own suggestions of articles he thought should be included in the bill, while at one time he apparently drew up an abortive scheme of his own. Thomas Forster, Rector of Halesworth and a member of Knights' Club, made an invaluable contribution at a crucial time when he steadied the members in the face of Buxton's dangerous reports and wrote the diplomatic letters to Knights and to Firebrace which scotched both the possibility of departure from the agreed course and Buxton's rumours.[1]

When the Act was on the statute book Buxton was assiduous in his attendance at the Angel meetings. He was certainly not short of funds and in 1761 when the Commissioners met with a very poor response to their appeal for more money his prompt readiness to top up his subscription and subsequently to put down his £10 for the first warehouse must have given them much encouragement.[2] In 1772 at young Sir John Rous's insistence Buxton had to leave Darsham Hall. He did so reluctantly although he eventually settled happily in Norfolk. His departure must have been a blow to the Commissioners for although he may well have been an irritating and pontifical colleague,

Halesworth Rectory as it looks today.

the fact remains that he was a man of substance who carried weight and lent authority to the Commission.

In the early days there was generally a sprinkling of clergy at the Navigation meetings – men like Martin Baylie, Rector of Kelsale and James Carter, Vicar of Sibton – but by the end of the seventies the only steady representatives of the cloth were Michael Driver Mease who had followed Buxton as Vicar of Darsham and the faithful Rector of Halesworth, Thomas Forster, who was still attending the Navigation meetings in 1782. Forster was a scholarly man with a reputation as a good preacher and he seems also to have been ready to lend his friendship and support to the business and professional men in Halesworth. The Reverend Isaac Avarne who succeeded him as Rector of Halesworth and Lord of the Manor of Halesworth Rectory was also Rector of Baddingham in Norfolk but he too was prepared to play his part as a Navigation Commissioner and often took the chair at the sparse gatherings of merchants and attorneys at the Angel meetings round the turn of the century.

Some clergy were integral members of the landowning class. Ralph Blois, who held the living of Blythburgh but lived first in Kelsale and then at Cockfield Hall, Yoxford, was certainly a cleric of this sort and another man in the same category was the Reverend John Leman of Wenhaston Hall. Ralph Blois and John Leman both served on the Navigation Commission in the early days and both were also Harbour Commissioners. Both were members of respected County families and as such would expect to be asked to take their place on important local boards.

The Harbour Commission was always more exalted than the Navigation Commission and apart from the two bailiffs of Southwold the list of Commissioners named in the first Harbour Act of 1746 consisted entirely of landed gentlemen who would certainly not contemplate shouldering the tasks of supervising construction and repair work. This was remedied in the years following by the additional appointment of some Southwold merchants together with two clergymen, Martin Baylie, Rector of Kelsale, and Christopher Smear, Vicar of Reydon and Curate of Southwold. Smear, who became a Commissioner in 1752, was repeatedly asked in 1754 as one of 'our three nearest resident members' to help oversee the work at the piers and he continued during this critical period when the new structures were faltering to work with the Southwold men. In October 1756 he, together with the Clerk, one of the bailiffs and Samuel Nunn, was thanked for constant attendance and great care in repairing and improving the piers.

Christopher Smear's readiness to accept this position beside the Southwold merchants and to share with them the burden of supervising the harbour work seems to reflect an old-fashioned early-eighteenth-century view of the social position of many of the clergy. The Harbour Commission did not again ask their clerical colleagues to dirty their boots in this way. Moreover the Act of 1789, which again is remarkable for its very grand list of Harbour Commissioners, named correspondingly grand clergy: John Ewen of Reydon Hall, Thomas Sheriffe of Uggeshall, Bence Sparrow, heir to Thorington Hall, the wealthy Henry Uhtoff whose wife was a Vanneck, and William Buckle, Rector of Wrentham, who was perhaps less in this social bracket but had wealthy relatives behind him.

There was always a large class of very poor clergy in England but by the late eighteenth century, as country gentlemen increasingly used livings in their gift to endow their younger sons and other relations and friends, the more affluent clergy became very much identified with the landowning class and for the most part were reliable supporters of landed interests. As we shall see, when Lord Stradbroke wished to pack the Harbour Commission, appointed under the Act of 1830, with his own loyal supporters he included fourteen parsons, much to the indignation of the Radical Joseph Hume.

HARBOUR BATTLES

CHAPTER 19

The Lord and the Merchant

TWO DETERMINED STIFF-NECKED MEN DOMINATE THE story of the River Blyth in the years leading up to the mid-nineteenth century. Each had complete faith in his own convictions and since these convictions were diametrically opposed a collision between the two men could hardly have been avoided. They saw the local scene from two very different standpoints which then existed in British society: on the one hand the standpoint of a complacent landed aristocracy and on the other that of the newly thrusting middle class. Their views met with a resounding clash and the noise of the impact and the written matter which their conflict produced have unfortunately obscured their very positive achievements, for both were able men and without their efforts the Blyth and its harbour might well have faded much earlier into insignificance.

John Edward Cornwallis Rous, second Lord Stradbroke, who succeeded his father in 1827, was the natural leader in the Blyth valley and he was accepted as such without question by a community which believed, as did most contemporary rural Englishmen, that ownership of land gave an inalienable right to lead and to dictate. Sheltered from the impact of ideas current in the manufacturing world, local men for the most part shared Stradbroke's own unquestioning conviction of his right to command. Stradbroke saw it not only as a right but also as a duty. Increased wealth and social success had made him more arrogant than his predecessors, certainly more so than his grandfather, but at the same time, like Sir John Rous in the mid eighteenth century and perhaps more so than his father, he had a paternalistic sense of obligation to the community and to his tenants.

Into this rural atmosphere there arrived an Edinburgh Scot, a confident, self-reliant man with capital and well-established as a corn merchant in Yarmouth. Patrick Stead was an educated man, a product of Perth Academy,[1] and his economic philosophy, like that of most prosperous middle-class merchants in the early nineteenth century, ran on Utilitarian lines. He believed in the benefits of Adam Smith's market economy and with him condemned old traditional rights and liberties which so often stood in the way of desirable economic expansion, an expansion which Smith considered could best be brought about by the pursuit of enlightened self-interest. C. J. Palmer, the Yarmouth historian, remarked on Stead's energetic promotion of 'mercantile improvements' in the town and by 1834 the Scotsman had achieved a considerable reputation both as a maltster and as a merchant. In that year he was chosen to represent maltsters in the region and to put their case before the Commissioners of Excise Enquiry on Malt and earlier in the same year he gave evidence as a corn merchant before the Select Committee on the Sale of Corn.[2]

The economic climate in which Lord Stradbroke and Patrick Stead were operating was very sombre. The long-term fall in corn prices which followed the wartime bonanza brought great distress to the farming community by the 1820s, and the distress continued through the 1830s and into the forties. Wheat prices dropped from an average of 102 shillings per quarter for the years 1810–14 to an average of 55 shillings for 1835–9. Barley, which was fetching nearly 80 shillings in August 1812, fetched an average of 33 shillings for the years 1830–33. James Cooper at Westwood Lodge was getting less than 25 shillings a quarter for his barley in 1835.[3] Many local farmers seem to have been unwilling or unable to adjust their farming practice to the changed circumstances. Judging by the amount of corn exported from Southwold harbour they seem to have tried for a long time to compensate for the poor prices by increasing the quantity of corn they sold. Over the eleven years from 1820 to 1830 the amount of corn sent to London from Southwold (even excluding the Halesworth trade) increased substantially and it was not till the thirties that the corn exports dropped (Table 2). James Cooper had the acreage and the capital to diversify, as we have seen (p.55). Many over-stretched farmers were less well placed. Agricultural wages of course fell and unemployment increased rapidly, but any relief which farmers obtained on these counts was more than offset not just by a tense atmosphere with intermittent riots and incendiarism but also by a rising bill for poor relief for which Cooper was paying out more than £254 a year in the mid thirties. In their turn landowners were faced with defaulting tenants and mounting arrears of rent and had to reduce their incomes by rent remissions and by increasing their own expenditure on tenants' repairs and farm maintenance. Even Coke's great agricultural estate at Holkham recorded a loss of over £11000 between 1817 and 1826.[4]

The slump affected all rural life and inevitably there was much selling and leasing of property in small country towns and villages particularly in the deflationary years of 1821–3. This, however, was opportune for a man like Patrick Stead who had accumulated capital and wanted to expand. In the early twenties he and his partner, John Robinson, another Scotsman, spread their business from their headquarters in Yarmouth into east Suffolk. In 1846 Stead stated that he had had malting establishments at various times in a list of country places: Ipswich, Woodbridge, Sibton, Ramsholt, Trimley, Bungay, Wainford, Beccles, Saint Olaves Bridge, Southwold, North Walsham as well as at Yarmouth. And he said that in 1824 or 1825 he had been malting in almost all these places.[5] His acquisitions included the maltings at Beccles bridge and the brewery in Bridge Street, Halesworth, which had been the basis of John Woodcock's business in the eighteenth century and had been acquired in 1809 by Dawson Turner, the Yarmouth banker, and his talented son-in-law, the botanist, William Hooker. Although he was not interested in brewing, Stead bought the brewery from Turner and Hooker and their partner Samuel Paget and he and John Robinson began some malting here in 1821.[6]

Patrick Stead's business in both barley and malt was widely spread. In 1834 he claimed to be shipping to almost every port in the United Kingdom but principally to London and the Humber (grain) and to London and Liverpool (malt).[7] In the twenties he began to supply malt to Messrs Truman, Hanbury and Buxton, who like other London brewers were coming increasingly to prefer the malt of Norfolk and Suffolk to that of Hertfordshire and Essex. From 1830 to 1836 Stead's supply to Trumans averaged nearly 12000 quarters a year and this was to increase so that in 1838 the Truman partners found that Patrick Stead was providing 16000 quarters that season and was their biggest supplier. His price at 55s. 3d. was also the cheapest and his extract ratio was very high. The partners felt 'disposed to encourage those whose Malt pays us best'.[8] Maltsters were not immune from the economic afflictions of the period and many small maltsters were in difficulties, but Stead had not only the benefit of the valuable Truman market but also the advantage of scale. Few maltsters made above 550 quarters a year but by 1834 Stead was making 15000 to 16000 quarters.[9]

Stead's headquarters were at Yarmouth and he had malting establishments scattered over the country but this did not prevent him from applying his energetic planning mind to the situation in Halesworth where he soon found he was up against obstacles to economic progress which were not easily swept aside. In the early twenties his attempts to link his recently purchased premises – the old brewery buildings – directly with Halesworth quay were frustrated by owners of intervening property and he was forced to rely on an awkward roadway carried along and over the river on posts and pilings. In 1826 he became a River Commissioner and strove with some success to have the Navigation improved and with less success to have the quay enlarged and wharves made for the 'encreased state of trade'.[10] This increase in the Halesworth trade shows up in the totals of dues collected by the River Commissioners which leapt from £781 for the five years from 1815 to 1819 to £1262 for the years 1820 to 1824 (Table 1). Already the Navigation was feeling the benefit of Stead's arrival in Halesworth and of the tolls from the wherries which carried his corn and malt down the river.

At the mouth of the river was Southwold harbour and inevitably Patrick Stead focused his attention on conditions there. He was evidently aware of the Report to the Harbour Commissioners written by John Rennie, an engineer with a considerable reputation, in January 1820. Rennie's Report commenced with the flat assertion that Southwold harbour had been gradually becoming more shallow 'owing to the embankment of the salt marshes over which the tide used to flow and the stopping of some of the creeks'; he went on to say that 'about 1100 acres of ground, over which the tides used to flow have been embanked' with the result that there was no longer adequate scour at the ebb tide to drive out shingle and sand; and he found that the greater part of the embankments were at Blythburgh, about four miles distant from the harbour. It was the marshes and flats on the north banks of the river at Blythburgh which Stradbroke's father had walled with so much enthusiasm.[11]

The irresolute Harbour Commissioners of the early twenties had laid John Rennie's Report on the shelf where it mouldered with other reports on the harbour (p.43). It was not a secret document, however, and Stead evidently knew of its contents and agreed with Rennie's attack on the embankments. None the less his main concern at this time was with the composition of the Harbour Commission itself and its dominance by the landed interest. He wanted the merchants and shipowners who paid the harbour dues to be adequately represented on the Commission as they were on many port authorities. He pinned his hopes of obtaining this goal on the prospect of a new Harbour Act since the Act of 1809 was due to expire in September 1829.

There was much amiss with the harbour administration in the early twenties but, following the death of his father, the second Earl of Stradbroke had rapidly put reforms in hand of which the most important was the appointment in June 1829 of Lieutenant Francis Ellis R.N. as Collector and Surveyor of Works at a salary which was eventually fixed at £100 a year. Although Ellis wrote to his cousin 'my interest and not my merit has prevailed' and also told him that he regarded the office as 'a stepping stone to something better' he proved an energetic and able adminstrator and settled down in Southwold where in 1844 he built Hill House at the top of Constitution Hill for himself and his family.[12]

The appointment of Ellis signalled the intention of Stradbroke and his fellow landowners to tackle the problems of Southwold harbour and they deeply resented the presumptuous merchant who was now trying to thrust his oar in. Stradbroke had an array of supporters, not least of whom was the County Member, Sir Thomas Gooch of Benacre Hall. Gooch's own encroachments on the river overflows were small but he was closely related to the Rous family since he had married Marianne Whittaker, sister to Charlotte, Countess of Stradbroke, so that his wife was aunt to the present Earl. Besides this, three

Halesworth in the 1840s

Also showing some places referred to in earlier chapters

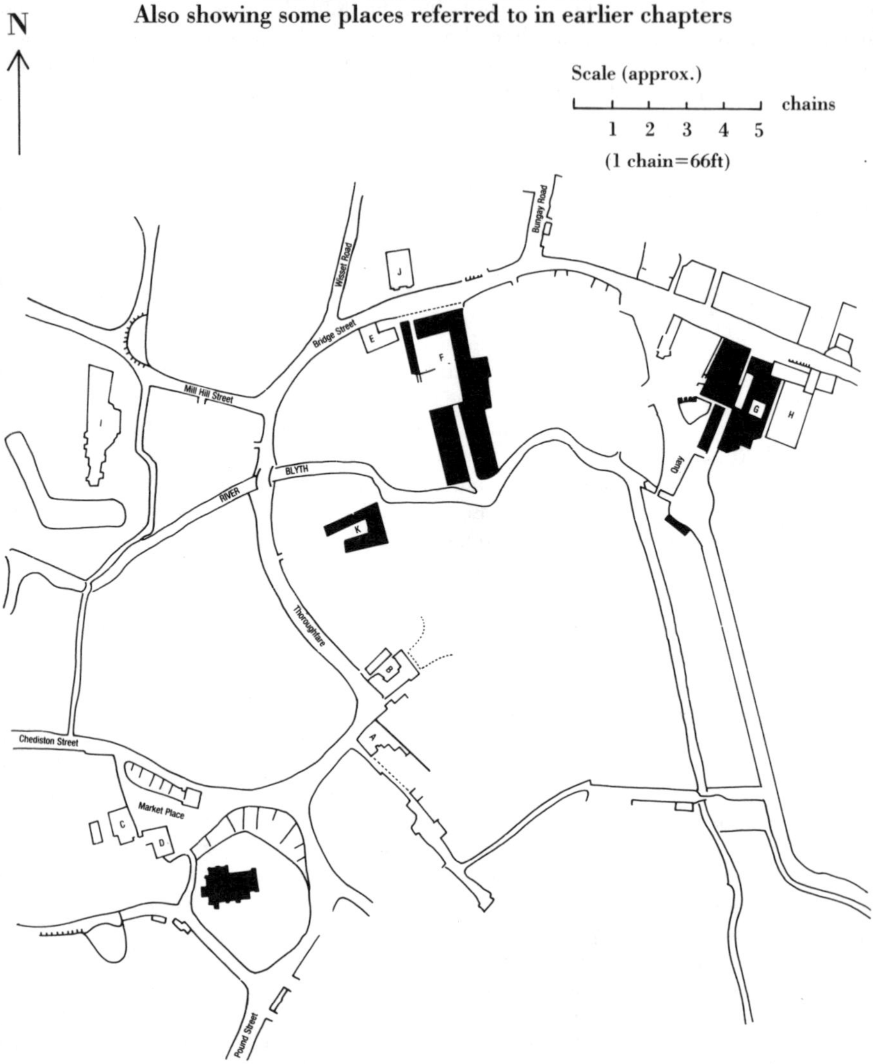

A. The Angel Inn
B. Peter Jermyn's house – later Crabtree's
C. The Three Tuns Inn
D. The house of Robert and James Reeve in the Market Place
E. Patrick Stead's house, 15 Bridge Street (now 15 Quay Street)
F. Stead's Bridge Street Maltings
G. Stead's Quay Maltings
H. Hammond Ringwood's house
I. The Rectory
J. The Independent Chapel, erected 1836
K. The Iron Foundry

generations of Gooch's family had served as Commissioners of Southwold harbour and like the Rous, Blois and Barne families he felt he had a possessive right to administer its affairs.

As County Member it fell to Sir Thomas Gooch to steer the new harbour bill through Parliament in 1830 and although when it came to affairs at Westminster Stead was no greenhorn, Gooch and Stradbroke, who also had the weight of opinion behind them, easily outmanoeuvred the Yarmouth merchant. According to Patrick Stead's own account Gooch originally discussed the bill amicably with him and agreed to provide for periodically elected Commissioners. But when the bill was in Committee the Commissioners' clause was delayed to the very last when it was disclosed that of the thirty-two men named for the office, all, apart from two Southwold merchants who were also the Southwold bailiffs in this year, were either members or friends of landowning families or else were clergymen, of whom there were fourteen named. Moreover no one was to serve as a Commissioner unless he was in receipt of rents from property of at least £100 a year.[13]

Petitions against the bill then had to be rushed through for the third reading. There were petitions from the bailiffs and Commonalty of Southwold; from the merchants, shipowners and shipmasters of Southwold; from bankers, merchants, shipowners and inhabitants of Halesworth; from the growers of grain and from Patrick Stead himself. All pleaded for the provision of Commissioners outside the landed class and the Halesworth petition in addition asked the House to enquire into the stopping-up of creeks and the embankment of land. Sir Thomas Gooch rose to fend off these petitions and his speech as reported by Barrow demonstrates the complete lack of comprehension with which he and his fellow landowners viewed Stead's interference.

> *Several of the Commissioners appointed by this Bill are gentlemen resident in the neighbourhood, who feel a strong interest in the prosperity of this harbour, as their tenants export their produce from it . . . .. Now the principal export of the port of Southwold is corn, and the merchants among whom Mr Stead classes himself are only the carriers of it. He has not a single foot of property of his own to stand on there – and it is not long since he has settled in that town.*

Gooch added with truth that 'there is not a Gentleman connected with that part of the country who would present such a petition' and indeed the petitions were presented by Radical and Whig Members from outside the county.

The petitions had no effect, but Stead who was staying in Covent Garden subsequently found he had a chance of having the bill defeated when the Lords sent it back to the Commons with an amendment. According to Stead's account, however, Lord Stradbroke then gave him to understand that he would ensure that four or five Commissioners from Halesworth would be appointed at the first meeting of the new Commission. Stead therefore wrote to Gooch and to his own particular ally in Parliament, the Radical, Joseph Hume, saying he would withdraw his opposition. Alas, the only Halesworth Commissioner that he was given was Hammond Ringwood (p.94), now comfortably established as a coal merchant and with little inclination to criticize the established order. Patrick Stead felt he had been tricked and he was left nursing a strong sense of grievance.[14]

This decisive defeat of his aspirations must surely have brought home to Stead the entrenched position of the landed gentry in east Suffolk. He had been made to feel their power in the local community and he had also come face-to-face with their ingrained beliefs and assumptions which were so different from his own. Yet despite this, seven years later he took the remarkable decision to move his business into the Blyth valley and to rely on the port of Southwold for his main shipments of barley and malt. In 1837 he decided to centre his business in Halesworth.[15] It was certainly well for the town that he did so for the malting business which he built up there flourished and buoyed up the economy of Halesworth and the surrounding district well into the twentieth century.

Stead had owned the capacious dwelling house and the old brewery in Bridge Street since the early twenties and had increased the malting capacity there. He was drawn to Halesworth by the quality of the barley grown on farms in the surrounding region – that same good malting barley of which many quarters had been shipped to London from Southwold harbour in the eighteenth century.

> *I found the advantage of having a malting establishment at Halesworth beyond all other places where I had carried on the business of a maltster on account of the quality of the water and also the quality of the barley which is often of a very fine kind and which is grown in the neighbourhood – in fact it is so good that I cannot find any so good anywhere else.*[16]

Plentiful supplies of best-quality barley were very strong attractions to a maltster of Patrick Stead's calibre and in addition he was presented in the late thirties with opportunities to buy land in Halesworth on which he could construct maltings to his own design and site them with excellent access both to the river and to the turnpike road. In 1837 he was able to purchase the land on the east and south of the old brewery in Bridge Street and he induced the River Commissioners to let him extend the Navigation at his own expense up river to this property with the aid of a new lock. Within a year he had built four new malt offices here and in the following year, taking advantage of Hammond Ringwood's retirement from business, he was able to buy land and buildings which stretched from the Holton Road down to the quay. Here he built his Quay Maltings, three further blocks of malt offices with a creek running into them for easy loading of his wherries. These splendid opportunities to plan and build just as he wanted must have been very enticing and especially perhaps because in the Quay Maltings he was able to incorporate his own revolutionary invention of a malting using steam for both damping and kilning. The four-floor tower which he built for kilning with steam created a sensation in the neighbourhood and for a time the experiment was remarkably successful. For about four years he was delivering appreciable quantities of 'hot air' and 'steam' malt to Trumans. Although about 1847 the apparatus failed, leaving him to face a considerable loss, the undertaking, so far in advance of current malting practice, helps us to realize that Stead was not only endowed with great technical imagination but also had the courage to put his ideas into practice.[17]

Patrick Stead was well able to face the loss from his steam project. Truman Hanbury were not his only customers for malt and from 1838 to 1851 they alone were paying him on average about £3800 a year for making their malt while they found the money for the barley and for freight and duty. Stead was very proud of the size of his malting business. In 1846 he told a Select Committee that he knew every town in England where there was a malting establishment but was not aware that anyone paid more malt duty than he did. 'Then yours is as large as any in the Kingdom?.' 'I should say almost the largest.'[18]

He was perhaps a little prone to exaggeration but it is at least quite certain that no other merchant or maltster in the Blyth valley came anywhere near the scale of his operations. In Halesworth the Reeve family who had achieved so much as merchants, brewers and maltsters in the eighteenth and early nineteenth centuries (p.86) were very badly hit by the agricultural distress around them. In the 1840s their large house in the south-west corner of the Market Place together with the Three Tuns and the brewery and maltings behind were sold to Thomas Cracknell of South Elmham.[19] Cracknell seems to have malted mainly for his own brewery, as did William Atmer, landlord of the Angel, who had now acquired the maltings in the Angel yard. One family of Halesworth farmers, Martin and Thompson George, who were engaged in trading activities on the pattern of

Stead's impressive Quay Maltings stand out in this photograph of a funeral procession about 1906.

The river access to Stead's Quay Maltings: a postcard of about 1907.

earlier general merchants and dealt in lime, corn, coal and malt, did increase their malting business in the thirties. They built and enlarged malt offices near the river (subsequently converted into the Halesworth Leisure Centre) and their malt was carried by wherry to Southwold and thence to London. We know that Trumans bought malt from them in 1844; however, their business was but a faint echo of Patrick Stead's.[20]

In taking his momentous decision to centre his business in Halesworth despite his failure to penetrate the Southwold Harbour Commission, Stead may well have been swayed by the improved condition of the harbour brought about by the efforts of Francis Ellis. When he commenced his duties as harbour surveyor in the summer of 1829 Ellis had been confronted by a formidable task. The harbour had been allowed to deteriorate into a deplorable state. Not only was the mouth frequently blocked but also the shoaling in the main channel of the river was so extensive that vessels could not find enough water to go up and down to the quays and had to be unloaded at a jetty just inside the harbour. By using a steam dredger Ellis cut through the shoals and cleared nearly a mile of river up to Blackshore quay. The results were very encouraging. The bar at the harbour mouth was opened by the force of the water now able to come down the channel so that the entrance went for nine years without closing up. Inside the harbour brigs and schooners were once again able to go up river not only to Blackshore but also to Reydon quay without having to be lightened. At Blackshore the improved conditions seem to have encouraged the rise of a boat-building industry which produced vessels for the coasting trade. In 1833 the *Sophia* and the brig *Effort* were built and launched, and in the next two years the *Vigilant* and the *Heart of Oak*. The industry was still in existence at Blackshore in 1846 when the *Two Friends* was built and launched at the quay.[21] There was also a decided increase in the late thirties in the number of vessels using the harbour (Table 3).

Ellis's operations were very expensive. The dredger with its steam engine cost over £1400 and although much of this money was recovered when it was sold, the dredging work itself had to be contracted and cost the Harbour Commission over £2000 in the years 1834 and 1835. Dues were bringing in about £1100 a year and £1400 had to be borrowed at five per cent interest. Certainly the Commissioners were very serious in their intention to improve the harbour.[22]

In addition to the dredging Francis Ellis put other work in hand, including repair of the piers, and it is clear that the funding of his improvements was made possible only by the new businesslike administration which Lord Stradbroke had initiated. The Earl himself frequently attended the main meetings at the Swan and in his absence he could rely on Sir Thomas Gooch or Sir Charles Blois to deputize for him. Joseph Berry Edwards, a prosperous and respected citizen of Southwold, had been appointed Treasurer in place of the devious James Jermyn and a Committee headed by Sir Thomas Gooch now met regularly to keep a sharp eye on accounts and on contracts which were correctly opened to public tender. The duties and remuneration of the Harbour Master and other officers had been defined.[23] Lord Stradbroke and his many friends and supporters could fairly claim credit for success. In 1828 the Earl had found an ineffective and probably corrupt administration and a harbour which was barely viable. Both had been transformed.

Stradbroke might also have claimed that there were at least some merchants on the Commission since, in addition to Joseph Berry Edwards, William Crisp served as a Commissioner and was a member of the Committee for many years, while the younger Francis Robinson was also appointed a Commissioner in the Act of 1830. All these men had mercantile interests but all of them seem to have been diverted by other enterprises in the difficult slump years of the twenties and thirties. One reason for this was the changing face of Southwold. The town was finding that commercial salvation rested in the delights of its smooth green turf and sea views. New settlers built genteel edifices and summer visitors were accommodated in handsome lodging houses. James Robinson spent some of his merchant father's fortune on 'an hotel on a very splendid scale'.[24] William

Crisp who, as we have seen above (p.81), had attempted to build up a large malting enterprise at the end of the war years, found himself overtaken by the depression and came to rely increasingly on brewing, a trade which was more likely to be profitable in nineteenth-century Southwold. The visitors and the gentry who enjoyed the Southwold air were happy to imbibe 'Crisp's Ale' which according to a contemporary chronicler was 'universally admired . . . for the purity and delicious flavour'. Joseph Berry Edwards whose father had been a miller and a merchant with a granary at Reydon quay turned to banking and no doubt the services of his banking house in Southwold High Street were appreciated by the occupants of the marine villas on Gunhill and the lushly designed Centre Cliff lodging houses.[25] Francis Robinson, whose energies were very much taken up with laying out for himself the Cliff estate at Dunwich, may also have limited or abandoned his mercantile activities by the thirties. All three men worked with and for the Harbour Commission and showed no desire to question the policies of Stradbroke and Francis Ellis. Robinson indeed did not agree at all with Rennie's indictment of the embankments and maintained that the lack of scour from the previously flooded flats and marshes had been compensated for by the height of the water flowing further upstream.[26]

In July 1835 another local merchant was elected a Commissioner. John Lay of Peasenhall dealt in corn and coal on a considerable scale. He had property at Walpole and a depot and coal bins at Blythburgh and he was also a Navigation Commissioner. On occasion he showed himself prepared to stand up for merchants' interests and at one time he gave some support to Stead, but he also co-operated with the Harbour Commission and like Crisp he served on the Committee for many years.[27]

This was not what Stead wanted. His demand was for the adequate representation of Halesworth and the representative he had in mind was of course himself. This ambition was eminently reasonable. During the thirties the wherries coming down river brought nearly sixty per cent of the grain shipped from Southwold harbour while over sixty per cent of the coal brought in by collier brigs was destined for Halesworth. (Tables 2,3.) Patrick Stead claimed in 1845 that he had been paying about a third of all the Southwold port dues and he was fully justified in asking for a proper voice in the management of the harbour. He was, however, never to be elected a Harbour Commissioner. As Lord Stradbroke expressed it in 1847 in a letter to the Lords Commissioners of the Admiralty, Stead's 'erratic flights' had 'repeatedly shewn to the Commissioners that his views were often at variance with those of the best practical authorities residing near to the Harbour'. These erratic flights included the firm belief that landlords' embankments would have to be pulled down and, as Stradbroke diplomatically explained, it was not 'deemed advisable to admit him into the Commission'.[28]

CHAPTER 20

Last Rounds and the Reckoning

PATRICK STEAD LEFT YARMOUTH IN 1838 AND MOVED his household into the brewery house in Bridge Street, Halesworth, a capacious house with a long garden facing south in which was the hothouse where William Hooker had coaxed his orchids during his temporary spell as a brewer. The maltings which Stead built beside the house have gone and the house and garden are greatly reduced in size but 'Hooker House' (now renumbered 15 Quay Street) remains one of the more handsome houses in Halesworth.[1]

Stead's energies were now concentrated on his Halesworth business which was so dependent on the Blyth and its harbour. It was particularly unfortunate that at this time the harbour was once again in trouble. The winds which for some time had been benign had changed to the north-east; soil was again being driven into the harbour and there was less water on the bar. Francis Ellis, who attributed most of his problems to the north-easterlies, warned the Commissioners in the summer of 1838 that conditions were rapidly deteriorating and obtained permission to hire the Lowestoft steam dredger, only to find that the dredger could not be spared till the following spring. The north-easterly gales raged at Southwold that winter and the bar was raised so high by shingle that as in 1827 even horses and carriages went across it. Vessels were detained inside the harbour for long periods while those inward bound could not get in and were forced to beat about for shelter. The *British Queen* was lost on the bar.[2]

In April and May 1839 the harbour was twice totally blocked by the bar despite the efforts of the Lowestoft dredger. Although in June Ellis reported that as a result of the dredging 'the interior of the harbour may be said to be at the present time in a far better state than it ever was known before in the memory of the present generation' the clearance inside had not this time had much effect on the bar. In the following January the *Lord Exmouth* bound for Cardiff with Stead's barley was imprisoned in the harbour and detained till April. Stead had been used to shipping from 10000 to 50000 quarters of barley a year from Yarmouth, Southwold and other ports but these delays forced him to give up exporting corn. As he explained in 1845:

> *The bar has been getting worse, and the complaints and losses which came upon me were so great, that I gave up the trade of shipping corn in 1840, and several merchants were ruined by the delay and loss of markets; they*

could not calculate what time would be occupied, and barley is of that perishable nature that after the month of April it is only fit for grinding.[3]

Stead was now galvanizing the Navigation Commissioners into action. At the Annual Meeting in June 1839 he poured out his grievances to the assembled company at the Angel and expressed his conviction that Southwold harbour had been reduced to a ruinous state by 'embankments of the Marshes and stopping of the Creeks'. He deluged the meeting with papers and reports and the indignation of the Halesworth men was aroused. They despatched a Memorial to Southwold and asked for the appointment of a Special Committee to hear their complaints and the evidence they proposed to bring. The Harbour Commissioners bowed to this demand.[4]

The Special Committee was chaired by Alfred Lillingston Esquire, the much respected mayor of Southwold, and apart from Colonel Bence of Thorington Hall, there was a noticeable absence of landowners among its members. Stead threw all the evidence he could muster at the committee and produced six Captains of vessels prepared to testify to the parlous situation at the harbour caused by the decrease of the back waters. The sessions at Southwold Town Hall continued all through August, with one in October. Later that month the Harbour Commissioners met to examine the proceedings of their Special Committee only to find themselves confronted at the meeting by a messenger from Stead complaining that he now had three vessels detained in the harbour.[5]

The relentless and public pressure which Stead had organized and the unhappy persistence of the bar at the mouth of the river did bring a positive result. The Harbour Commissioners decided to call in James Walker C.E. provided that the Halesworth men would share his very heavy fees. The Navigation Commissioners declared that they had full confidence in the engineer but when Stead came to read Walker's Report in the summer of 1841 he must have done so with disappointment. The acreage of marsh enclosed and the cubic feet of water excluded were carefully set out in a table, and John Wright, Walker's surveyor, mapped the drained land. Walker lamented that the owners of estates when reclaiming land 'were not advised of the injury they were about to do to the public and themselves by the reduction of the backwater upon which their harbour is dependent', but he considered that it was too late to destroy the banks, 'practically out of the question'. He was concerned to make peace and, while making various structural suggestions, he recommended that a first step to a solution would be 'a perfect understanding between the Harbour and River Commissioners'. Seizing on this the Harbour Commissioners proposed a bill to amalgamate the two Commissions with clauses guaranteeing the rights of landowners to their marsh lands. They could be sure that the Navigation Commissioners would never accept the offer.[6]

Stead now abandoned any hopes of local action. He turned away from stuffy Suffolk to London and Westminster where the commercial middle classes with their faith in liberalism and the virtues of free competitive enterprises were challenging the powers of the landed and aristocratic classes. He had privately obtained Counsel's opinion to the effect that the embankments were 'public nuisances' and 'illegal' and he now wrote to the Commissioners of Woods and Forests and to the Board of Trade; he petitioned the House of Commons; he induced the Admiralty to send down Captain Washington, one of their surveyors, to look at the position and was rewarded by a Report condemning the embankments in the strongest terms.[7]

His last great hope lay in the Tidal Harbour Commission whose members visited Southwold harbour as a result of his pleas in 1845. The Commission had been set up following a campaign for a national takeover of tidal harbours; and the radical reformer Joseph Hume used the survey to mount a violent attack on the landed interest who in the case of Southwold formed the chief vested obstruction to commercial freedom. Hume had the rest of the Commission and its chairman, Admiral Bowles, behind him. They reported forthrightly that in some southern ports the landed, fishing, and corporation interests had

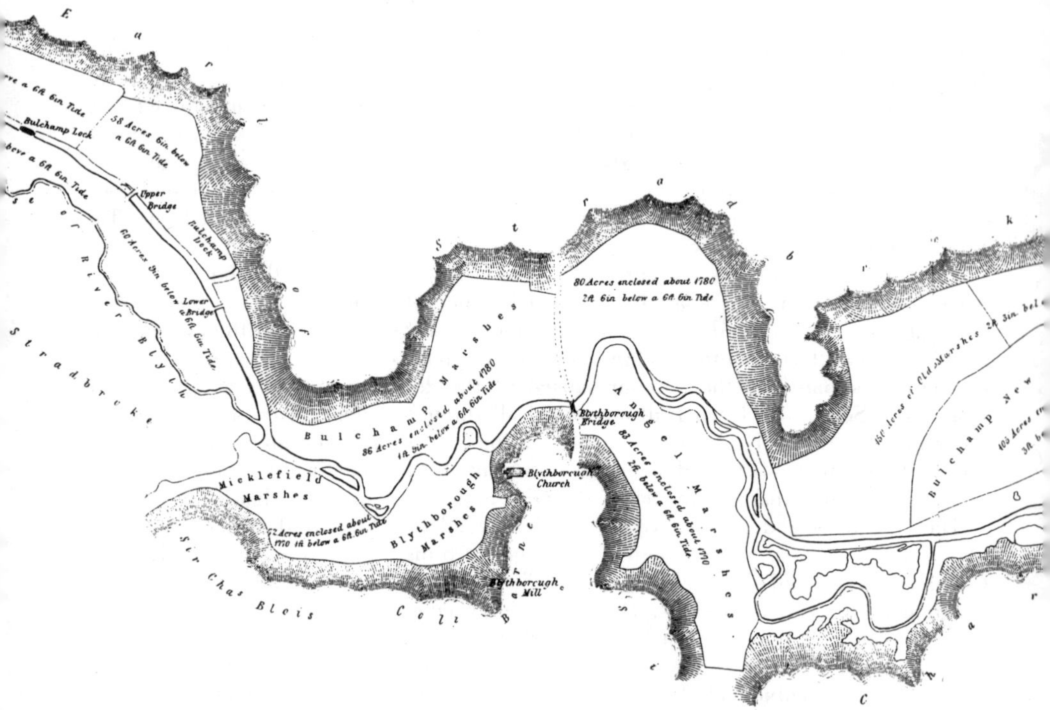

SOUTHWOLD HARBOUR,

AND THE

RIVER BLYTH.

SURVEYED BY JOHN R WRIGHT,

under the direction of

JAMES WALKER. F.R.S.

1840.

The space over which the River used to flow is tinted Green.

Area of the embanked Lands.

Nº of Acres	Cubic Feet of Water excluded
1504	148. 296, 490
1200	Dunwich, Dingle and Westwood Marshes.
2704	Total Area in Acres.

Mr Walker's Report in 1841. p. 22

Scale of One Nautic Mile

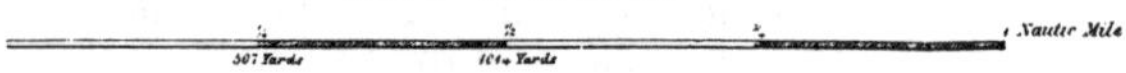

Reduced from Mr Walker's large Plan,
by
E. K. CALVER,
Master and Assistant Surveyor.
H. M. S. Blazer,
1844

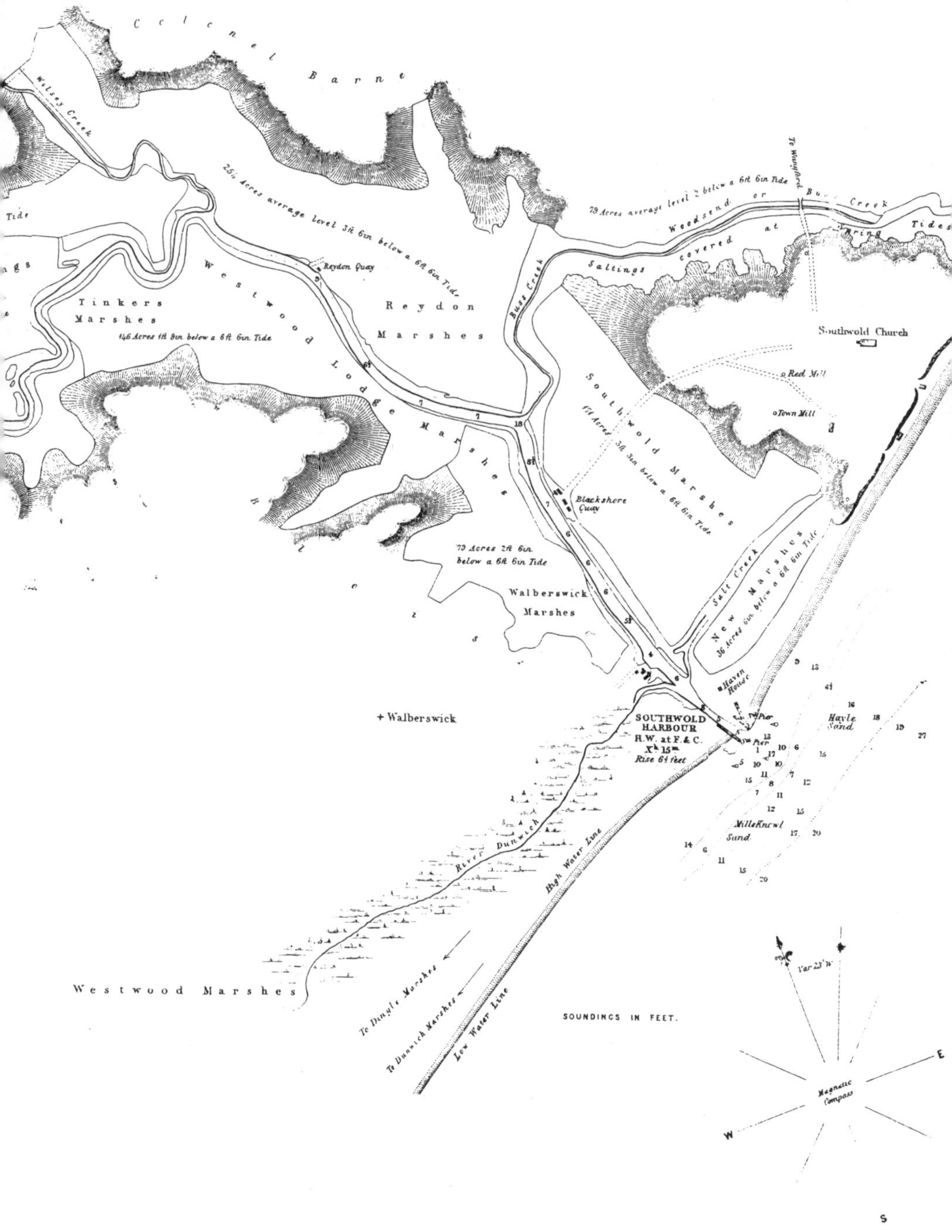
Colonel Barne
Welsey Creek
254 Acres average level 3ft 6in below a 6ft 6in Tide
Reydon Quay
Reydon Marshes
Tinkers Marshes
146 Acres 1ft 9in below a 6ft 6in Tide
Westwood Lodge Marshes
79 Acres average level 2 below a 6ft 6in Tide
To Wangford
Woodsend or Buss Creek
Saltings covered at Spring Tides
Buss Creek
Southwold Church
Red Mill
Town Mill
Southwold Marshes
174 Acres 3ft 3in below a 6ft 6in Tide
Blackshore Quay
79 Acres 2ft 6in below a 6ft 6in Tide
Walberswick Marshes
Salt Creek
New Marshes
36 Acres 6in below a 6ft 6in Tide
Haven House
Pier
SOUTHWOLD HARBOUR
H.W. at F. & C.
Rise 6¼ feet
Havle Sand
Walberswick
MilleKnowl Sand
River Dunwich
High Water Line
Low Water Line
Westwood Marshes
To Dingle Marshes
To Dunwich Marshes
SOUNDINGS IN FEET.
Var 23° W
Magnetic Compass
E
W
S

proved too powerful and that 'the consequence has been in several cases a dry bar, a deserted port, and all-but ruin to the ship-owner and merchant'. 'The river Blyth and the port of Southwold on the east coast of Suffolk offer strong proof of the correctness of these statements.' Southwold at this time was certainly not a deserted port; in the year 1844–5, 487 merchant vessels went in or out of the harbour. But if this statement was hyperbole the evidence brought out in the proceedings was not. Expertly questioned by Hume, Stead was able both to set forth the many opinions he had collected condemning the embankments and to impress on his audience the high-handed treatment he had received from the Harbour Commissioners, despite the fact that he was the main shipper from the port and the main contributor to its finances.

Q *Do you and the inhabitants with whom you have communicated, consider that the injury done to the Navigation . . . has been caused by these lands on each side of the river being embanked, so as to exclude the flood tide?*
A *Yes; we do believe that is the cause of the harbour being so bad.*

Q *Do you know under what authority these lands have been enclosed?*
A *I never heard of any authority whatever . . ..*

Q *What do you consider ought to be done to remedy the present state of the harbour?*
A *The same remedy that was applied at Wells, that is to take the banks down . . ..*

Q *You complain of the expenses being high, have any books of account of the receipts and expenditure been given to you?*
A *I have never been able to see the proper books which the Act [Southwold Harbour Act, 1830] requires, and I have never been able to check the accounts . . ..*

Q *Have you as a merchant, paying upwards of £300 a-year towards these revenues had access to books in order to ascertain whether the credits were proper and expenditure regularly entered?*
A *I have not . . ..*

Q *Did you ever present yourself at any . . . annual meetings and were you refused?*
A *I presented myself in the year 1840, and wrote a respectful letter asking to be admitted, and I was admitted then, but I understood by the address that I got, it was by courtesy . . ..*

Q *You did not apply in any subsequent year to be admitted?*
A *No, I did not, because I thought it was not the proper way to go.*

Q *Did you consider yourself entitled under the Act to attend?*
A *I did, but the only way, and that is the hardship of the case, would have been to go to law.*

The Commissioners gave Francis Ellis a fair hearing and the harbour surveyor stood up well to some of Hume's loaded questions and was able in his turn to quote some respectable authorities who did not place the blame for the harbour's problems on the embankments. The Tidal Harbour Commissioners did pay a rather grudging tribute to Ellis's work; 'under the direction of the present harbour Surveyor the lower part of the harbour has been somewhat improved; yet as the Act [1830] did not touch the embankments, the bar has been at times since that period dry at high water so that no vessel could get in or out'.[8]

Though it must have given Stead much emotional relief to pour out his complaints to the Commission, their Reports failed to result in any legislation affecting Southwold, while in the meantime the position of the riparian owners was bolstered by the General Enclosure Act of 1845. The Harbour Commissioners proposed an Act to establish a national harbour conservancy board and in 1848 Stead, backed by Thompson George of Halesworth and other merchants, sent a supporting petition to the House of Commons. The opposition to the proposal was, however, altogether too strong and Stead cannot have had much hope that it would succeed.[9]

This was his last fling. Already his fertile forward-looking mind had foreseen the impact of the railways. He was among the first directors of the Ipswich line and in 1846 he told a Royal Commission: 'my thorough belief is that the effect of railways will be to do away with the small ports'.[10] His Halesworth maltings were deliberately built for easy river transport and it may well have been the shadow of the railways which decided him to sell out at what was a very shrewd time. He was also nearing retiring age and he was over sixty when in April 1849 the Truman partners decided to offer him £18000 for all his property in Halesworth, including his shares in the Navigation. He accepted the offer and in less than two years he had returned to Scotland where he enjoyed a ripe old age.

He was eighty-one when he died and he left nearly £56000, of which £25000 eventually went at his bequest to build and endow the Patrick Stead Hospital in Halesworth. The hospital, however, was not his greatest contribution to Halesworth. The business he had built flourished under Trumans till well into the twentieth century and encouraged other brewers to look to Halesworth for their malt.[11]

He was right in foreseeing that the railways would take over the transport of malt to London and would bring down the coal from the north-east. Although Robert Burleigh, his successor at Hooker House and Truman's agent, must have used wherries for some time and still owned three wherries and a ketch-barge when he died in 1883, the railways had dealt a death blow to the Navigation long before then.[12]

Francis Ellis continued to wrestle with the harbour's problems till his retirement in 1858 and he must have been thankful to be away from the harbour in the following year when once again people were strolling across the entrance. His many improvements and his efforts to keep the harbour viable deserve recognition, as does the practical sense of Lord Stradbroke who put him into office and backed him. It is well to remember that during the ten years from 1831, 4250 merchant ships passed in or out of the harbour, and that the numbers increased in the following decade (Table 3). Lord Stradbroke and his fellow landowners have been heavily condemned by some modern writers for their natural refusal to contemplate the destruction of their embankments and for their hostile attitude to Stead. But the Scotsman was an alien presence in east Suffolk. Stradbroke and his friends were men of their time and place and they carried most local contemporaries with them. They did their best with the finances that they had and without the management they established at the harbour Patrick Stead's affairs could not have prospered as they did.

Stead's remarkable achievements provided a fitting finale to a hundred years of mercantile activity at the harbour and on the river. That mercantile activity had been made possible by the initiative and dogged determination of local men over the years. They were not all merchants: landowners, lawyers, clergymen, all made contributions. In the face of uncontrollable winds and waves and even more baffling economic fluctuations, some of them at least showed the courage and enterprise which was found in so many British people at this period, and of which enterprise the embankments were after all another manifestation. In the later years of the nineteenth century river and sea transport were replaced by road and rail but the pattern of trade, particularly in barley and coal, which had been engendered by Southwold harbour and the Blyth Navigation remained. Seventy years before Patrick Stead came to Halesworth barley and malt had been the main cargo sent coastwise from the Blyth valley. Seventy years after he built his maltings, horses and carts were still bringing barley to be roasted at Halesworth and newly erected maltings dwarfed even his ambitious structures. Depression enveloped the agricultural community in the early years of the twentieth century, but the tasselled red caps of the Halesworth maltsters must have been a heartening and encouraging sight.

A Note on Weights and Measures

THE GRAIN TRADE traditionally conducted its business by measure, not weight. The basic unit for corn and malt was the quarter (8 bushels). A 'last', which was used early in the eighteenth century, was the equivalent of 10 quarters.

East Suffolk farmers and merchants reckoned their corn and malt in coombs. There were two coombs to a quarter and one coomb filled a sack. Conversion into weight is hazardous and varied according to the type of grain. However, towards the end of the nineteenth century quarters were of fixed weight: 448 lb for barley and 336 lb for malt. In earlier years the weight equivalent seems to have been considerably less.

COAL was measured in chaldrons. Both the measure and the weight equivalent varied according to the district but by the eighteenth century the imperial chaldron, used in London, had settled down to the equivalent of 1.32 tons. At Southwold in 1840 the equivalent was taken to be 1.25 tons.

TABLE 1

YEARS	TOLLS PAID ON RIVER £	HARBOUR DUES PAID £
1750–54		1187
1755–59		1681
1760–64		2494
(1762–64	376)	
1765–69	699	3028
1770–74	707	2966
1775–79	750	2966
1780–84	454	2300
1785–89	585	2582
1790–94	789	3063
1795–99	760	3583
1800–04	1145	3929
1805–09	915	3170
1810–14	903	3898
1815–19	781	4738
1820–24	1262	5613
1825–29	1986	6126
1830–34	1941	5677
1835–39	1830	5576
1840–44	2117	5235
1845–49	1976	5361

Sources: NRO,EAW 9/1, 9/24
STH, SHCB, H9, H10, H14.

TABLE 2

COMPARATIVE STATEMENT of the HARBOURS DUES paid by the Southwold and Halesworth Trade, 1810–40, from Parliamentary and Harbour Returns

Dates	*Southwold Trade*		*Dues* £.	s.	d.	*Halesworth Trade*		*Dues* £.	s.	d.
1810	190 790	Qrs Corn	2011	6	8	39 482	Qrs Corn	380	9	0
1819	36 165	Chals Coal	2976	8	8	26 897	Chals Coal	2236	0	0
			4987	15	4			2616	9	0
1820	243 302	Qrs Corn	3041	5	6	71 843	Qrs Corn	898	0	9
1830	34 221	Chals Coal	3421	13	0	36 947	Chals Coal	3694	14	0
			6462	18	6			4592	14	0
1831	105 262	Qrs Corn	877	3	8	152 185	Qrs Corn	1268	14	2
1840	23 295	Chals Coal	1811	16	8	46 397	Chals Coal	3608	13	6
			2689	0	4			4877	7	8

Source: PP 1845XVI, Appx 18,165.

TABLE 3

SOUTHWOLD HARBOUR: YEARLY TRADE FIGURES
Midsummer to Midsummer – 1829/30–1865/6

Year	*Dues £*	*Tons of Coal imported (in '00s)*	*Qrs of Corn exported (in '000s)*	*Vessels in and out*
1829/30	1315	104	25	338
1830/31	1025	80	19	309
1831/32	1267	103	22	394
1832/33	1228	90	26	411
1833/34	1098	81	22	378
1834/35	1059	80	18	357
1835/36	1145	88	29	472
1836/37	1063	98	32	434
1837/38	1050	100	28	425
1838/39	1045	100	29	418
1839/40	1273	132	32	523
1840/41	1054	111	24	440
1841/42	1157	124	26	501
1842/43	968	106	19	450
1843/44	959	100	24	415
1844/45	1097	123	23	487
1845/46	1077	112	26	–
1846/47	1046	112	22	483
1847/48	1194	131	21	460
1848/49	1003	106	24	426
1849/50	1041	119	25	414
1850/51	987	121	28	398
1851/52	934	118	19	412
1852/53	911	107	26	380
1853/54	1015	125	23	411
1854/55	921	101	30	393
1855/56	547	75	18	361
1861/62	543	78	9	251
1865/66	362	47	9	170

Source: Southwold Harbour Ledgers, 1829–66, Southwold Town Hall, H9, H10, H12

REFERENCES

For details of published and unpublished sources used see Bibliography.

Where no specific repository is given the document is in the Suffolk Record Office, Ipswich Branch.

Abbreviations used

BL	British Library
DED	D. E. Davy, Suffolk Collections: Collections for the History of Suffolk by Hundreds & Parishes; Pedigrees; Original Letters addressed to Eleazar Davy & D. E. Davy; Misc. Collections; Legal documents. BL Add. MSS
H14	Southwold Haven Cash Book, 1824–60, Southwold Town Hall
KPB	Thomas Knights' Pocket Book, NRO MS 362 T1310
NRO	Norfolk Record Office
PRO	Public Record Office
PSIA	Proceedings of the Suffolk Institute of Archaeology and History
RBCI	Minute Book of the River Blyth Commissioners & Committee, 1757–1839, NRO EAW 9/1
RBCII	Minute Book of the River Blyth Commissioners & Committee, 1839–1856, NRO EAW 9/2
SCA	Minutes of Southwold Corporate Assemblies, 1713–1800, Southwold Town Hall
SHCI	Minutes of Southwold Harbour Commissioners, 1747–1804, Southwold Town Hall
SHCII	Minutes of Southwold Harbour Commissioners, 1804–1859, Southwold Town Hall
SHCB	Southwold Harbour Cash Book, 1747–1824, Southwold Town Hall
SRB	Minutes of Evidence, Commons Select Committee on Railway Bills (Group 22), HC 1846 vol. 42, House of Lords Record Office
SRO(L)	Suffolk Record Office, Lowestoft Branch
STH	Records in Southwold Town Hall

Prologue – Then and Now

1. J. Armstrong & P. Bagwell, 'Coastal Shipping', 141–158, G. Jackson, 'The Ports', 194–200, B. Duckham, 'Canals & River Navigations', 100–1, 109, 128–30, all in Aldcroft & Freeman (eds.), *Transport in the Industrial Revolution*
2. STH, H8, H9, H10, H11 (Harbour ledgers & log books); PP1845XVI, 51; Maggs, *Handbook*, xviii
3. Clark, *Black Sailed Traders*, 48, 58–63, 112–114; Malster, *Wherries & Waterways*, 55–6 and generally on Norfolk and Suffolk wherries

Chaper 1 Thomas Gardner's World

1. A. Young, *General View of the Agriculture of the County of Suffolk*, 4–5; La Rochefoucauld, *A Frenchman's Year in Suffolk*, 137,147
2. A. Bottomley, *A Short History of the Borough of Southwold*, 2–3, 6–11; Thomas Gardner, *An Historical Account of Dunwich, Blithburgh, Southwold*, 120–1, 145–176, 191–5
3. 20 Geo II. cap. 14: 30 Geo II. cap. 47
4. Gardner as (2), 'Dedication', 120-1, 145–176, 196–9, 252–7
5. J. Kirby, *The Suffolk Traveller*, 138; Daniel Defoe, *Tour through the Eastern Counties*, 80; *Ipswich Journal*, 7 Sept. 1751; A. Young as (1), 141, 199–203; N. Evans, *The East Anglian Linen Industry*, 1–11
6. NRO, EAW9/34
7. PP1845XVI, 50
8. *Ipswich Journal*, 15 June 1754; Wright, 'Survey of the River Blyth' 1840; HA53/359/286/6; SCA 1719
9. G. Crabbe, *The Borough*, Letter 16
10. L. S. Presnell, *Country Banking*, 36–37; RBCI, 27 Sept. 1759; HB26/412/182, 191, 202, 239, 772

Chapter 2 The Harbour Initiative

1. Quoted by Defoe, *Tour through the Eastern Counties*, 1724, 76
2. J. Armstrong & P. Bagwell, 'Coastal Shipping' in Aldcroft & Freeman (eds.), *Transport in the Industrial Revolution*, 142–4
3. SCA, 31 Jan. 1741; Maggs, *Handbook*, ix, x
4. SHCI, Lists of subscribers, 4 Dec. 1747, 1 Sept. 1749, 2 Sept. 1751
5. SCA, 20 Aug. 1745
6. G. Jackson, 'The Ports' in Aldcroft & Freeman as (2), 199; SHCI, 1747–51
7. SHCI, 23 Oct. 1751, 27 May 1754
8. SHCI, 1753–56
9. 30 Geo II. cap. 58

Chapter 3 The Launch of the Navigation

1. RBCI, 27 Sept., 14 Nov. 1759, 22 Sept., 22 Oct. 1760; NRO, EAW/9/43; 30 Geo II. cap. 47
2. B. Duckham in Aldcroft & Freeman (eds.), *Transport in the Industrial Revolution*, 100–1; Boyes & Russell, *The Canals of Eastern England*, 79–83, 179–80, 183–4, 111–12; KPB, Yates to Knights, 23 Nov. 1756
3. HB/8/50/1/1–60; HA 30/50/22/4, 48
4. KPB, Buxton to Knights, 25 Nov. 1753
5. DED 19080, 383
6. KPB, Jermyn to Knights, 26 Feb. 1757
7. RBCI, 26 Nov. 1757, 6 June 1759, 30 Jan. 1760, 3 June 1761, 25 Sept. 1834; NRO, EAW 9/41
8. Crabbe, *The Borough*, Letter 1
9. KPB, Forster to Knights, 13 Feb. 1757, Hay to Knights, 14 Feb. 1757
10. KPB, Norford to Knights, 23 Feb. 1757, Hay to Knights, 21 Feb. 1757
11. KPB, Rous & others to Vernon, 10 Jan. 1757, Jermyn to Knights, 26 Feb. 1757; *House of Commons Journals*, Vol. 27, 1 Feb., 8 Feb., 4 March, 23. March 1757
12. *Ipswich Journal*, 1 Aug. 1761; KPB, Nunn to Knights, 4 Dec. 1759
13. RBCI, 6 June 1764

Chapter 4 Creating the Waterway: Frustrations and Delays

1. RBCI, 6 June, 13 July, 27 Sept., 31 Oct., 14 Nov., 1759
2. RBCI generally to 5 June 1771
3. RBCI, 30 July, 20 Aug., 3 Sept., 10 Sept., 22 Sept., 22 Oct., 1760
4. RBCI, 22 Oct. 1760, 14 Jan. 1761, 15 Feb., 21 Feb., 13 May, 1761
5. RBCI, 23 July, 6 Aug., 11 Sept., 1761; *Ipswich Journal*, 1 Aug. 1761
6. RBCI, 3 June 1761 et seq.; NRO, EAW 9/41
7. RBCI, 9 Dec. 1761, 6 Jan., 2 June 1762
8. RBCI, 6 June, 4 July 1764; NRO, EAW 9/41, 9/43; Cross Ram, 'Abstract of title to lands held of Manor of Halesworth, late P. Jermyn'
9. RBCI, 11 Sept. 1761; SHCI, 26 June 1762, 9 May 1764
10. RBCI, 5 June 1776, 2 June 1784

Chapter 5 The Commissioners at Work: Theory and Practice

1. NRO, EAW 9/41
2. RBCI, 4 June, 9 July 1777
3. DED 19080, 424
4. 29 Geo III. cap. 77, 1789
5. SHCI, 24 Feb. 1779 – 24 Aug. 1781; Maggs, *Handbook*, xi
6. P. Homer in *Suffolk Garland*, 1818, 221
7. Maggs, *Diary*, I, 27; SHCB, May 1796
8. Mathias, *Industrial Nation*, 43–44
9. SHCII, 8 Sept. 1814
10. Maggs, *Handbook*, xii

Chapter 6 Rous of Henham: Portrait of a Landowner

1. Alfred Suckling, *History & Antiquities*, 354–5; DED 19081, 2, 8
2. HA11/C6/1/1–3
3. DED 19215, 18–19, corresp. Rous/Buxton, 1773
4. As (2)
5. HA11/C7/1/1–4
6. HA11/C6/1/1, HA11/C7/1/2–18
7. Gardner, *An Historical Account of Dunwich, Blithburgh, Southwold*, 257; HA11/C7/1/3–14; HA11/C6/1/1
8. HA11/C6/1/1; HA11/C6/1/2
9. HA11/C6/1/1
10. DED 19223, 33, Rous to Davy, 9 June 1788
11. DED 19223, 37–8, Rous to Davy, 15 Dec. 1788
12. DED 19213, 91, 93, Thomas Holt to Davy, 13 May, 6 July 1790
13. DED 19223, 164–5, Rous to Davy, 29 Dec. 1791; Stone, *An Open Elite?*, 37–40
14. DED 19223, 176–7, 185, Rous to Davy, 16 Jan., 20 Feb. 1792
15. Thompson, *English Landed Society in the Nineteenth Century*, 212–215
16. HB26/371/127, 128; HA11/C6/28; HA11/C7/1/48
17. HA11/C46/65; Robson, *Georgian Model Farms*, 126
18. DED 19223, 164, Rous to Davy, 29 Dec. 1791

Chapter 6 – *continued*

19. HA11/C6/1/3; HA11/C7/1/27–31
20. Jane Austen, *Mansfield Park*, 53–58
21. HA11/C46/64
22. HB/26/412/191

Chapter 7 Rous and the River Blyth

1. HA11/C7/1/48
2. HA11/C6/1/6–7
3. HA11/C7/1/22–49
4. HB26/371/128
5. KPB; RBCI, 6 June 1759, 3 June 1761
6. HA11/C6/1/2, 'Debts 1785'
7. HA11/C7/1/9–38
8. HA11/C7/1/32–42; PRO, CUST97/348(9), 2 Feb. 1798
9. HA11/C7/1/7–51
10. SHCI, 29 March 1758
11. SHCI, 24 Feb., 28 May 1779; HA11/C6/1/1, Dec. 1779
12. Beckett, *The Aristocracy in England*, 357–8
13. HA11/C6/1/8–9
14. SHCI, 1807–9
15. La Rochefoucauld, *A Frenchman's Year in Suffolk*, 190
16. SHCI, April 1799–1813; Bottomley, *A Short History of the Borough of Southwold*, 13–14
17. Maggs, *Handbook*, xiii–xv; SHCI, 30 July 1812 – Sept. 1827
18. PRO, CUST 97/350, 1805

Chapter 8 Cockfield Hall, a Distracted Estate

1. Parr, 'Yoxford Yesterday', Vol. II, 172–195; Burke's *Peerage*
2. HA30/312/419
3. Parr, as (1), 193–222
4. HA30/50/22/7, 25
5. RBCI, 1757–1761
6. SHCI, 29 March 1758, 29 May 1760, 31 May 1769
7. HA30/50/22/3, 16; HA30/324/4; SCA, 11 Oct. 1764, 12 Sept. 1800
8. Kirby, *The Suffolk Traveller*, 146
9. Parr, 'Yoxford Yesterday', Vol. V, 230; HA30/50/22/3, 8; PRO, E190/562/25, 563/9
10. HA30/312/419; HA30/369/271–80; HA30/50/22/3, 41, 4, 48
11. Becker, *Blythburgh*, 60
12. HA30/50/22/1, 12; RBCI, 26 Nov. 1757–1767
13. HA30/324/25; HA30/312/65; HA30/50/22/5, 17
14. HB26/412/244
15. HA53/359/106, Mary Barne to Miles junior, 22 Sept. 1762
16. HA30/50/22/3, 16, 3, 17
17. HA30/50/22/1, 2 & 3, 17
18. DED 19083, 257
19. La Rochefoucauld, *A Frenchman's Year in Suffolk*, 44–5, 133; Stone, *An Open Elite?*, 350; Parr, 'Yoxford Yesterday' Vol. II, 225–229; HA30/324/4
20. HA30/50/22/3, 8; HA30/324/4

Chapter 8 – *continued*

21. HA30/50/22/3, 10, 'An Epistle from a Lady in the Country'
22. HA30/312/64, 65
23. As (22); HA30/50/22/3, 9, 3, 41
24. Parr as (19), 240; HA30/50/22/5, 16, 6, 11; Scarfe, 'Whitney and Read', PSIA xxviii (2), 191–2
25. HA30/324/17; HB26/412/244

Chapter 9 Westwood Lodge

1. A. Young, *General View of the Agriculture of the County of Suffolk*, 13
2. HA30/50/22/3, 40, Watling to Gooch, 19 Nov. 1769
3. HA30/50/22/1, 12, 3, 10, 3, 40, 7, 25; DED 19186, 37–40, 19189, 26–8
4. HA53/359/114, letter to Sir John Blois, 2 Oct. 1763
5. HA30/50/22/1, 12, 3, 40, 4, 85
6. DED 19083, 258; HA11/C6/1/1
7. HA53/359/72, Read to Barne, 2 July 1818
8. Thirsk & Imray (eds.) *Suffolk Farming*, 92–3
9. HA30/50/22/5, 17
10. PP1836(189)VIII, 62–71; E. R. Cooper's Notes; HA30/50/22/3, 18
11. Parr, 'Yoxford Yesterday', Vol. V, 230; A. Young as (1), 34
12. SRB, 132–141
13. PRO, E190/580/20
14. DED 19188, 54
15. HA30/50/22/1, 12, 3, 40, 4, 87, 5, 7(1)
16. HA30/50/22/1, 12, 3, 40
17. HA30/50/22/5, 17
18. Southwold Museum, J. Rennie C. E., 'Report of Southwold Harbour', 6 Jan. 1820; HA30/50/22/3, 18, 5, 17

Chapter 10 Barne of Sotterley

1. HA53/407/156
2. Pickard, *Dunwich – The Rotten Borough*
3. As (1)
4. HA53/359/318, 617, 704
5. HA53/359/119, Mary Barne to Miles junior, 12 Feb. 1764
6. HA53/359/106, 107, 119, letters, Mary Barne to Miles junior
7. HA53/359/114, Sayers to Barne, 5 Nov. 1746; HA53/359/286/6, 359/704
8. HA53/359/330
9. HA53/359/130/xi, Case for Counsel's Opinion, 1752
10. HA53/359/114/i, Levins to Barne, 9 Feb. 1747
11. PRO, CUST97/356, Board to Collector, 13 June 1752; as (9)
12. SCA, 6 Dec. 1754
13. SHCI, 23 Oct. 1751, 27 May, 23 July 1754
14. SHCI, 30 May 1755, 30 May 1757; HA53/359/607
15. SHCI, marked minutes 1754–55; PRO, C/33/403–7; 30 Geo II. cap. 58
16. SHCI. 30 May 1757
17. Jenkins, *Bygones and Local Characters*, 36
18. HA53/359/67, 72, 318, 330

Chapter 10 – *continued*

19. Burke's *Landed Gentry* II
20. SHCI, 25 May 1781 et seq.
21. HA30/50/22/3. 18; Maggs, *Diary* I, 52–3
22. HA53/359/107, B. Barne to Miles u/d; HA53/359/330
23. HA53/359/830, 1824

Chapter 11 The Role of the Middleman

1. N. J. Williams, *The Maritime Trade of the East Anglian Ports 1550–90*, Oxford, 1988; DED 19198, 121; HA11/C7/1/5 & 7; see note on chaldrons on p. 128
2. Flinn, *History of the British Coal Industry*, 1–2, 231–245
3. Crabbe, *The Borough*, Letter 1
4. As (3), Letter 8

Chapter 12 The Caretakers of the Harbour: Southwold Merchants

1. Bottomley & Hutchinson, *Discovering Southwold*, 28; SRO(L), Loftus, 'History of Brewing in Southwold'; information from Bottomley
2. PRO, E190/534/6, 17, 554/14, 559/3, 560/3
3. Loftus as (1); *Ipswich Journal*, 24 May 1755; PRO E190/512/25, 563/9
4. RBCI, 30 Jan., 4 June 1760, 3 June 1761
5. FC 202/D1/1; PRO, PROB11/1444
6. Maggs, *Diary* I, 39–40, 47
7. DED 19083, 58, 61
8. Adnams' records
9. PRO, E190/559/5, 560/1, 562/25, 563/9, 568/14; SCA, 12 June 1760; KPB, Nunn to Knights, 4 Dec. 1759
10. SHCI, 5 Sept. 1753 et seq.; SHCB, Oct. 1756
11. Bottomley & Hutchinson as (1), 26, 28
12. PRO, E190/560/3, 562/25, 567/14, 573/8, 580/20
13. Bottomley, *Short History of Borough of Southwold*, 13
14. HA11/C7/1/2–32; HA30/50/22/4, 87; HA30/324/4
15. SHCI, 30 May 1770, 31 May 1776; SHCB 1776 et seq.; SHCB May 1796
16. RBCI, 4 June 1760, 6 Aug. 1761, 6 June 1770, 5 June 1771
17. PRO, E190/570/3, 573/9, 580/11

Chapter 13 The Village Merchants: Reydon and Wangford; Walberswick and Dunwich

1. HB26/412/612, 615; HA53/359/330
2. Gardner, *An Historical Account of Dunwich, Blithburgh, Southwold*, 256–7
3. PRO, E190/555/14, 559/3
4. SHCI, 1747–51
5. HA53/359/286/6
6. PRO, E/190/559/3, 562/25, 563/9, 567/14, 568/14, 570/10, 19, 573/8, 574/2; R. Bloomfield, 'Suffolk Cheese' in *Suffolk Garland*, 1818, 374

Chapter 13 – *continued*

7. KPB; RBCI, 8 June 1762, 11 July 1767; Adnams' records, 'Harbour Inn'; RBCI, 7 June 1769
8. PRO, E190/555/14 et seq. to 585/25; Mathias, *Brewing Industry*, 392–7, 403; SRB 25 May 1846, 60–2
9. HA11/C7/1/5–50; HB26/412/776, 777; HA11/C3/9; PRO, E190/580/20, 581/23
10. HB/26/412/227–238
11. F. A. Crisp, *Collections* Vol. III; Charlotte Primrose, 'Reminiscences' 1885; Browne, *History of Congregationalism*, 432
12. PRO, E190/559/3, 560/3, 573/8, 574/2, 580/20, 581/23; F. A. Crisp, *Collections* Vol. I
13. J419/9(1860); HA11/C7/1/30/51; Adnams' records, sales 1795, 1809; *Ipswich Journal*, 3 Aug. 1799; information from Bottomley
14. G. Crabbe, 'The Frank Courtship' in *Tales*, 1812
15. Adnams' records, sale 18 Sept. 1814; sale brochure, Southwold brewery, 11 April 1844; Parr, 'Yoxford Yesterday' Vol VI, 167; HA53/359/67
16. Mathias, *The Brewing Industry*, 548
17. Adnams' records, sale brochure as (15), Conveyance of Malting Office, 20 July 1844; Loftus, 'History of Brewing in Southwold'
18. HA11/C9/74; as (10)
19. HB26/371/8, 1792; DED 19146, 215–16, Will of Robert Reeve
20. 1851 Census; White, *Directory of Suffolk*, 1844, 402
21. PRO, E190/562/25, 563/9, 567/14, 568/14, 570/10, 570/19, 573/8, 574/2, 580/20, 581/23
22. RBCI, 8 June 1762; HA11/C7/1/9–24; PRO, E190/570/3, 580/11; PRO, CUST 97/348 (38), 21 June 1797
23. E. R. Cooper, *Brief History of Southwold Haven*, xiii
24. SHCII, 12 July 1810, 8 Sept. 1814, 29 April 1824

Chapter 14 Halesworth: A New Economy and a Changing Society

1. *Ipswich Journal*, 1 Aug. 1761
2. RBCI, 8 June 1762; PRO, CUST 97/350, 86; E. R. Cooper 'Suffolk Coast' in EADT, 2 May 1934
3. Cross Ram, Manor of Halesworth General Court, 9 Jan. 1738, 7 June 1762
4. HB26/412/49, 7 April 1750; *Ipswich Journal*, 28 Sept. 1751
5. PRO, C33/411, May 1759, 335, C12/2310/15, C38/579, 23 June 1761, C33/417, 1762, 276; as (3) 7 June 1762; *Ipswich Journal*, 17 Aug. 1764
6. RBCI, 30 Jan. 1760, 2 June 1762, 5 June 1765
7. RBCI, 26 Nov. 1757 et seq., 3 June, 13 Oct. 1772, 6 June 1792; *Universal British Directory* III, 1794; *Ipswich Journal*, 24 June 1809
8. HB26/412/107; Cross Ram, Manor of Halesworth General Court, 18 Dec. 1772; KPB; RBCI, 14 Oct. 1761
9. FC190/D1/1; Cross Ram as (8), 1758, 2 Aug. 1827
10. Cross Ram as (8), 3 Aug. 1772, 29 Oct. 1777, 15 Aug. 1778; NRO MS18622/252, Sale of Halesworth Brewery 1855
11. RBCI, 4 June 1766, 3 June 1778, 20 Sept. 1810; DED 19146, 215–16, Will of Robert Reeve; HA11/C6/1/3–4
12. RBCI, 13 Oct. 1772; Clarke, *Black Sailed Traders*, 114
13. Newby, *Independency in Halesworth & District*, 46; KPB; RBCI, 26 Nov. 1757, 7 June 1769
14. NRO, EAW 9/41; Cross Ram, Will of Peter Jermyn; RBCI, 8 June 1762
15. PRO, E190/562/25, 568/14, 570/19, 574/2; PRO, CUST 97/348; HB26/371/8

Chapter 14 – *continued*

16. NRO, Harleston Parish Registers; *Ipswich Journal*, 16 May 1752; Halesworth Parish Registers; Watney, Combe Reid & Truman, Halesworth Maltings Indenture, 1849; NRO, EAW9/42; *Ipswich Journal*, 25 May 1811
17. HB/26/412/915; NRO, MS18622/252; Adnams' records, 1795; SRO(L), Halesworth Rectory Manor Court, 9 Nov. 1793
18. Parr, 'Yoxford Yesterday' Vol V, 45; DED 19083, 142–4, 151; *Ipswich Journal*, 22 Sept. 1810; Watney, Combe Reid & Truman as (16)
19. HA11/B19/4; Deeds of Magnolia House, Halesworth; *Universal British Directory* III, 1794; *Ipswich Journal*, 27 April 1799; Adnams' records, John Woodcock's will
20. Parr, 'Yoxford Yesterday' Vol V, 85–88; D. E. Davy, *Journal of Excursions*, 5; *New Suffolk Garland*, 302; DED 19223, 87, Rous to Davy u/d 1790
21. *Ipswich Journal*, 13 July, 3 Aug. 14 & 21 Sept. 1799
22. Wrentham Parish Register; DED 19216, 186
23. *Ipswich Journal*, 5 June, 25 Sept., 23 Oct. 1790; Bidwell, *Annals of an East Anglian Bank*, 322
24. Tolls Table (1); RBCI, 1 June 1774, 18 March 1775
25. RBCI, 2 June 1784, White's Directory, 1874, gives 1803 as the date when the iron foundry was established
26. Evans, *East Anglian Linen Industry*, 162–3; *Universal British Directory* III, 1794

Chapter 15 The French Wars and Shadows of Post-war Slump

1. DED 19224, 41–55, corresp. March–April 1804 re the Blything Hundred Volunteers; Bottomley, *Short History of Borough of Southwold*, 13–14
2. Mathias, *First Industrial Nation*, 218; Woodforde, *Diary*, 25 Feb. 1797; HA11/C7/1/31, 40, 48; Chambers & Mingay, *The Agricultural Revolution*, 109–13
3. *Ipswich Journal*, 7 Sept. 1799, 4 June, 17 Sept. 1808, 22 June 1811
4. HA11/C7/1/25–43; PRO, CUST97/349, Collector to Board, 8 Aug. 1800
5. DED 19083, 142–4; qS929, 2, Jermyn & Davy, 290
6. RBCI, 5 June 1799; *Holden's Annual London & Country Directory*, 1811; Tolls Table (1)
7. Guildhall Library MS 10270; Adnams' records
8. HA11/C7/1/34–51; Guildhall Library as (7)
9. Watney, Combe Reid & Truman, Halesworth Maltings Indenture, 1849
10. PP1845XVI, 57; White, *Directory of Norfolk*, 1836
11. Maggs, *Handbook*, xii–xiii; SHCI, 23 June 1803; PP1845XVI, 62, 167
12. HA53/359/67; HA11/C3/8
13. PRO, CUST97/348, Collector to Board, 3 Jan. 1798, CUST97/349, Collector to Board, 10 June, 27 Oct. 1802
14. Bottomley, *Short History of Borough of Southwold*, 13; PRO, CUST97/348, Collector to Board, 24 Oct. 1798
15. PRO, CUST97/350, Collector to Board, 12 Aug. 1806, 28 Oct. 1805
16. SHCI, 25 April, 14 June, 23 Aug. 1799
17. HA11/B7/1, P. Jermyn to Rous, 5 June 1802
18. SHCI, 17 June 1802
19. Maggs, *Diary* I, 80
20. PRO, CUST97/350, Collector to Board, 12 Aug. 1806; Bottomley as (14), 14
21. SHCII, 26 Aug. 1808, 18 March, 31 July et seq.; Maggs, *Handbook*, xiii–xv; Maggs, *Diary* I, 2–3

Chapter 15 – *continued*

22. SHCB & H14; SHCII, 8 Sept. 1814; Wake, *Southwold*, 271
23. SHCII, 25 Sept, 1828, 19 March, 28 April, 25 June 1829

Chapter 16 Pullyn of Halesworth; Ingham of Yoxford

1. Rev. J. B. Clare, *Wenhaston & Bulcamp*, 50
2. P. Mathias, 'The lawyer as businessman in eighteenth century England' in *Enterprise & History*, ed. Coleman & Mathias, 152–162
3. SCA, 20 Aug. 1745, 4 April 1746; SHCI, 1 May, 31 July, 1747, 5 Aug., 21 Oct., 1748
4. HB26/412/561
5. R.Robson, *The Attorney in Eighteenth Century England*, 134–5; Boswell, *Life of Johnson* II,126,1770
6. qS929, 2, Jermyn & Davy, 362
7. DED19080, 397, 19083, 241, 254–7, 19218, 129; Parr, 'Yoxford Yesterday' V, 13–14
8. DED19083, 254; Robson as (5), 134–146
9. RBCI, 10 Aug., 26 Nov., 1757, 27 Sept., 31 Oct., 1759, 23 July, 6 Aug., 9 Dec., 1761, 6 June 1764
10. HA30/50/22/3, 8, corresp. & accounts, 1765–1769
11. As (10); HA30/50/22/3, 9, Blois to Ingham 27 Jan. 1770
12. HA30/324/4; HA30/50/22/5, 7(1–6); HA30/369/121
13. DED19083, 260

Chapter 17 Peter Jermyn of Halesworth; Eleazar Davy of the Grove, Yoxford

1. RBCI, 26 Nov. 1757, 6 Jan., 8 June, 1762; Cross Ram, Abstract of title to lands held of Manor of Halesworth, late P. Jermyn
2. PRO, CUST97/348(61); *Ipswich Journal*, 27 Nov. 1790; RBCI, 6 June 1792
3. RBCI 2 June 1790
4. DED19225, 80–81, Jermyn to Davy 7 Dec. 1788
5. SCA 8 April 1774; SHCI, 25 May 1781, Aug. 1787, 16 July 1789
6. HA11/B7/1, Jermyn to Rous, 5 June 1802
7. DED19217, 45, G. Vanneck to Davy, 8 Jan, 1778
8. HB26/371/127, Account Book, Rous Manors
9. DED19223, 55, 61, 96, 134, 178, corresp. Rous to Davy, 1789–1792
10. As (8)
11. DED19223, 108, Rous to Davy, 14 Jan. 1791
12. DED19223, 134, Rous to Davy, 9 June 1791
13. DED19220, 80–94, corresp. H. Jermyn to D. E. Davy, 9–19 June 1810
14. SRB, 25 May 1846, 173
15. DED19080, 121–2, 19083, 81–2, 85
16. qS929, 2, Jermyn & Davy, 336, 347; Parr, 'Yoxford Yesterday' IV, 272; DED19083, 257
17. DED19083, 3, 8–9, 19198, 4–7
18. DED19083, 8, 19188, 50; HA30/50/22/3, 11; HA30/369/271–280; Parr, 'Yoxford Yesterday' II, 193–5, IV, 272–5
19. DED19214, 140–1, Golding to Davy, 11 March 1777
20. DED19217, 41, 45–6, G.Vanneck to Davy, 8 Jan. 1778, to Hon. Mrs Davy u/d
21. DED19213, 15–91, corresp. Davy/Rowland & Thomas Holt, 1776–90

Chapter 17 – *continued*

22. Stone, *An Open Elite?*, 246–7; Beckett, *The Aristocracy in England*, 385
23. DED19185, 231, Knights to Davy, 24 Nov. 1756; RBCI, 6 June 1759; NRO, EAW9/41, EAW9/42
24. SHCI, 30 May 1755, 31 May 1769, 30 May 1777
25. DED19223, 2–203, corresp, Rous to Davy, 1786–1792; HB26/412/353–4
26. Parr, 'Yoxford Yesterday' V, 114; Davy, *Journal of Excursions*, 6–8

Chapter 18 The Clergy: a Postscript

1. Above pp.19–20; Buxton to Knights 26 July 1758
2. RBCI, 23 July, 9 Dec. 1761
3. RBCI, 14 Aug. 1749, 9 Jan. 1752 to 4 Oct. 1756

Chapter 19 The Lord and the Merchant

1. Newby, *The Patrick Stead Hospital*, 2; NRO D51/1978
2. Palmer, *The Perlustrations of Great Yarmouth*, III, 275; PP1835XXXI, Appx 61; PP1834VII, 50
3. Mathias, *The First Industrial Nation*, 474; Chambers & Mingay, *The Agricultural Revolution*, 113; PP1835XXXI, Appx 34; PP1836(189)VIII, 64
4. PP1836(189)VIII, 65; Beckett, *The Aristocracy in England*, 163
5. SRB, 25 May 1846, 59
6. Watney, Combe Reid & Truman, Halesworth Maltings Indenture, 1849; PP1845XVI, 57
7. PP1834VII, 60
8. Greater London Record Office, Ac73, 36, Truman, Hanbury & Buxton, Malting & Barley Ledgers 1818–1836, 'Thursday's Private Memoranda', 12 April 1838
9. Ford, *A Practical Treatise on Malting & Brewing*, 292; PP1835XXXI, Appx 61
10. RBCI, 1824–26, 13 March 1829
11. Southwold Museum, J.Rennie, 'Report of Southwold Harbour', 6 Jan. 1820, 1–2
12. SHCII, 25 June 1829, 4 Sept, 1830; Ellis to Elliott, 29 June 1829; Bottomley & Hutchinson, *Discovering Southwold*, 12
13. RBCI, 5 June 1839; PP1845XVI, 57–8; 11 Geo IV. cap. 48
14. RBCI, 5 June 1839; NRO, EAW9/5, EAW9/57; PP1845XVI, 58; J. H. Barrow, *The Mirror of Parliament* II
15. RBCI, 31 May 1837
16. SRB, 25 May 1846, 60–2
17. RBCI, 31 May 1837 – 5 June 1839; Watney Combe Reid & Truman, Halesworth Maltings Indenture, 1849; Lawrence, 'An Early Nineteenth Century Malting Business, in East Suffolk'. PSIA XXXVI(2), 121–4
18. Greater London Record Office, Ac 73, 36, Truman, Hanbury & Buxton barley ledgers 1835–55; SRB 25 May 1846, 99
19. Cross Ram, Manor of Halesworth Courts, 13 June 1840, 12 June 1846
20. Halesworth Tithe Map, 1840; barley ledgers as (18). 1835–44
21. PP1845XVI, 63; SHCII, 13 July 1834; Maggs, *Diary* I, 78, 81, 82, 92, 104, 122, 132
22. STH, H14
23. SHCII, 25 June, 28 July 1829; STH, H5, Minutes of Committee of Harbour Commissioners
24. *An Interesting History & Topographical Description of Southwold & its Vicinity*, 1818; *Ipswich Journal*, Dec 1833

Chapter 19 – *continued*

25. Wake, *Southwold & its Vicinity*, 27; Bottomley & Hutchinson, *Discovering Southwold*, 26, 28
26. SHCII, 7 March 1845
27. White, *Directory of Suffolk* 1844, 358, 385; SHCII, 14 July 1835, 23 July 1836 et seq.; STH, H5, Minutes of Committee of Harbour Commissioners, 19 July 1839
28. PP1845XVI, 58; Southwold Museum, Stradbroke to Admiralty, 13 Jan. 1847

Chapter 20 Last Rounds and the Reckoning

1. PP1845XVI, 57; Allan, *The Hookers of Kew*,74
2. Ellis,'Report on Southwold Harbour', 22; SHCII, 14 July, 14 Aug, 1838; SHT, H5, Minutes of Committee of Harbour Commissioners, 28 Feb., 16 March, 1839; PP1845XVI, 53
3. STH, H5, Minutes of Committee, 30 May 1839; Ellis 'Report on Southwold Harbour', 22; PP1845XVI, 56–7
4. RBCI, 5 June, 8 July, 1839
5. STH, H5, Minutes of Committee, 19 July 1839; PP1845XVI, 55; SHCII, 26 Oct. 1839
6. SHCII, 26 Oct. 1839; RBCII, 6 Nov, 1839, 7 April 1840; Walker's Report in PP1845XVI, Appx 20a; SHT, John Wright, 'Survey of River Blyth from Blyford Lock to Southwold Harbour'
7. PP1845XVI, 55, 58, Appx 20; NRO EAW9/36
8. PP1845XVI, viii-ix, 53, 54, 58, 59 and generally; Table 3
9. PP1845XVI, 67; BL8775d4, Reports of the Crown etc, on Embankments upon the Crown Lands of the River Blyth etc., 3
10. SRB, 25 May 1846, 102
11. Greater London Record Office, Ac73, 36, Truman Hanbury and Buxton,'Thursday's Private Memoranda', 23 April 1849, 28 March 1851; RBCII, 4 June 1851; Newby,*The Patrick Stead Hospital*, 7–8
12. Roy Clark, *Black Sailed Traders* , 114-115

BIBLIOGRAPHY

Unpublished Sources

Adnams PLC, Southwold, business records

E. R. Cooper, papers and notes

F. A. Crisp, Ed. *Collections relating to the family of Crispe, Abstracts of Wills and Administrations 1454–1800*, Vol III, 1884, Printed for private circulation

Cross Ram, Solicitors, Halesworth, archives

Customs Board and Collector, Port of Yarmouth (Southwold), corresp, PRO CUST97/ 346–358

D. E. Davy, Suffolk Collections: Collections for the History of Suffolk by Hundreds and Parishes; Pedigrees; Original Letters addressed to Eleazer Davy and D. E. Davy; Misc. Collections; Legal documents. BL Add. MSS 19080–19225 (19080-19083, Blything Hundred, on microfilm, Ipswich Record Office)

East Anglia Port Books, 1701–1798, PRO E190

F. W. Ellis (Lieut.) 'A Brief Historical Report on Southwold Harbour', 1839, HA56: 373/182

F. W. Ellis to Henry Elliott, 29 June 1829, lent by Miss K. Richmond

Halesworth Tithe Map, 1840 and Apportionment of Rent Charges, 1842, P461/117 and FDA117/A1/1a

Jermyn, G. B. and Davy, D. E., Suffolk genealogies, arms and church notes, 1830-40, qS929, 2

Thomas Knights' Pocket Book, NRO MS 362 T1310

S. Loftus, 'History of Brewing in Southwold', typescript, SRO(L)

Magnolia House, Halesworth, deeds lent by Mrs Turner

Manor of Rectory of Halesworth, Court Records, SRO(L)

Minute Book of the River Blyth Commissioners and Committee, 1757–1839, NRO EAW9/1

Minute Book of the River Blyth Commissioners and Committee, 1839–1856, NRO EAW9/2

Minutes of Southwold Corporate Assemblies, 1713–1800, Southwold Town Hall

Minutes of Southwold Harbour Commissioners, 1747–1804, Southwold Town Hall

Minutes of Southwold Harbour Commissioners, 1804–1859, Southwold Town Hall

Minutes of Committee of Southwold Harbour Commissioners, 1832–1846, Southwold Town Hall, H5

MS Minutes of Evidence, Commons Select Committee on Railway Bills (Group 22), Ipswich, Norwich, Yarmouth and Halesworth Bills, House of Lords Record Office, HC 1846 Vol, 42

Norfolk Record Office, mainly papers relating to Blyth Navigation under EAW9/

R. T. L. Parr, 'Yoxford Yesterday', typescript, 8 vols., c1950, qS Yoxford 9

Messrs Prest, Cornfactors, papers 1790-1819, Guildhall Library, MSS 10270–1
Charlotte Primrose,'Reminiscences', 1885, lent by Mrs G. Spriggs
John Rennie C. E. 'Report of Southwold Harbour', 6 Jan, 1820, Southwold Museum
Reports of the Crown, etc, on the Embankments and Encroachments upon the Crown Lands of the River Blyth and Harbour of Southwold, BL 8775 d4
Southwold Haven Cash Book, 1747–1824, Southwold Town Hall
Southwold Haven Cash Book, 1825–1860, Southwold Town Hall, H14
Southwold Harbour Ledgers, 1829–1866, Southwold Town Hall, H9, H10, H12
Southwold Harbour Log Books, 1811–1823, Southwold Town Hall, H7, H8
Southwold Harbour Log Book, 1840–1846, Southwold Town Hall, H11
Stradbroke to Admiralty, 13 Jan. 1847, Southwold Museum
Suffolk Record Office (Ipswich Branch): papers particularly used are Barne papers (HA53), Blois papers (HA30), Cross Ram records (HB26), Rous papers (HA11)
Truman, Hanbury and Buxton records, Greater London Record Office, Ac 73, 36
Watney, Combe Reid and Truman PLC, Halesworth Maltings Indenture, 1849
John R. Wright,'Survey of River Blyth from Blyford Lock to Southwold Harbour . . . under the direction of James Walker, 1840' (Map), Southwold Town Hall

Published Sources

Official Publications

House of Commons Journals, Vol. 27, 1757

Parliamentary Papers:

First Report of the Tidal Harbours Commission, 1845 (PP 1845 XVI)
Fifteenth Report of Commissioners of Excise Enquiry /on Malt/, 1835 (PP1835 XXXI)
Second Report of Select Committee on Agricultural Distress, 1836 (PP 1836(189)VIII)
Report of Select Committee on the Sale of Corn, 1834 (PP 1834 VII)
Second Report of Tidal Harbours Commission, 1846, (PP 1846 XVIII)

Journals

East Anglian Daily Times, 'Suffolk Coast' articles by E. R. Cooper, 25 April, 2, 9, 16 May 1934
Ipswich Journal

Books, Pamphlets and Articles

Aldcroft, D. H. & Freeman, M. J. (eds.) *Transport in the Industrial Revolution*, Manchester, 1983
Allan, Mea, *The Hookers of Kew*, London, 1967
Anon. *An Interesting History & Topographical Description of Southwold and its Vicinity*, Halesworth, 1818
Austen, Jane, *Mansfield Park*, 1814, Everyman, London
Barrow, J. H., *The Mirror of Parliament* II, London, 1830
Becker, M. Janet, *Blythburgh*, Halesworth, 1935
Beckett, J. V., *The Aristocracy in England 1660–1914*, Oxford, 1986
Bidwell, W. H., *Annals of an East Anglian Bank*, Norwich, 1900
Boswell, James, *Life of Johnson*, II, Hill's editn (revised)
Bottomley, A. F., *A Short History of the Borough of Southwold*, Southwold 1974

Bottomley, A. F. & Hutchinson, J., *Discovering Southwold*, Southwold 1986
Boyes, John & Russell, Ronald, *The Canals of Eastern England*, Newton Abbot, 1977
Browne, John, *History of Congregationalism in Norfolk and Suffolk*, London, 1877
Burke's *Landed Gentry* II, 8th Edition, London 1969
Burke's *Peerage, Baronetage & Knightage*, 101st Edition, London, 1956
Chambers, J. D. & Mingay, G. E., *The Agricultural Revolution 1750–1880*, London, 1966
Clare, Rev. J. B., *Wenhaston & Bulcamp: Curious Parish Records*, Halesworth, 1903
Clarke, Roy, *Black Sailed Traders*, London, 1961
Coleman, D. C. & Mathias, P. (eds.) *Enterprise & History*, Cambridge, 1984
Cooper, E.R., *A Brief History of Southwold Haven*, Southwold, 1907
Crabbe, G., *The Borough*, London, 1810
George Crabbe, Tales 1812 & Other Selected Poems, ed. H. Mills, Cambridge, 1967
Davy, David Elisha, *A Journal of Excursions through the County of Suffolk 1823–1844*, ed. John Blatchly, Suffolk Records Society, 1982
Defoe, Daniel, *Tour through the Eastern Counties*, 1724, Republished Ipswich, 1949
Evans, Nesta, *The East Anglian Linen Industry*, Pasold Studies in Textile History 5, 1985
Flinn, M. W. *The History of the British Coal Industry* II, 1700–1830, Oxford, 1984
Ford, William, *A Practical Treatise on Malting and Brewing*, London, 1862
Gardner, Thomas, *An Historical Account of Dunwich, Blithburgh, Southwold*, London, 1754
Hodskinson, Joseph, *The County of Suffolk Surveyed*, 1783, ed. D. P. Dymond, Suffolk Records Society, 1972
Holden's Annual London & Country Directory, London, 1811
Jenkins, A. B., *A Photographic Collection of Bygones and Local Characters of Southwold*, Southwold 1985
Kirby, John, *The Suffolk Traveller*, 2nd Edition, London, 1764
La Rochefoucauld, Francois de, *A Frenchman's Year in Suffolk*, 1784, ed. and trans. Norman Scarfe, Suffolk Records Society, 1988
Lawrence, Rachel, 'An Early Nineteenth Century Malting Business', PSIA XXXVI (2). 1986
Maggs, James, *Handbook to the Port & Shipping of Southwold*, Halesworth, 1842. (Although published under Maggs' name, the Handbook was probably written by James Jermyn)
Maggs, James, *Southwold Diary*, Vol. I, 1818–1848, Vol.II, 1848–1876, ed. A. F. Bottomley, Suffolk Records Society, 1983, 1984
Malster, Robert, *Wherries and Waterways*, Lavenham, 1971
Mathias, Peter, *The Brewing Industry in England, 1700–1830*, Cambridge, 1959
Mathias, Peter, *The First Industrial Nation*, London, 1969
Mingay, G. E., *English Landed Society in the Eighteenth Century*, London, 1963
New Suffolk Garland, collected by John Glyde Junior, Ipswich, 1866
Newby, J. W. *Independency in Halesworth & District, Halesworth*, 1936
Newby, J. W., *The Patrick Stead Hospital*, Halesworth 1964
Ordnance Survey, Reprint of first edition of one-inch survey, 1837, Newton Abbot, 1980
Palmer, C. J., *The Perlustrations of Great Yarmouth*, Great Yarmouth, 1874
Pickard, O. G., *Dunwich – The Rotten Borough*, Dunwich, 1988
Presnell, L. S., *Country Banking in the Industrial Revolution*, Oxford, 1956
Priestley, Joseph, *Navigable Rivers and Canals*, 1831, David & Charles reprint, Newton Abbot, 1969
Robinson, J. M., *Georgian Model Farms*, Oxford, 1983
Robson, Robert, *The Attorney in Eighteenth Century England*, Cambridge, 1959
Scarfe, Norman, *The Suffolk Landscape*, revised edition, Bury St Edmunds, 1987

Scarfe, Norman, 'Whitney and Read', PSIA XXVIII (2), 1959
Stone, L., *An Open Elite? England 1540–1880*, Oxford, 1985
Suckling, Rev. Alfred, *The History & Antiquities of the Hundreds of Blything and Part of Lothingland in the County of Suffolk*, London 1847
Suffolk Garland, Ipswich 1818
Thirsk, Joan & Imray, J. M. (eds.), *Suffolk Farming in the Nineteenth Century*, Suffolk Records Society, 1958
Thompson, F. M. L., *English Landed Society in the Nineteenth Century*, London, 1963
The Universal British Directory Vol III (Country), 1794
Wake, Robert, *Southwold and its Vicinity*, Yarmouth, 1839
White, William, *Directory of Norfolk*, 1836
White, William, *Directory of Suffolk*, 1844, 1874
Woodforde, James, *The Diary of a Country Parson 1758–1802*, Passages selected and edited by John Beresford, Oxford, 1978
Wren, Wilfrid, *Ports of the Eastern Counties*, Lavenham, 1976
Young, Arthur, *General View of the Agriculture of the County of Suffolk*, 1813, David & Charles reprint, Newton Abbot, 1969

INDEX